RULES AND PRINCIPLES IN EUROPEAN CONTRACT LAW

European Contract Law and Theory Series, Volume 1

# RULES AND PRINCIPLES IN EUROPEAN CONTRACT LAW

*Edited by*

Jacobien RUTGERS
Pietro SIRENA

intersentia
Cambridge – Antwerp – Portland

Intersentia Ltd
Sheraton House | Castle Park
Cambridge | CB3 0AX | United Kingdom
Tel.: +44 1223 370 170 | Email: mail@intersentia.co.uk

*Distribution for the UK:*
NBN International
Airport Business Centre, 10 Thornbury Road
Plymouth, PL6 7 PP
United Kingdom
Tel.: +44 1752 202 301 | Fax: +44 1752 202 331
Email: orders@nbninternational.com

*Distribution for the USA and Canada:*
International Specialized Book Services
920 NE 58th Ave. Suite 300
Portland, OR 97213
USA
Tel.: +1 800 944 6190 (toll free)
Email: info@isbs.com

*Distribution for Austria:*
Neuer Wissenschaftlicher Verlag
Argentinierstraße 42/6
1040 Wien
Austria
Tel.: +43 1 535 61 03 24
Email: office@nwv.at

*Distribution for other countries:*
Intersentia Publishing nv
Groenstraat 31
2640 Mortsel
Belgium
Tel.: +32 3 680 15 50
Email: mail@intersentia.be

Rules and Principles in European Contract law
Jacobien Rutgers and Pietro Sirena (eds.)



ISBN 978-1-78068-257-0
D/2015/7849/77
NUR 822

British Library Cataloguing in Publication Data. A catalogue record for this book is available from the British Library.

# CONTENTS

*Table of Cases* . . . . . . . . . . vii
*List of Authors* . . . . . . . . . . xi

**Introduction**
Jacobien RUTGERS and Pietro SIRENA . . . . . . . . . . 1

**Principles versus Rules in the Emerging European Contract Law**
Yehuda ADAR and Pietro SIRENA . . . . . . . . . . 7

I. Introduction . . . . . . . . . . 8
II. The Substantive Content and Analytical Structure of a Principle: A Critique of the Common View . . . . . . . . . . 13
III. Principles and Rules . . . . . . . . . . 20
IV. Principles of European Law . . . . . . . . . . 23
V. Principles in the Evolving European Contract Law . . . . . . . . . . 26
VI. The Balance between Principles and Rules . . . . . . . . . . 29

**The ECJ and General Principles Derived from the *Acquis Communautaire***
Elise POILLOT . . . . . . . . . . 33

I. General Principles as a Remedy to Limits on European Legislature Competences in Contract Law . . . . . . . . . . 35
II. General Principles as a Tool of Court Policy Making in Contract Law . . 42

**The Principle of Effectiveness and EU Contract Law**
Norbert REICH . . . . . . . . . . 45

I. A Constitutional Starting Point: Article 47 of the Charter . . . . . . . . . . 46
II. Effectiveness versus Procedural Autonomy . . . . . . . . . . 49
III. Some Examples Applying the Effectiveness Test in Mandatory EU Contract Law . . . . . . . . . . 53
IV. Some General Conclusions . . . . . . . . . . 63

**The Principle of Proportionality and European Contract Law**
Caroline CAUFFMAN . . . . . . . . . . 69

I. The 'Classic' Content of the 'Principle of Proportionality' in EU Law . . . 72
II. Expressions of the Principle of Proportionality in EU Contract Law . . . . 73

III. The Principle of Proportionality as an Autonomous General Principle of EU Contract Law . . . . . 81
IV. Conclusion . . . . . 97

**'General Principles' and 'Underlying Principles' in the Proposed Common European Sales Law and their Role in its Interpretation**
Simon Whittaker . . . . . 99

I. The Evolution of 'Principles' in the DCFR . . . . . 100
II. Two Types of 'Principles' in the CESL? . . . . . 105
III. Conclusion . . . . . 120

**Contractual Autonomy and European Private Law**
Salvatore Patti . . . . . 123

I. Freedom of Contract as a Principle of European Private Law . . . . . 123
II. Limits of the Freedom of Contract in the Tradition of the European Civil Codes . . . . . 124
III. New Limits of the Freedom of Contract . . . . . 126
IV. 'Aims' to be Realised by Means of Private Law and the Increase of Mandatory Rules . . . . . 128
V. New Techniques of Distribution and New Rules of Concluding the Contract . . . . . 129
VI. Sufficient Information as a Condition of the Freedom of Contract . . . . . 131
VII. 'Petrification' of the Law or a New Conception of the Freedom of Contract . . . . . 132

**Good Faith and Reasonableness in European Contract Law**
Emanuela Navarretta . . . . . 135

I. The General Issue . . . . . 135
II. The European Perspective . . . . . 139
III. The Policy Dimension . . . . . 142
IV. Coordination between Good Faith and Reasonableness . . . . . 146
V. The Politics of Harmonisation and a Final Remark . . . . . 148

**Benefits to the Defendant as a Measure for Relief: Toward a Specific Rule in European Contract Law?**
Carlos Gómez Ligüerre . . . . . 151

I. Restitution and Unjust Enrichment . . . . . 151
II. Profits as Enrichment . . . . . 154
III. Disgorgement of Profits Made by Breach of Contract . . . . . 157

# TABLE OF CASES

## EUROPEAN COURT OF JUSTICE


*Alexandros Kefalas and others v. Elliniko Dimosio (Greek State) and Organismos Oikonomikis Anasygkrotisis Epicheiriseon AE (OAE)* (C-367/96) [1998] ECR I-2843 . . . . . 91–92, 95

*Annelore Hamilton v. Volksbank Filder eG* (C-412/06) [2008] ECR I-2383 . . . . . 9, 117

*Asturcom v. Christina Rodrigues Nogueria* (C-40/08) [2009] ECR I-9579 . . . . . 40, 57, 64

*Audiolux v. Bertelsmann* (C-101/08) [2009] ECR I-9823 . . . . . 1, 24

*Bernhard Pfeifer and others v. Deutsches Rotes Kreuz* (C-397/01) [2004] ECR I-8835 . . . . . 48

*Brennet v. Paletta* (C-206/94) [1996] ECR I-2357 . . . . . 91

*Comet* (45/76) [1976] ECR 2043 . . . . . 49–51

*Commission of the European Communities v. Council of the European Communities* (218/82) [1983] ECR 4063 . . . . . 84

*Commission v. France* (C-52/00) [2002] ECR I-3827 . . . . . 114

*Commission v. Greece* (C-154/00) [2002] ECR I-3879 . . . . . 114

*Coote v. Granada Hospitality* (C-185/97) [1998] ECR I-5199 . . . . . 55

*Crailsheimer Volksbank eG v. Klaus Conrads and others* (C-229/04) [2005] ECR I-9293 . . . . . 66

*Criminal proceedings v. Lodewijk Gysbrechts and Santurel Inter BVBA* (C-205/07) [2008] ECR I-9947 . . . . . 70

*DEB Deutsche Energiehandels- und Beratungsgesellschaft mbH v. Bundesrepublik Deutschland* (C-279/09) [2010] ECR I-13849 . . . . . 47

*Dekker v. Stichting Vormingscentrum voor Jong Volwassenen (VJV-Centrum) Plus* (177/88) [1990] ECR I-3941 . . . . . 55

*Dionysios Diamantis v. Elliniko Dimosio (Greek State) and Organismos Ikonomikis Anasygkrotisis Epicheiriseon AE (OAE)* (C-373/97) [2000] ECR I-1705 . . . . . 92

*Draehmpaehl v. Urania Immobilienservice OHG* (C-180/95) [1997] ECR I-2195 . . . . . 54–56

*E. Friz GmbH v. Carsten von der Heyden* (C-215/08) [2010] ECR I-2947 . . . . . 9, 117

*E.M.M. Claro v. Centro Movil Milenium* (C-168/05) [2006] ECR I-10421 . . . . . 40, 57

*Einfuhr- und Vorratsstelle für Getreide und Futtermittel v. Köster, Berodt & Co.* (25/70) [1970] ECR 1161 . . . . . 8

*Ekro* (327/82) [1984] ECR 107 . . . . . 114

*Elisabeth Schulte and Wolfgang Schulte v. Deutsche Bausparkasse Badenia AG* (C-350/03) [2005] ECR I-9215 . . . . . 66–67

*Emsland-Stärke GmbH v. Hauptzollamt Hamburg-Jonas* (C-110/99) [2000] ECR I-11569 . . . . . 93

*Eva Martín Martín* (C-227/08) [2009] ECR I-11939 ................................ 43
*Freiburger Kommunlbauten* (C-237/02) [2004] ECR I-3403 ..................... 37, 149
*General Milk Products v. Hauptzollamt Hamburg-Jonas* (C-8/92) [1993]
ECR I-779 ....................................................................... 91
*Gonzàlez Sanchez v. Medicina Asturiana SA* (C-183/00) [2002] ECR I-3901 ......... 114
*Götz Leffler v. Berlin Chemie AG* (C-443/03) [2005] ECR I-9611 .................... 114
*Grimaldi (Salvatore) v. Fonds des maladies professionnelles* (C-322/88) [1989]
ECR 4407 ........................................................................ 60
*Halifax plc, Leeds Permanent Development Services Ltd, County Wide Property Investments Ltd Commissioners of Customs & Excise* (C-255/02) [2006]
ECR I-1609 ...................................................................... 93
*Hauer v. Land Rheinland-Pfalz* (44/79) [1979] ECR 3727 .......................... 24
*Heininger v. Bayrische Hypo- und Vereinsbank* (C-481/99) [2001] ECR I-9945 ..... 65, 67
*Hoechst AG v. Commission* (46/87) [1989] ECR 2859 ............................... 30
*Internationale Handelsgesellschaft mbH v. Einfuhr- und Vorratsstelle für Getreide und Futtermittel* (11/70) [1970] ECR 1134 ..................................... 24, 70
*Invitel* (C-466/11), judgment of 26 April 2012 ................................. 37, 39
*K. Adeneler and others v. ELG* (C-212/04) [2006] ECR I-6057 ...................... 49
*Kadi and others v. Council of the EU* (C-402 + 415/05 P) [2008] ECR I-6351 .......... 47
*Kingdom of Spain v. Commission of the European Communities* (C-135/93)
[1995] ECR I-1651 ............................................................... 84
*Kledingverkoopbedrijf de Geus en Uitdenbogerd v. Robert Bosch GmbH, Maatschppij tot vnoortzetting van de zaken der Firma Willen van Rijn*
(13/61) [1962] ECR 45 ............................................................ 8
*Kušinova v. SMART cap.* (C-34/13), judgment of 10 September 2014 ................. 47
*Lair v. Universität Hannover* (39/86) [1988] ECR 3161 ............................ 91
*Leclerc and others v. 'Au Blé Vert' and others* (229/83) [1985] ECR 1 .................. 91
*Linster* (C-87/98) [2000] ECR I-6917 ........................................... 114
*Marthe Klensch and others v. Secrétaire d'État à l'Agriculture et à la Viticulture*
(201 + 202/85) [1986] ECR 3477 .................................................. 84
*Masdar (UK) v. Commission* (C-47/07 P) [2008] ECR I-9761 ...................... 9, 47
*Mono Car Styling SA, in liquidation v. Dervis Odemis and others* (C-12/08)
[2009] ECR I-6653 ................................................................ 47
*Nemzeti Fogyaszróvédelni Hatóság v. Invitel* (C-472/10), judgment
of 26 April 2012 .......................................................... 57–58, 63
*Nold v. Commission* (4/73) [1974] ECR 491 ........................................ 24
*Océano Grupo ed. v. Quintero and others* (C-240–244/98) [2000] ECR I-4941 ... 39–40, 57
*Panagis Pafitis and others Trapeza Kentrikis Ellados A.E. and others* (C-441/93)
[1996] ECR I-1347 ................................................................ 91
*Pannon v. Erzsébet Sustikné Győrfi* (C-243/08) [2009] ECR I-4713 .................. 57
*Penzügyi Lizing v. Ferenc Schneider* (C-137/08) [2010] ECR I-10847 .......... 40, 57, 149
*Pia Messner v. Firma Stefan Krüger* (C-489/07) [2009] ECR I-7315 ............. 9, 41, 43, 82–84, 117, 148
*R. Prigge and others v. Lufthansa* (C-447/09) [2011] ECR I-8003 .................... 56
*Rampion* (C-429/05) [2007] ECR I-8017 ........................................... 43
*Rewe Central Finanz* (33/76) [1976] ECR 1989 ................................. 4, 49–51

*Roda Golf* (C-14/08) [2009] ECR I-5439 .......... 114
*Rosalba Alassini and others v. Telecom Italia* (C-317/08) [2010] ECR I-2213 .......... 46, 48, 59–60, 63–64
*Rutili v. Minister des Inneren* (36/75) [1975] ECR 1219 .......... 24
*San Georgio* (199/82) [1983] ECR 3595 .......... 50
*Seda Kücükdevici v. Swedex GmbH* (C-555/07) [2010] ECR I-365 .......... 56, 63
*Simmenthal (II)* (106/77) [1978] ECR 629 .......... 95
*Simone Leitner v. TUI Deutschland* (C-168/00) [2002] ECR I-2631 .......... 40, 54
*Societé thermal d'Eugénie-les-Bains v. Ministère de l'Économie, des Finances et de l'Industrie* (C-277/05) [2007] ECR I-6415 .......... 9
*Tanja Kreil v. Germany* (C-285/98) [2000] ECR I-7403 .......... 55
*Test-Achat* (C-236/09) [2011] ECR I-773 .......... 38
*TV 10 v. Commissariaat voor de Media* (C-23/93) [1994] ECR I-4795 .......... 91
*Unibet v. Justiekanslern* (C-432/05) [2007] ECR I-2271 .......... 47
*Van Binsbergen v. Bedrijfsvereniging Metaalnijverheid* (33/74) [1974] ECR 1299 .......... 91
*Van Schijndel and Van Veen v. Stichting Pensioenfonds* (C-430–432/93) [1995] ECR I-4705 .......... 58
*Veedfald v. Århus Amtskommune* (C-203/99) [2001] ECR 1–3569 .......... 114
*Von Colson and Kamann v. Land Nordrhein-Westfalen* (14/83) [1984] ECR 1891 .......... 53–55, 63
*Weber and Ingrid Putz* (C-65 + 87/09) [2011] ECR I-5257 .......... 41, 61–63, 65 67, 85–87, 90, 93–94
*Werner Mangold v. Rüdiger Helm* (C-144/04) [2005] ECR I-9981 .......... 24, 56, 65

## GENERAL COURT

*Citymo SA v. Commission* (T-271/04) [2007] ECR II-1375 .......... 93, 95, 98
*Distilleria F. Palma SpA v. Commission of the European Communities* (T-154/01) [2004] ECR II-1493 .......... 71, 98

## GERMANY

*Heininger II*, BGH, XI ZR 91/99, judgment of 9 April 2002 (2002) *NJW* 1881 .......... 65
*Quelle*, BGH, VIII ZR 2008/05, judgment of 26 November 2008 (2009) *NJW* 427 .......... 62
*Putz/Weber II*, BGH, VIII ZR 70/08 (2012) *NJW* 1073 .......... 62

## ISRAEL

*Klemer v. Guy* (CA 986/93) [1996] IsrSC 50(1) 185 .......... 14

## UNITED KINGDOM

*Attorney General v. Blake* [2000] UKHL 45 . . . . . . . . . . . . . . . . . . . . . . . . . . . . . . . . 154–155
*Magor & St. Mellos R.D.C. v. Newport Corporation* [1952] AC 189. . . . . . . . . . . . . . . . . . 119

## UNITED STATES

*Riggs v. Palmer*, 115 NY 506 (1889). . . . . . . . . . . . . . . . . . . . . . . . . . . . . . . . . . . . . . . . . . . . . . . . 14
*Snepp v. United States*, 444 U.S. 507 (1980). . . . . . . . . . . . . . . . . . . . . . . . . . . . . . . . . . 154–155

# LIST OF AUTHORS

**Yehuda Adar**
Assistant Professor of Private Law, University of Haifa, Israel

**Caroline Cauffman**
Associate Professor of Private Law, Maastricht University

**Carlos Gómez Ligüerre**
Professor of Private Law, Universitat Pompeu Fabra, Barcelona

**Emanuela Navarretta**
Full Professor of Private Law and European Private Law,
Law Faculty, University of Pisa

**Salvatore Patti**
Full Professor of Private Law, Sapienza University of Rome

**Elise Poillot**
Professor of droit civil, University of Luxembourg

**Norbert Reich**
Emeritus Professor, Law Faculty, University of Bremen

**Jacobien Rutgers**
Reader in Private Law and Private International Law,
Free University (VU) Amsterdam

**Pietro Sirena**
Full Professor of Private Law and European Private Law,
University of Siena

**Simon Whittaker**
Professor of European Comparative Law, University of Oxford,
and Fellow of St. John's College, Oxford

# INTRODUCTION

Jacobien RUTGERS and Pietro SIRENA

> 'The general principles of Community law have constitutional status while the principle proposed by Audiolux is characterized by a degree of detail requiring legislation to be drafted and enacted at Community level by a measure of secondary Community law. Therefore, the principle proposed by Audiolux cannot be regarded as an independent general principle of Community law.'[1]

These words are part of the ruling of the European Court of Justice in *Audiolux*, in which the question at stake was whether a minority shareholder in a company under Luxembourg law could rely on the general principle of equal treatment in EU law to secure its position. According to the decision rendered by the Court, general principles of EU law should be distinguished by a constitutional relevance. Examples of this are fundamental rights, equal treatment, non-discrimination, effective judicial protection and proportionality. For similar reasons, general principles of EU law should not be restricted to a certain area of the legal order, but rather should be applicable in all its possible branches.[2]

More recently, however, the European Court of Justice has increasingly acknowledged and applied 'general principles of civil law', relying upon values which are traditionally rooted in and pertain to the domain of private law. Examples of this are full compensation, good faith and restitution of unjustified enrichment.

The principles of EU law have been used by the Court of Justice for many a purpose.[3] First, they are an aid to interpretation with respect to EU and national law falling within the scope of EU law. Both national law and EU law must be

---

1 Case C-101/08, *Audiolux SA v. Groupe Bruxelles Lambert SA (GBL) and Bertelsmann AG* [2009] ECR I-9823, ECLI:EU:C:2009:626. See about this case: J. BENGOETXEA (2010) 47 *Common Market Law Review* (*CMLR*) 1173 et seq.; M.W. HESSELINK, 'The General Principles of Civil Law: Their Nature, Roles and Legitimacy', SSRN.com/abstract=1932146, 23 (also published in: D. LECZYKIEWICZ and S. WEATHERILL (eds.), *The Involvement of EU Law in Private Law Relationships*, Hart Publishing, Oxford and Portland 2013, pp. 131 et seq.).

2 Opinion, V. TRSTENJAK, case C-101/08, *Audiolux SA v. Groupe Bruxelles Lambert SA (GBL) and Bertelsmann AG* [2009] ECR I-9823, ECLI:EU:C:2009:410, nos. 87, 94.

3 K. LENAERTS and J.A. GUTIÉRREZ-FONS, 'The Constitutional Allocation of Powers and General Principles of EU Law' (2010) 47 *CMLR* 1629 et seq.

interpreted in the light of those principles. Secondly, they can be applied to fill gaps in EU law, and finally they may be a ground for judicial review.

The Commission has long started a discussion about the future of European contract law,[4] in order to overcome the piecemeal approach that had until that point been followed by harmonising national laws through sectorial directives. This led to the Draft Common Frame of Reference (DCFR),[5] which is referred to by some authors as a European Civil Code in disguise. A proposed Regulation on a Common European Sales Law (CESL) has also been advanced,[6] although it has been now withdrawn by the Commission, as reported in the annex to the Work Program for 2015, presented to Parliament on 16 December 2014.[7]

Both these projects (one 'soft' law and the other 'hard' law) make use of principles of European private law.

In fact, the final *Outline Edition* of the DCFR provides for a self-contained section of four 'underlying principles', namely freedom, security, justice and efficiency. The drafters have thus followed the French model of the *Principes contractuels communs.*[8]

The CESL project also opened with a separate chapter dedicated to the 'General Principles' (freedom of contract, good faith and cooperation) which were meant to govern the interpretation and implementation of this instrument.

The pervasive use of principles, both in the case law of the Court of Justice and in projects of 'soft' and 'hard' law, challenges legal scholarship. Although the concepts of 'principles' and 'rules', as well as the very sense of their distinction, have already been widely discussed with regard to national legal orders, they now need to be rethought at the European level.

First, in EU law the commonly purported connection of principles with morality seems possible, but only accidental, and sometimes seems not to be the case at all. In any event, such connection is not necessary.

Secondly, principles of European law are not always vague and generic attitudes of legal thought, but rather are sometimes very specific and precise norms which are capable of direct application in individual cases.

---

4 Communication from the Commission to the European Parliament and the Council – A more coherent European contract law – An action plan [COM (2003) 68 final].

5 C. von Bar, E. Clive and H. Schulte-Nölke et al. (eds.), *Principles, Definitions and Model Rules of European Private Law. Draft Common Frame of Reference (DCFR). Outline edition*, Sellier, Munich 2009.

6 11 October 2011 [COM (2011) 635 final]. See also the Communication from the Commission to the European Parliament, the Council, the European Economic and Social Committee and the Committee of the Regions – A Common European Sales Law to facilitate cross-border transactions in the Single Market [COM (2011) 636 final].

7 The reason thereof is reported as follows: 'Modified proposal in order to fully unleash the potential of e-commerce in the Digital Single Market' (the document is available at http://ec.europa.eu/atwork/pdf/cwp_2015_withdrawals_en.pdf).

8 *Principes contractuels communs. Projet de cadre commun de référence*, edited by B. Fauvarque-Cosson, D. Mazeaud and by G. Wicker, J.-B. Racine, L. Sautonie-Laguionie and F. Bujoli, Société de Législation Comparée, Paris 2008.

Even more importantly, the traditional view of what a principle is turns out not to be completely consistent with the Union's unique constitutional architecture, which is not comparable to that of any single Member State.

By acknowledging general principles of civil law, the European Union pushes forward the core of the common tradition of national laws. Coordination and competition among the Member States and their laws are however not spontaneous, but are rather the output of a supranational framework of strong rules, designed and enacted by the Union in order to prevent the risks of market failure.

Therefore, the division between principles and rules raises in essence the question of an optimal equilibrium between them, to be achieved by adjusting the level of regulation from a national to supranational dimension.

Law-making through principles derived from national laws shall be restricted in view of the risk of a democratic deficit, because it undermines the legislature in favour of the judicature. Conversely, law-making through rules designed and enacted by the European Union shall be restricted in view of the risk of failure of legislative power, because at the supranational level decisions are not taken under significant pressure from the market as well as from public opinion (including legal scholarship).

EU general principles and their distinction from rules were the topic of the annual Secola conference in Messina in June 2012. This book is composed of papers presented during that conference.

Yehuda Adar and Pietro Sirena propose to take principles 'seriously', by understanding them in the framework of the well-known Dworkinian theory of law. As showed by their constitutional link to human rights and fundamental freedoms, 'principles' would therefore have an anti-positivistic nature and thus would be opposed to 'rules'. At the European level particularly, principles would encapsulate the common core of the laws of the Member States and (especially with regard to subsidiarity and proportionality) would set the conditions for it to be applied by the Court of Justice. 'Principles' would promote the goal of European legal unity by reinforcing what national laws already have in common, while 'rules' enacted by the Union would do so by elimination of national divergences.

In her contribution Elise Poillot elaborates on the relationship between general principles that can be derived from the *acquis communautaire* and European contract law. She focuses on the principles of non-discrimination, proportionality and effectiveness. She discerns a development from general principles to structural principles in European contract law and in particular with respect to remedies. She argues that the three principles are used as a gap-filling device to balance economic interests with more social interests. Her final conclusion is that general principles derived from the *acquis* do not play a very important role, since EU legislation in the area of contract law is restricted to sector-specific legislation. Only in the case of more general legislation in the area of contract law will the role of principles derived from the *acquis* become more important.

Norbert Reich analyses the effects of the principle of effectiveness on European contract law in more detail. His starting point is Article 47 of the Charter on Human Rights, where it is stated that everyone who has a right guaranteed by EU law has the right to an effective remedy. Thus, it requires an individual to have a right based on European law; most frequently, this will involve matters relating to non-discrimination and consumer contracts, which must consequently be ensured by an effective remedy. This remedy involves substantive and procedural aspects. In his view, only mandatory rules of EU contract law classify for the effectiveness test. This effectiveness test follows from the *Rewe* case law and is laid down in Article 47 of the Charter, which enhances the constitutionalisation of European private law. This principle of effectiveness has a negative side, namely that some national rules render the enforcement of a right based on EU law ineffective or practically impossible. On the other hand, Reich deduces the positive side of the principle of effectiveness from what he calls the hybridisation of remedies; in other words national remedies are reshaped by means of the doctrine of consistent interpretation, which is also referred to as indirect effect. Reich discusses a number of cases in which the ECJ within the room of the national remedies adopts those national remedies.

The proportionality test is the subject of Caroline Caufmann's contribution. Cauffman discusses the role of the proportionality principle in European contract law. Within EU law the principle of proportionality is developed by the ECJ and it consists of three elements: the proportionality test *stricto sensu*, necessity and suitability. After analysing European legislation in the area of contract law, for instance the Unfair Terms Directive and Anti-Discrimination Directives, she draws the conclusion that proportionality plays a role in European contract law, in particular in balancing interests. She also discusses to what extent proportionality could be an independent principle within European contract law.

In relation to the CESL, two types of principles are discerned: general principles and underlying principles. Freedom of contract, good faith and fair dealing, and cooperation are general principles, which are laid down in specific rules. Underlying principles play a role in interpreting the CESL provisions (Article 4 CESL). After analysing freedom of contract, good faith and fair dealing, and cooperation, Simon Whittaker draws the conclusion that the general principles are at the same time underlying principles. Moreover, he distinguishes three roles played by the principles, namely a political, a cultural and a normative role. The political role involves a balance between a non-interventionist market on the one hand and a more social view of the market on the other hand. The cultural role relates to the civil law tradition on the European continent and in particular to good faith. The normative role refers to the imposition on the courts to rule in conformity with the principles underlying CESL.

Salvatore Patti discusses freedom of contract in relation to its limits. He argues that, due to the mandatory rules in European contract law, old principles such as good faith have been given a new lease of life. He inquires into the idea of freedom of contract and what its limits are today in the European context. He describes the mandatory rules and information duties. The latter serve to provide both parties an equal power to negotiate in theory. In addition, he also focuses on an evolution to a less obvious role for freedom of contract due to the role of good faith.

Emanuela Navarretta also deals with the issue of good faith and reasonableness in European contract law. She argues that the success of these principles is mainly based on the politics of harmonisation. The notions of good faith and reasonableness work really well in the context of harmonisation since they are not very detailed and leave room for national and regional preferences.

Carlos Gómez Ligüerre elaborates on restitution and unjust enrichment, and more particularly disgorgement for profit. These concepts all refer to the situation where someone holds an asset or profits without being entitled to it. These notions seem to be universally recognised, although the legal technique differs. A requirement is that the plaintiff must suffer a loss due to the defendant's behaviour. However, there are also other situations that fall within the scope of unjust restitution but where the plaintiff does not suffer a loss. This situation could arise if someone profits from someone else's non-performance under a contract. If the principle of unjust enrichment is used in this situation, it will be an effective threat against opportunistic non-performance. By punishing opportunistic behaviour, there is an incentive for the wrongdoer to start negotiations with the other party.

The papers which are collected here make clear that even the most traditional concepts of private law, when used at the European level, should not be defined and discussed on the basis of their national dimension, but rather rethought and made consistent with the unique architecture of the Union and the nature of its law.

Scholars may hope to contribute to the goal of European unity only if they dare to depart from the reassuring paths of legal nationalism and to develop concepts of private law that might be able to prove to be truly European.

# PRINCIPLES VERSUS RULES IN THE EMERGING EUROPEAN CONTRACT LAW

Yehuda ADAR and Pietro SIRENA

CONTENTS

I. Introduction ... 8
II. The Substantive Content and Analytical Structure of a Principle: A Critique of the Common View ... 13
1. The Common View ... 13
2. A Critique of the Common View ... 15
a) The Substantive Level: Are Principles Necessarily 'Moral'? ... 16
b) The Analytical Level: The Formal Structure of Principles and Rules ... 18
III. Principles and Rules ... 20
1. The Distinction Redefined ... 20
2. The Political Role of Principles as Legitimising Instruments of a Legal Order ... 21
IV. Principles of European Law ... 23
1. A Formal Perspective ... 23
2. A Substantive Perspective ... 24
V. Principles in the Evolving European Contract Law ... 26
1. The Principles of European Contract Law ... 26
2. The Draft Common Frame of Reference ... 27
3. The Directives on European Contract Law and the Project of a 'Common European Sales Law' ... 27
VI. The Balance between Principles and Rules ... 29
1. The Law which is Common to the Member States ... 29
2. The Risk of a Democratic Deficit as a Restriction on Law-Making through Principles ... 31

3. The Risk of Regulatory Failure as a Restriction on Law-Making through Rules . . . . . . . . . . 31
4. The Principle of Subsidiarity as a Tool for Adjusting the Level of Regulation . . . . . . . . . . 32

# I. INTRODUCTION

Principles of law play an important role in any legal system. Both in common law and civil law jurisdictions, courts not only plead 'principles' to interpret statutory provisions, but also apply them while adjudicating specific cases.[1] Academics often attempt to describe or explain the essence of a certain field of law by reference to a number of underlying 'principles'. Lawyers frequently construct legal arguments, either positive or normative, relying on presumably established 'principles'. Finally, and more recently, legislators have come to accept that their power is restricted by 'principles' of law. In particular, in the wake of the Second World War, 'general principles' have been formally acknowledged and solemnly embraced by many national constitutions,[2] as well as by international conventions on human rights.[3]

At the European level, the Court of Justice has, in recent decades, developed a rich jurisprudence of 'principles', which at first have solely concerned the definition and limits of the Union's powers (i.e. the principles of primacy, effectiveness, proportionality, etc.).[4]

---

1 See e.g. A. Scalia, 'The Rule of Law as a Law of Rules' (1989) 56 *UChiLRev (University of Chicago Law Review)* 1175, 1185: 'the establishment of broadly applicable general principles is an essential component of the judicial process'. In his famous *Discours preliminaire*, Jean-Étienne-Marie Portalis, one of the fathers of the French *Code civil*, made this illuminating statement: '*Peu de causes son susceptibles d'être decides par un texte précis; c'est par les principes généraux, par la doctrine, par la science du droit qu'on a toujours prononcé sur la plupart des contestations. Le Code civil ne dispense pas de ces connaisances; au contraire il les suppose*'.

2 See e.g. Constitution of the Republic of South Africa (the terms 'principles' or 'principle' appearing 14 times); Canadian Charter of Rights and Freedoms (3 times); Constitution of the Italian Republic (17 times); France Constitution (14 times); Basic Law for the Federal Republic of Germany (25 times); Constitution of the Republic of China (7 times); Constitution of the Argentine Nation (9 times).

3 See e.g. Universal Declaration of Human Rights (1948); European Convention on Human Rights (1950); Charter of Fundamental Rights of the European Union (2000).

4 E.g. case 25/70, *Einfuhr- und Vorratsstelle für Getreide und Futtermittel v. Köster, Berodt & Co.* [1970] ECR 1161, 1175 (principle of proportionality); case 13/61, *Kledingverkoopbedrijf de Geus en Uitdenbogerd v. Robert Bosch GmbH, Maatschppij tot voortzetting van de zaken der Firma Willen van Rijn* [1962] ECR 45, 52 (principle of legal certainty).

Such principles have therefore been depicted by scholars as 'institutional',[5] being understood as rooted in and pertaining to the domain of public law.[6] Not surprisingly, most of them have later on found their way into the Treaties of the Union.[7]

Starting from the 1970s, however, the Court of Justice has declared and enforced more substantive principles, which concern the protection of human rights (i.e. dignity, equality, freedom of religion, etc.) and are (at least partly) applicable to the sphere of private law.[8]

More recently, the Court of Justice has even shown an increasing willingness to acknowledge and declare 'general principles of civil law', relying upon values which traditionally have been thought of as strictly inherent to private law.[9] Relevance has been therefore given to the principles of full compensation, good faith, restitution of unjustified enrichment, etc.[10]

In the meanwhile, important 'soft' law instruments, which aim at streamlining the 'common core' of European private law, have made explicit reference to 'principles', shared by all or at least most European legal systems. Indeed, the *Principles of European Contract Law* (PECL) were given by their drafters such a denomination to emphasise that they consist of a set of rules which are not in themselves legal norms *stricto sensu*,[11] but may nonetheless be chosen by contracting parties as the law governing their transaction.[12] Beyond

---

5 B. de Witte, 'Institutional Principles: A Special Category of General Principles of EC Law' in U. Bernitz and J. Nergelius (eds.), *General Principles of European Community Law*, Kluwer International Law, The Hague 2000, p. 143.

6 J. Usher, *General Principles of European Community Law*, Longmann, Edinburgh 1998, pp. 52 et seq., pp. 72 et seq., pp. 199 et seq.

7 Treaty on European Union (1992) ('principles' mentioned 28 times); Treaty on the Functioning of the European Union (2007) (61 times).

8 See section IV.1 below.

9 See M.W. Hesselink, 'The General Principles of Civil Law: their Nature, Roles and Legitimacy' in *Centre for Study of European Contract Law Working Paper Series* No. 2011–14, available at: http://ssrn.com/abstract=1932146; C. Mak, 'Hedgehogs in Luxemburg? A Dworkinian Reading of the CJEU's Case Law on Principles of Private Law and Some Doubts of the Fox' (2012) 20 *ERPL* 323; K.P. Purnhagen, 'Principles of European Private or Civil Law? A Reminder of the Symbiotic Relationship between the ECJ and the DCFR in a Pluralistic European Private Law' in *Centre for Study of European Contract Law Working Paper Series* No. 2011–04, available at: http://ssrn.com/abstract=1652039.

10 Case 277/05, *Societé thermal d'Eugénie-les-Bains v. Ministère de l'Économie, des Finances et de l'Industrie* [2007] ECR I-6415, para. 24; case C-412/06, *Annelore Hamilton v. Volksbank Filder eG* [2008] ECR I-2383, para. 24; case C-47/07 P, *Masdar (UK) v. Commission* [2008] ECR I-9761, para. 47; case C-489/07, *Pia Messner v. Firma Stefan Krüger* [2009] ECR I-7315, para. 29; case C-215/08, *E. Friz GmbH v. Carsten von der Heyden* [2010] ECR I-2947, paras. 48–49.

11 See section V.1 below.

12 Therefore, such an instrument does not represent a mere scholarly exercise, but an existing body of law, although not consisting of rules in a positivistic sense. On the point, see S. Grundmann, *Europäisches Schuldvertragsrecht. Das europäische Recht der Unternehmensgeschäfte*, de Gruyter, Berlin 1999, pp. 1 et seq. It has been emphasised that soft law is relevant not only in order to interpret the provisions of the European Union's legislative

the European context, something of the kind happened with the *UNIDROIT Principles of International Commercial Contracts* (PICC).[13]

The notion of 'underlying principles' has played a significant role in the unification instrument known as the *Draft Common Frame of Reference* (DCFR). This project collects *Principles, Definitions and Model Rules of European Private Law*. Its final *Outline Edition*, published in 2009, differs from its predecessor, the *Outline Interim Edition,* in that it includes a self-contained section of four 'underlying principles', namely freedom, security, justice and efficiency.[14] They represent the underpinning of the whole body of rules contained in the following section of the DCFR.[15]

Last but not least, the project of a *Common European Sales Law* (CESL) opened with a separate chapter dedicated to 'General Principles' (freedom of contract, good faith and cooperation),[16] which were meant to govern the interpretation and implementation of this proposed instrument.[17]

The pervasive use of principles, both in judicature of the Court of Justice and in projects of 'soft' or 'hard' law, has given rise to a wide literature, which over time is naturally growing.[18] Although they had already been widely discussed

---

acts, but also to fill their gaps. In a more general perspective, see A. Hartkamp, 'Principles of Contract Law' in A. Hartkamp et al. (eds.), *Towards a European Civil Code*, 3rd ed., Ars Aequi Libri, Nijmegen 2004, p. 129.

13 See section V.1 below.

14 C. von Bar, E. Clive and H. Schulte-Nölke et al. (eds.), *Principles, Definitions and Model Rules of European Private Law. Draft Common Frame of Reference (DCFR). Outline edition*, Sellier, Munich 2009, pp. 57 et seq. For a strong criticism against that choice see M.W. Hesselink, 'If you don't like our principles we have others. On core values and underlying principles in European private law: a critical discussion of the new "principles" section in the draft CFR' in R. Brownsword, H.-W. Micklitz, L. Niglia and S. Weatherill (eds.), *The Foundations of European Private Law*, Hart, Oxford 2011, p. 59.

15 In the 2009 *Outline Edition* of the DCFR has been thus implemented the model, in the meantime proposed, of the *Principes contractuels communs. Projet de cadre commun de référence*, edited by B. Fauvarque-Cosson, D. Mazeaud and by G. Wicker, J.-B. Racine, L. Sautonie-Laguionie and F. Bujoli, Société de Législation Comparée, Paris 2008. See section V.2 below.

16 The project had been drafted in the Proposal for a Regulation of the European Parliament and of the Council on a Common European Sales Law, 11 October 2011 [COM (2011) 635 final]. See also the Communication from the Commission to the European Parliament, the Council, the European Economic and Social Committee and the Committee of the Regions – A Common European Sales Law to facilitate cross-border transactions in the Single Market [COM(2011) 636 final]. However, in the annex to the Work Program for 2015, which on 16 December 2014 the European Commission presented to Parliament, such proposal of a regulation is listed among those which have been withdrawn by the Commission. The reason thereof is reported as follows: 'Modified proposal in order to fully unleash the potential of e-commerce in the Digital Single Market' (the document is available at http://ec.europa.eu/atwork/pdf/cwp_2015_withdrawals_en.pdf).

17 See section V.3 below.

18 R. Schulze, 'Allgemeine Rechtsgrundsätze und europäisches Privatrecht' (1993) *ZEuP (Zeitschrift für Europäisches Privatrecht)* 442 et seq.; J. Basedow, 'The Court of Justice and Private Law: Vacillations, General Principles and the Architecture of the European Judiciary' (2010) 18 *ERPL (European Review of Private Law)* 462 et seq.; M.E. Storme, 'Une question

with regard to national legal orders,[19] in fact, the concepts of 'principles' and 'rules', as well as the very sense of their distinction, need rethinking at the European level.

This happens because the Union's law has a unique constitutional architecture, which is not comparable to that of any single Member State. In fact, it deals with a *supra*-national legal order, which includes in itself a part (or eventually even most) of Member States' private law, but at the same time sets a general framework into which this European 'common core' is put and made consistent with a new and self-standing point of view.[20]

de principe(s)?' in A. Fuchs (ed.), *European Contract Law - ERA Forum Special Issue 2008*, in *ERA Forum* scripta iuris europei, Springer, Heidelberg 2008, p. 72; A. Hartkamp, 'The General Principles of EU Law and Private Law' (2011) 75 *RabelsZ (Rabels Zeitschrift für ausländisches und Internationales Privatrecht)* 241, 255–256; G. Alpa, 'CESL, Fundamental Rights, General Principles, Rules of Contract Law' (2012) *Diritto del commercio internazionale* 837 et seq.; N. Reich, *General Principles of EU Civil Law*, Intersentia, Antwerp-Oxford 2014, passim. The second issue of 2012 of the *European Review of Private Law* collected most of the papers presented at a conference on 'Principles and the Law', held on 25 May 2011 by the University of Utrecht; particularly relevant is the editorial of E. Hondius, 'Principles and the Law' (2012) 20 *ERPL* 289 et seq.

19 In Europe, the pioneering work of J. Esser, *Grundsatz und Norm in der richterlichen Fortbildung des Privatrechts*, 1st ed., Mohr, Tübingen 1956, raised an intense debate, mainly in German scholarship, over the appropriate distinction between principles and rules. The Anglo-American literature dealing with the interrelationship between the different types of legal norms is also rich and versatile. See e.g. R. Pound, 'Juristic Science and Law' (1918) 31 *HarvLRev (Harvard Law Review)* 1047, esp. 1061–1063; R.M. Dworkin, 'The Model of Rules' (1967) 35 *UChiLRev* 14, esp. 22–40; D. Kennedy, 'Form and Substance in Private Law Adjudication' (1967) 89 *HarvLRev* 1685, esp. 1687–1713; P. Schlag, 'Rules and Standards' (1985–1986) 33 *UCLALRev (University of California Los Angeles Law Review)* 379; L. Kaplow, 'Rules *Versus* Standards: An Economic Analysis' (1992–1993) 42 *DukeLJ (Duke Law Journal)* 557; E.A. Posner, 'Standards, Rules, And Social Norms' (1997–1998) 21 *HarvJL&PublPol (Harvard Journal of Law & Public Policy)* 101; K.M. Sullivan, 'Foreword: The Justices of Rules and Standards' (1992–1993) 22 *HarvLRev* 106. Notably, however, many of these sources equate 'principles' with 'standards', contrasting them with rules, rather than distinguishing between these two concepts. Much attention to the role of principles has been paid by scholars of comparative law. Outstanding in this context is the 6th Annual Conference of the *Académie International de Droit Comparé*, which took place in Hamburg in 1962: in a session specifically devoted to general principles of law, twelve national reports were presented (Buch for Belgium, Janneau for France, Wolf for Germany, Péteri for Hungary, van der Ven for Holland, Wroblenski for Poland, Gilliard for Switzerland, Elias de Tejada, Garcia Valdecasas, Legaz Lacambra for Spain, Prodanović for Yugoslavia). The general report was given by Rudolf B. Schlesinger.

20 The concept of 'common core' has been developed by Rudolf Schlesinger during the famous Cornell Law School seminars of the 1960s. See R. Schlesinger, 'On the General Principles of Law Recognized by Civilized Nations' (1957) 51 *American Journal of International Law* passim; R. Schlesinger (ed.), *Formation of Contracts. A Study of the Common Core of Legal Systems. Conducted under the Auspices of the General Principles of Law Project of the Cornell Law School*, Oceana Publ, Dobbs Ferry NY 1968, 2 vols. In a specifically European scale, the same concept has been later on assumed as a starting point by the Trento Common Core Project. See M. Bussani and U. Mattei (eds.), *Making European Law. Essay on the Common Core Project*, Università degli Studi di Trento, Trento 2000, passim.

Therefore, the commonly accepted (or better, presumed) view of 'principles', as it has been mainly developed at the national level,[21] will be critically discussed in section II.

Then, in section III, a theoretical descriptive model of the nature of principles will be developed. The proposed model argues that, while principles do often differ from rules in their normative content and analytical structure (moral versus neutral evaluations of human behaviour; general and vague versus specific and sharp norms), these common distinctions fail to capture the most essential difference between principles and rules. Instead, the proposed model claims that the distinctive trait of principles is that they are acknowledged by a legal order as preceding the legislative power. Therefore, principles are here understood as having an anti-positivistic nature, in that they impose an external (or a self-imposed) limitation on the legislative power (national or supranational). While some norms are the expression of a fairly concrete will of the legislator ('rules'), other norms ('principles') represent instead the declaration and recognition by the political sovereign of certain legal (or constitutional) limits to that will. Such limits dwell in assumptions of human rationality, as historically embodied and reflected in the social experience of a given time.

Section IV applies this general thesis in the context of the multi-level architecture of the Union's law and comes to the conclusion that principles of European law are the legal norms which are common to the Member States (*ius commune Europaeum*), notwithstanding whether they are classified as 'principles' or 'rules' at the national level.

In section V, European contract law (both 'soft' and 'hard') will be scrutinised on the basis of the previous discussion.

Finally, in section VI, are sketched the subtle and challenging implications that the 'principles'-versus-'rules' distinction might have on the future development of European law. In particular, the use of rules and principles is seen as enabling dynamic shifts from legislature to judicature (or vice versa), as well as the fine-tuning of the level of regulation between the national and the supranational level. The role played by the 'principle of subsidiarity' is deemed crucial in this context.

[21] For a still valuable survey, see N. Bobbio, 'Principi generali di diritto', in *Novissimo Digesto Italiano*, U.T.E.T., Turin 1966, pp. 887 et seq.

# II. THE SUBSTANTIVE CONTENT AND ANALYTICAL STRUCTURE OF A PRINCIPLE: A CRITIQUE OF THE COMMON VIEW

## 1. THE COMMON VIEW

According to a widely accepted opinion, principles represent the underpinning of a whole set of norms, or of a certain branch, of the legal system (e.g. restitution of unjustified enrichment).

Principles traditionally consist of unwritten maxims,[22] which in civil law are oft rooted in the legacy of thought, practise and sometimes language of Roman law.[23] Also because of this historical origin, they have been meant to cast light on the norms set by the legislator, but not to be themselves in force as norms (at least, not applicable to single cases).[24]

Therefore, the primary function attributed to principles has traditionally been to assist courts in the interpretation of legislative rules.[25] Nevertheless, it has been widely acknowledged that they may also have a creative function,[26] as when they serve to remove inconsistencies between sources of law or to fill gaps in the formal body of rules.[27] To a lesser extent, they have played a more

22 T. Tridimas, *The General Principles of EC Law*, 2nd ed., Oxford University Press, Oxford 2006, p. 1: 'such reference [to general principles of law] usually connotes principles which are unwritten'. See also B. de Witte, n. 5 above, p. 143, defining the general principles of EC law as 'unwritten principles, recognized by the European Court of Justice'.

23 Several civilian principles stem from the compilation by Justinian, known in the Middle Ages as *Corpus iuris civilis*. See P. Stein, Regulae iuris. *From juristic rules to legal maxims*, Edinburgh University Press, Edinburgh 1966, passim. Even after the birth of national laws, such principles have been resorted to by lawyers and scholars of each European State and even regarded as tenets of some kind of (possibly eternal) natural law. See H. Coing, *Grundzüge der Rechtsphilosophie*, 4th ed., de Gruyter, Berlin 1985, pp. 206–207; Id., *Naturrecht als wissenschaftliches Problem*, Steiner, Wiesbaden 1965, pp. 22 et seq.

24 See J. Esser, n. 19 above, pp. 132–133, and after him C.-W. Canaris, *Systemdenken und Systembegriff in der Jurisprudenz. Entwickelt am Beispiel des deutschen Privatrechts*, 3rd ed., de Gruyter, Berlin 1987, p. 57.

25 See T. Tridimas, n. 22 above, p. 1: 'a principle of law, as opposed to a rule, underlies a rule and explains the reasons for its existence [... principles] provide justification for concrete rules.' See also Sir G. Fitzmaurice, 'The General Principles of International Law' (1957) 7 *Collected Courses of the Hague Academy of International Law* 92. The role of principles as interpretive instruments is discussed in J. Raz, 'Legal Principles and the Limits of Law' (1972) 81 *YaleLJ (Yale Law Journal)* 823, 839–840.

26 T. Tridimas, n. 22 above, p. 1: 'a principle is a general proposition of law of some importance from which concrete rules derive.' See also J. Raz, n. 25 above, pp. 840–841.

27 The connection between general principles of law and lack of completeness of legal systems is already evident in the national civil codes of the 19th century, which strive to reduce this problematic issue to the familiar device of analogy. At the first level, gaps of legislation shall be therefore filled through the application of legal rules relating to similar cases (*analogia legis*); when not possible, through the direct application of general principles of law (*analogia iuris*); see A. Falzea, 'Relazione introduttiva' in *I principi generali del diritto. Atti del convegno linceo del 27–29 maggio 1991*, Accademia dei Lincei, Roma 1992, p. 11, esp. p. 18. The forerunner

aggressive role, as when they are used to challenge the validity of a certain legal rule (often by shrinking its scope of application).[28]

After the Second World War, the normative nature of principles has been increasingly admitted. Predominant scholarship has therefore come to focus on the distinction between them and the remaining norms, which in this respect have been denominated as 'rules'.[29]

From a substantive point of view, principles are widely supposed to contain normative imperatives which overlap considerably with basic moral or social values respected by most citizens in a given society.[30]

---

of this tendency has been the Austrian ABGB of 1811, whose §7 refers to the principles of nature law as the final criteria to decide a case not taken into consideration by specific legal provisions (*'Läßt sich ein Rechtsfall weder aus den Worten, noch aus dem natürlichen Sinne eines Gesetzes entscheiden, so muß auf ähnliche, in den Gesetzen bestimmt entschiedene Fälle, und auf die Gründe anderer damit verwandten Gesetze Rücksicht genommen werden. Bleibt der Rechtsfall noch zweifelhaft; so muß solcher mit Hinsicht auf die sorgfältig gesammelten und reiflich erwogenen Umstände nach den natürlichen Rechtsgrundsätzen entschieden werden*'). That model has been followed by the *Codice civile degli Stati di Sua Maestà il Re di Sardegna* of 1838 (Article 15 of the introductory chapter), later by the first Italian Civil Code of 1865 (Article 3 of the preliminary provisions) and finally by the actual Italian Civil Code of 1942 (Article 12, paragraph 2, of the preliminary provisions: '*Se una controversia non può essere decisa con una precisa disposizione, si ha riguardo alle disposizioni che regolano casi simili o materie analoghe; se il caso rimane ancora dubbio, si decide secondo i principî generali dell'ordinamento giuridico dello Stato*'); see R. Sacco, 'I principi generali nei sistemi giuridici europei', in *I principi generali del diritto*, this n. above, pp. 163 et seq. Much more outspoken is the *Código civil español* of 1889, whose *Título preliminar*, art. 1, mentions the general principles among the sources of Spanish law (paragraph 1: '*Las fuentes del ordenamiento jurídico español son la ley, la costumbre y los principios generales del derecho*'), although immediately adding that they are applicable only when a specific legal rule or a specific use are lacking (paragraph 4: '*Los principios generales del derecho se aplicarán en defecto de ley o costumbre, sin perjudicio de su character informador del ordenamiento jurídico*'). Interestingly, the Government lead by Mussolini attempted to make general principles of law enumerated in a preliminary chapter of the drafting of the Italian Civil Code of 1942, because they were meant to become more consistent with the tenets of Fascist doctrine and the precepts of the dominant ideology. However, in the 1940 Congress of Pisa 'Formulazione legislativa dei principi generali del Diritto', the opposite position was successfully advocated by a young (but already authoritative) scholar, namely Francesco Santoro-Passarelli. He was later to become one of the most influential Italian scholars of the 20th century. See P. Rescigno, 'Conclusioni' *I principi generali del diritto*, this n. above, pp. 331 et seq.

28 See J. Raz, n. 25 above, p. 840. In the celebrated American case of *Riggs v. Palmer*, 115 NY 506 (1889), the moral principle that no man shall profit from his own wrong led the Court to restrict the application of a specific rule which apparently governed the question, and which led to a manifestly unjust result. Compare CA 986/93, *Klemer v. Guy* [1996] IsrSC 50(1) 185, where the Supreme Court of Israel relied on the principle of good faith to enforce an oral agreement to sell a parcel of land, notwithstanding a statutory requirement that such agreements be made in writing.

29 Ground-breaking has been R.M. Dworkin, *Taking Rights Seriously*, 1st ed., Bloomsbury Academic, London 1977, passim. For a critical reaction, see L. Alexander and K. Kress, 'Against Legal Principles' in A. Marmor (ed.), *Law and Interpretation: Essays in Legal Philosophy*, Oxford University Press, Oxford 1995, pp. 279 et seq. See sections III.1 and III.2 below.

30 A. Hartkamp, n. 18 above, pp. 241–242: '[The general principles of EU law] constitute deeply rooted principles, without which a civilized society would not exist.' With regard to national

From a structural (or analytical) point of view, principles are assumed to be relatively vague,[31] while rules are expected to usually contain rather specific normative imperatives.[32] Closely related to the last feature is the common presumption that the normative message conveyed by a legal principle is often vague and uncertain, compared to that of other legal norms.

Furthermore and closely related to the features mentioned above, principles are often thought of as having a high normative status within the legal system.[33] Describing a certain legal norm or institution as a 'principle' will most often reflect an underlying presumption that for some reason or another the norm concerned is highly regarded compared to other legal norms within the legal system. This may be either because principles are deemed to embody a fundamental moral or social value, because they reflect a time-honoured and thus entrenched legal norm or practice, or because of the belief that they have an important impact on other legal norms.

This consensus over the common traits of legal principles does not exempt jurists from further investigations regarding the nature of principles, both at the national and the supranational European level. In fact, while evident in many principles, these purported characteristics are by no means universal or necessary.

## 2. A CRITIQUE OF THE COMMON VIEW

In what follows, a critique of the common view of principles is proposed. First, the proposed model claims that the most commonly accepted attributes of principles (namely vagueness, conclusiveness and moral content) do not capture their most essential quality. Second, the proposed model explains as well why, notwithstanding this claim, the conventional view of principles is quite entrenched. The reason is that, in a national legal order, a strong affinity or correlation will very often exist between the essential feature of a principle and the other presumed attributes of it. This common correlation obscures the fact that moral content, abstractness and conclusiveness are only typical but not essential attributes of legal principles.

---

law, see F. Bydlinski, *Fundamentale Rechtsgrundsätze. Zur rechtsethischen Verfassung der Gesellschaft*, Springer, Vienna 1988, passim and esp. p. 128. See section II.2.a) below.

31 J. Boulanger, 'Principes généraux du droit et droit positif' in *Le droit prive français au milieu du XX^e siècle – Études offertes à Georges Ripert*, I, *Études generales – droit de la famille*, LGDJ, Paris 1950, p. 56; E. Betti, *Interpretazione della legge e degli atti giuridici*, Giuffrè, Milan 1949, pp. 209 et seq. See section II.2.b) below.

32 A. Hartkamp, n. 18 above, p. 242: 'They [the principles] possess a *general, comprehensive character* which is naturally inherent in general principles of law.'.

33 'The General Principles of EC law [...] have a status of *higher law*, by the fact that they may be invoked as a standard for the review of Community acts.' B. de Witte, n. 5 above, p. 143.

### a) *The Substantive Level: Are Principles Necessarily 'Moral'?*

In the common understanding of national lawyers, to rely on a 'principle' is to justify a decision by reference to a pre-existing moral ideal of society, rather than by reference to any desirable future outcome which may result from that decision (e.g. deterrence, economic growth, social stability, etc.).[34]

In that way, principles are supposed to reflect time-honoured and entrenched legal norms or practices, which are allegedly derived from basic moral values of a given society.[35]

If principles were to be identified with social traditions or habits or beliefs, however, their own nature and function would be evidently put in jeopardy, by reducing law to a fact. On the contrary, principles are the arena in which social traditions and habits and beliefs shall be critically and rationally revised under the force of legal norms.

At a first glance, the possible divergence between morality (in the strict sense of moral deontology) and the concept of a legal principle emerges in the domain of public administrative law. In most Western states, administrative law (and often constitutional law as well) restricts the government's freedom of action by subjecting it to norms such as proportionality, equal treatment, transparency, and various norms of procedural justice (i.e. the right to be heard). While these norms are often perceived as legal principles, they do not necessarily flow from any deontological moral value. This example also demonstrates that while a strong correlation definitely exists between principles and morality, morality is but one of the substantive sources of legal principles.

The lack of necessary connection of 'principles' to morality is evident as well when we move from the national to the supranational level. Take for example the so-called principles of subsidiarity, primacy and sincere cooperation. Notwithstanding their vital importance for the proper functioning of the European Union and their comprehensive character, it would seem unintuitive, if not altogether artificial, to conceptualise them as shreds of fundamental moral or social values.[36]

---

34 H.H. Wellington, 'Common Law Rules and Constitutional Double Standards: Some Notes on Adjudication' (1973) 83 *Yale L.J.* 221.

35 The question of which moral values a principle should or could legitimately reflect is a difficult and controversial one. A non-positivist will clearly prefer the view that it is only the common morality of society rather than the personal morality of the agent employing the principle that is relevant (see e.g. H. Wellington, n. 34 above, p. 244). Some positivists, on the other hand, may prefer the view that when a court is asked to rely on a moral principle, this process inevitably requires it court to employ its own morality (see e.g. J. Raz, n. 25 above, p. 847: 'What is "unjust" or "for the general good" is a matter of opinion and the courts or officials concerned *are instructed by law to act on their own views.* The law does not impose its own views of justice or the common good.').

36 Some authors suggest viewing these principles as setting a distinct category of 'institutional principles'. See B. de Witte, n. 5 above. On our understanding of subsidiarity, primacy and sincere cooperation and their role in the European Union see section V.3 below.

Coming closer to the field of private law, (almost) all the norms provided by national civil codes could be well depicted as 'moral', but conversely this fact proves that 'morality' is not able to provide for a distinctive feature of principles as such.

Even beyond the famous claim against a possible '*Tyrannei der Werten*' (tyranny of values),[37] it is evident that describing a certain legal norm or institution as a 'principle' will most often reflect an underlying presumption (by a judge, by an academic, even by a legislator) that, for some reason or another, that norm is highly regarded, compared to others within the same legal system.

In modern societies, especially if governed by a liberal democracy, people are allowed – and even encouraged – to hold radically different views, beliefs and practices. It is therefore quite impossible to identify and formulate the core values or goals endorsed by all or most members of such a society.[38] Any conventional morality is therefore compelled to co-exist with many other moralities, without one of them having the upper hand.

The deontological content of the principles shall be therefore understood only from a formal (not substantive) point of view, in the sense that they do not serve as tools of the legislator to pursue a specific goal (may it be social, or economic, or even moral). Instead, principles stand as self-evident tenets of human rationality, and for this reason are acknowledged by law as norms (*non ratione imperii, sed imperio rationis*).

Principles of law are therefore to be distinguished from legal policies, that is, social or political or even moral goals. When a rule or a specific decision is justified by consequentialist reasoning (e.g. by reference to notions of deterrence or even the desire to strengthen certain moral values), the reasons or justifications employed are never truly legal principles, but rather policies.[39] They are decided by the will of the competent agent, irrespective of the inherent rationality of its decision (*stat pro ratione voluntas*).

This assumption implies that legal principles might not be elected or even examined from a moral point of view. It implies as well that they are equally binding notwithstanding the conventional morality of a single person or group.

---

37 C. Schmitt, *Die Tyrannei der Werte*, 3rd ed., Duncker & Humblot, Berlin 1967, *passim*.

38 To some the idea that such a common morality ever exists is pure fiction. See e.g. J. Raz, n. 25 above, p. 850, describing as a 'harmful myth' the belief 'that there is a considerable body of specific moral values shared by the population of a large and modern country'.

39 Admittedly, a certain rule or a certain judicial decision may often be justified by reference to both deontological and consequentialist reasoning. In such cases, the rule or decision will reflect both a principle and a policy. H. Wellington, n. 34 above, pp. 222–223. The correlation principles-deontology and policy-teleology is recognised by that author at p. 223, n. 4. It was clearly presumed by Dworkin. See R.M. Dworkin, n. 19 above, p. 22 ('I call a "policy" that kind of standard that sets out a goal to be reached, generally an improvement in some economic, political, or social feature of the community [...] I call a "principle" a standard that is to be observed, not because it will advance or secure an economic, political or social situation deemed desirable, but because it is a requirement of justice or fairness or some other dimension of morality.').

To put it differently, the discussion about legal principles may be only approached on the basis (not of their morality, but) of their rationality. This does not mean that they are eternal and immutable, since in the field of social experience human rationality is not self-evident, but shows itself through a never-ending quest for the truth.[40]

To conclude, the connection of principles to conventional morality, however strong and frequent, is nevertheless not necessary or inevitable, and therefore not an essential feature of the concept of a 'principle'.

### b) *The Analytical Level: The Formal Structure of Principles and Rules*

As noted above,[41] it is a commonplace that principles differentiate from rules in so far as they give vague directives of law, which as such are not applicable to single cases.[42]

Intuitive as it may sound, however, such assumption does not (at least entirely) correspond to the actual state of European laws, nor (and even less) to the trend of their developments.

In fact, many a principle is not less specific than rules and, similarly to the latter, capable of direct application in single cases. Take the duty to compensate for loss wrongfully caused (sometimes known as full compensation or of *restitutio in integrum*), which is considered a basic tenet of tort law in most legal systems. It is also fairly abstract, as its scope of application depends on vague concepts such as 'unlawfulness', 'reasonableness', 'damage', etc. On the other hand, the norm does include a relatively concrete command (to pay compensation) and defines, if only in very broad terms, the conditions under which this command becomes operative. In this respect, the norm seems more a general rule (or a standard) rather than a principle.

The same consideration may be advanced for the principle of restitution of unjustified enrichment, which integrate compensation for damages in order to satisfy the Aristotelian demand of corrective (rectificatory) justice.[43]

---

40 H.G. Gadamer, *Wharheit und Methode. Grundüge einer philosophischen Hermeneutik*, Mohr, Tübingen 1960, passim; P. Häberle, *Wahrheitsprobleme im Verfassungsstaat*, Nomos Verlagsgesellschaft, Baden-Baden 1995, passim.

41 See section II.1 above.

42 See e.g. F. Schauer, *Playing by the Rules: A Philosophical Examination of Rule-Based Decision-Making in Law and in Life*, Clarendon Press, Oxford 1991, p. 13: 'For many, a principle is a principle and not something else just because it is general rather than specific'. An important philosopher who based the distinction between rules and principles on their relative degree of specificity is Joseph Raz. See J. Raz, n. 25 above, p. 838: 'Rules prescribe relatively specific acts; principles prescribe highly un-specific actions.' Notably, Raz admits that the distinction is not a sharp one, but one of degree (ibid.). Compare N. MacCormick, *Legal Reasoning and Legal Theory*, Clarendon Press, Oxford 1978, p. 155, noting that 'the difference is exaggerated'.

43 Aristotle, *Nicomachean Ethics*, Book V, ch. 4 (W.D. Ross tr., 350 BCE, 1908), also available at: http://classics.mit.edu/Aristotle/nicomachaen.5.v.html.

In turn, some norms which are regarded like 'rules' are somewhat as vague as principles and their application to singles cases depends on a very wide discretion by courts.

This may happen because any of the requirements of (even traditional) norms stands as an unfixed criterion of technical or material assessment of a fact, which may widely vary in single cases.

Take the common rule pursuant to which the breach of contract by one of the parties triggers the other's termination remedy only if it is 'fundamental' (or 'essential'). The question whether a breach of contract is or not fundamental (or 'essential') is a question of fact which is assessed by the judge according to criteria which have not been fixed in advance by the legislator.

Furthermore, some norms which are regarded as rules (and not as principles) give courts the power of balancing interests normally entrenched in the exercise of a right or a freedom and therefore doomed to collide (e.g. freedom of contract of each contracting party is potentially in contrast with the other's). According to the German tradition, such norms are defined as 'general clauses' (*Generalklauseln*) and the most prominent among them is notoriously that of 'good faith' which is embodied in §242 BGB.[44]

---

44 It would be fairly impossible to give an account of relevant literature, which is huge. For a recent valuable collection of essays with regard to European law, see S. Grundmann and D. Mazeaud (eds.), *General Clauses and Standards in European Contract Law: Comparative Law, EC Law and Contract Law Codification*, Kluwer Law International, The Hague 2006. On German law, see particularly the brief account by P. Schlechtriem, 'The Functions of General Clauses. Exemplified in Regarding German Law and Dutch Law' in S. Grundmann and D. Mazeaud (eds.), this n. above, p. 41. In Italian literature the most classical and influential works have been those of A. Falzea, 'Gli standards valutativi e la loro applicazione' (1987) I *Riv. dir. civ. (Rivista di diritto civile)* 1; L. Mengoni, 'Spunti per una teoria delle clausole generali' (1986) *Riv. crit. dir. priv. (Rivista critica di diritto privato)* 5, followed by C. Castronovo, 'L'avventura delle clausole generali' (1986) *Riv. crit. dir. priv.* 21; P. Rescigno, 'Appunti sulle clausole generali' (1998) I *Riv. dir. comm. (Rivista di diritto commerciale)* 1; S. Rodotà, 'Il tempo delle clausole generali' (1987) *Riv. crit. dir. priv.* 709, and already S. Rodotà, *Le fonti di integrazione del contratto*, Giuffrè, Milan 1969, passim. For a detailed exposition of the previous debate and the new trends of its development, see M. Libertini, 'Clausole generali, norme di principio, norme a contenuto indeterminato. Una proposta di distinzione' (2011) *Riv. crit. dir. priv.* 345; S. Patti, 'La ragionevolezza nel diritto civile' (2012) *Riv. trim dir. proc. civ. (Rivista trimestrale di diritto procedura civile)* 1; F. Denozza, 'Norme, principi e clausole generali nel diritto commerciale: un'analisi funzionale' (2011) *Riv. crit. dir. priv.* 379; G. D'Amico, *'Clausole generali' I rapporti civilistici nell'interpretazione della Corte Costituzionale*, Edizioni Scientifiche Italiane, Naples 2007, I, p. 429 and the monography by V. Velluzzi, *Le clausole generali. Semantica e politica del diritto*, Giuffrè, Milan 2010, passim. Less relevant has been the concept of general clauses for the development of French law. See C. Jauffret-Spinosi, 'Théorie et Pratique de la Clause Générale en Droit Français et dans les Autres Systemes Juridiques Romanistes' in S. Grundmann and D. Mazeaud (eds.), this n. above, p. 23.

# III. PRINCIPLES AND RULES

## 1. THE DISTINCTION REDEFINED

The distinction between principles and rules represents the opposition of two kinds of norms, which are not only different, but also mutually exclusive, thus embracing the whole legal order.

In this framework, it has been pointed out that rules are to be applied according to an 'all-or-nothing' logic:[45] either they are fully applicable to a case, or they are not such at all. Instead, principles are capable of a discrete application and, in a sense, require it necessarily, since each of them always needs balancing with (one or more of) the others.[46] For this reason, principles have been defined as 'mild',[47] none of them logically excluding the others or setting them aside.

The single most important feature of legal principles has to do neither with their analytical structure, nor with their substantive content. Rather, it has to do with their distinctive function within a legal system and with their source.

*Principles are norms which are acknowledged by a legal system as pre-existing the exercise of the legislative power.* They are not the expression of a distinctive will of the legislator, but they precede it and, when constitutionally relevant, may also bind it.

At the European level, the principles consist of the core which is common to the constitutional traditions of the Member States (human rights) and to the entirety of their private law (good faith, restitution of unjustified enrichment, etc.).

Rules represent a radically different technique of legislation. Unlike a principle, announcing a rule is *not* merely an act of declaration. Rather, by its very nature, *a rule represents an imposition.* By enacting a rule, the political sovereign, through its authorised representatives, constitutes a new binding norm, *regardless of the degree to which that norm has already been accepted by*

---

45 Unless, of course, for some reason the rule is not a valid rule, or an exception to the rule applies to the particular case under consideration.

46 R.M. Dworkin, n. 19 above, pp. 22–28, esp. pp. 23, 24, 25: 'Rules are applicable in an all-or-nothing fashion. If the facts a rule stipulates are given, either the rule is valid, in which case the answer it supplies must be accepted, or it is not, in which case it contributes nothing to the decision'; '[principles] do not set out legal consequences that follow automatically when the conditions provided are met. [...] A principle [...] does not even purport to set out conditions that make its application necessary.' Dworkin's sharp distinction between principles and rules was further deepened and formally elaborated as a constitutional theory of law. See e.g. the classical and most influential works of R. Alexy, 'Rechtsregeln und Rechtsprinzipien' (1985) 25 *ARSP (Archiv für Rechts- und Sozialphilosophie) Beihefte* 13; R. Alexy, 'Zum Begriff des Rechtsprinzips' (1979) 1 *Rechtstheorie Beiheft* 59; R. Alexy, 'Zur Kritik des Rechtspositivismus' (1990) 37 *ARSP Beihefte* 9.

47 G. Zagrebelsky, *Il diritto mite*, Einaudi, Torino 1992, passim; Id., *Principî e voti. La Carta costituzionale e la politica*, Einaudi, Torino 2005, passim.

*the community subject to the ruler's laws.* Put differently, a rule may be defined as the product of a process through which a competent agent (typically a legislator or a court) manifests its will to impose on its subjects a norm which may well contradict their practices, customs, values and beliefs.

A brief look at the semantics and etymology of the terms 'rule' and 'principle' renders some support for the propositions just made. To 'rule', in the English language, is to govern, to reign or to control other people.[48] A principle, on the other hand, is a word of Latin origin ('*principium*'), which means an origin or a beginning.[49] The close semantic connection between the literal meaning and the definition we here proposed is almost self-evident. To enact a principle is to look *backwards* at the origins of the norm merely restated by the principle. To rely on a principle is merely to approve and acknowledge what is presumably already a recognised truth. Enacting a rule, on the other hand, is a *forward*-looking process. It reflects the sovereign will not to declare, but rather to dictate and impose a constitutive norm upon the subjects. A rule is not primarily intended to reinforce an existing norm or practice, but rather to bring about a change in the conduct of those subject to the sovereign's laws.

## 2. THE POLITICAL ROLE OF PRINCIPLES AS LEGITIMISING INSTRUMENTS OF A LEGAL ORDER

Human law-making is a social process through which a sovereign political entity aims to achieve certain goals by influencing the conduct of those subject to its laws. In order to do so, the political sovereign must lay down effective norms of conduct, in other words, normative imperatives that will be widely obeyed by those at which they are directed.

The simplest and most direct way to affect human conduct by legal norms is to formulate and enforce what H.L.A. Hart called 'primary rules' or 'rules of duty'. Rules of duty are specific conditional orders or norms defining the circumstances or conditions under which a certain person (or class of persons) is required to act (or to refrain from acting) in a certain predetermined way. A more sophisticated method by which a legal system may influence human conduct is to lay down 'secondary rules' or 'rules of power'. These norms do not demand action (or inaction). Rather, they enable agents (either private or public) to bring about an effective change in their own legal position or the legal position of others, provided that certain requirements are met. Thus, while the tort duty to compensate for wrongfully caused loss is a primary rule or a rule of duty, the

48 See e.g. Oxford on Line Dictionary, available at: http://oxforddictionaries.com/definition/english/rule?q=rule.

49 See e.g. Latin Dictionary, Perseus Digital Library, available at: www.perseus.tufts.edu/hopper/resolveform?type=begin&lookup=principium&lang=la.

norm limiting the power of termination to fundamental breach is a secondary rule or a rule of power.[50]

To achieve obedience and effectiveness, both duty norms and norms granting legal power must be backed with a corresponding legal outcome, which will create a sufficiently strong incentive to fulfil the duty imposed or to take into account the relevant rules of power. In regard to duty rules, most frequently the outcome will be a negative sanction, ideally imposed for any failing to fulfil one's duties.[51] Similarly, certain outcomes must attach to one's following – or one's failing to follow – the rules of power. For example, failing to follow the rules on formation of contracts will result in a failure to bring about a voluntary change in one's legal position, while following these rules of power will enable contracting parties to create or modify enforceable rights and duties.

In practice, however, no sanctioning system is ever perfect. The incentives created by the sovereign's norms and by the operation of the mechanisms established for their enforcement are often insufficient to guarantee a satisfactory level of compliance. A legal system, especially one based on a liberal philosophy, cannot rely solely on deterrence. It must look for additional ways to encourage obedience to and reliance on the law. One such technique is to install a sense of respect for the law in general, as well as for its concrete imperatives in the society (i.e. the primary and secondary rules).[52]

From a political point of view, the principles attain this sense of respect and legitimacy towards the legal system, because they establish a highly visible link between the legislator's will and the 'good reasons' which lay behind it. In other words, principles do not only link a number of scattered, single decisions by the competent agent (rules) into a consistent and organic whole (legal order), but provide also that they are reasonable, i.e. rationally acceptable by citizens.

A citizen bound solely by an effective system of rules will probably obey those rules, if only for fear of being sanctioned for not doing so. When such system is rationalised by way of principles of law, instead, a citizen may feel less obliged

50 For an authoritative discussion of the distinction between primary and secondary rules see H.L.A. Hart, *The Concept of Law*, 1st ed., Clarendon Press, Oxford 1961, pp. 27–28, 78–79, 89–96. Cf. F. Schauer, n. 42 above, pp. 3–6 (distinguishing mandatory rules, which exert normative pressure to act on those subject to them from 'rules of thumb', which merely present options, which can either be followed or ignored under specific circumstances).

51 This is not to imply that the sanction will necessarily be defined *ex ante* in the rule itself. Thus, the concrete sanction for a certain violation of a rule may be defined only *ex post*, in which case often a principle will be invoked in order to justify the imposition of the sanction (e.g. the principle of '*nullum crimen sine poena*'). The key role of sanctions in any theory of law was emphasised by eminent philosophers such as John Austin and Hans Kelsen, which defined law as a system of coercive orders backed with organised social sanctions.

52 This insight, namely, that law requires legitimacy and general acceptance by those subject to it lies at the heart of H.L.A. Hart's criticism of John Austin's command theory, which defined law as a system of commands backed with threats. H.L.A. Hart, n. 50 above, esp. ch. 4 (pp. 49–76).

– and more obligated – to obey the rules and to accept the social institutions creating, modifying and enforcing them.

This legitimising function of legal principles represents the political reason why modern legal orders have come to acknowledge them as limits to legislative power. If not linked to some basic tenets of human reason, the legislator's will would become arbitrary and, in the long run, lose its capacity of obedience by citizens. Only if such will is rationally 'understandable' is it proved to citizens that it is reasonable as well and therefore worth social respect.[53]

Conversely, this fact explains the comprehensiveness and abstractness which commonly affect principles, as well as their tendency to converge with highly regarded moral or social values, because such features prevent norms which declare principles from (frequent) modifications.

Indeed, in order to achieve the goal of legitimising a legal order, the norms declaring principles shall be as stable and firm as possible.

Changing 'rules' of a legal order is not only ordinary, but even desirable in due course, because it serves to provide for the modernity and the efficiency of legislature.

Changing 'norms' declaring principles, instead, is a traumatic event, because it generally marks a crisis of legitimacy or effectivity of a legal order (as a consequence of a revolution, a civil war, etc.).

## IV. PRINCIPLES OF EUROPEAN LAW

### 1. A FORMAL PERSPECTIVE

In order to examine the question of principles in the framework of European law, the starting point is the Treaty on European Union. Indeed, together with the Treaty on the Functioning of the European Union and some key decisions rendered by the Court of Justice, it represents the constitutional underpinning of the entirety of the European legal order.

In the Preamble of the Treaty on European Union, it is explicitly declared the '*attachment to the principles of liberty, democracy and respect for human rights and fundamental freedoms and of the rule of law*'.

This hint as to the status and nature of European principles finds its decisive elucidation in Article 6(3) of the same Treaty, which acknowledges human rights and fundamental freedoms as general principles of law and derive them from the European Convention of 1950, as well as from the '*constitutional traditions common to the Member States*'. This legislative provision consists of a plain

53 About the connection between reasonableness and legitimacy of a legal order, see J. Esser, *Grundsatz und Norm in der richterlichen Fortbildung des Privatrechts*, Mohr, Tübingen 1956, passim.

rewording of statements on protection of human rights, which are to be found in the jurisprudence of the Court of Justice.

Particularly, the reference by the Court of Justice to the 'constitutional traditions common to the Member States' dates back to the 1970s.[54] In later decisions, regarding the principle of non-discrimination, the Court added a reference to the international treaties binding the Member States to respect human rights,[55] and particularly to the above-mentioned European Convention.[56]

## 2. A SUBSTANTIVE PERSPECTIVE

It follows from the foregoing general part of this work that the multi-level architecture of the Union's law is highly relevant to the issue of its general principles, both in order to identify and to define them.[57]

The constitutional foundation of general principles, which is to be found in the Preamble and in Article 6(3) of the Treaty on European Union, tells a lot not only about their nature, but also about their roots.

---

54 The first statement of the kind may be traced in case 11/70, *Internationale Handelsgesellschaft mbH v. Einfuhr- und Vorratsstelle für Getreide und Futtermittel* [1970] ECR 1134, para. 4: 'In fact, respect for fundamental rights forms an integral part of the general principles of law protected by the Court of Justice. The protection of such rights, whilst inspired by the constitutional traditions common to the Member States, must be ensured within the framework of the structure and objectives of the Community'.

55 It should be noted that Article 38(1)(c) of the Statute of the International Court of Justice, which is annexed to the Charter of the United Nations, of which it forms an integral part, foresees that the Court shall apply 'the general principles of law recognized by civilized nations'.

56 Leading precedents in this context are case 4/73, *Nold v. Commission* [1974] ECR 491, para. 13; case 36/75, *Rutili v. Minister des Inneren* [1975] ECR 1219, para. 32; case 44/79, *Hauer v. Land Rheinland-Pfalz* [1979] ECR 3727, paras. 17 et seq.; for a general survey, see H.G. Schermers, 'Human Rights as General Principles of Law' in U. Bernitz and J. Nergelius (eds.), n. 5 above, pp. 61 et seq.; X. Groussot, *General Principles of Community Law*, Europa Law Publishing, Groningen 2006, pp. 56–58. Recently the most important (and fiercely debated) cases have been definitely case C-144/04, *Mangold v. Helm* [2005] ECR I-9981 and case C-101/08, *Audiolux v. Bertelsmann* [2009] ECR I-9823. Both relate to the application of the non-discrimination principle, the former in the field of labour law and the latter in that of company law. For an insightful comment, see A. Metzger, 'Allgemeine Grundsätze in Europa – dargestellt am Beispiel des Gleichbehandlungsgrundsatzes' (2011) 75 *RabelsZ* 845 et seq.

57 In the same sense, see A. Metzger, *Extra legem, intra ius: Allgemeine Rechtsgrundsätze im Europäischen Privatrecht*, Mohr, Tübingen 2009, p. 109 (also for a challenging comparison with the federal legal system of the United States); S. Grundmann, 'General Standards and Principles, Clauses Générales and Generalklauseln in European Contract Law – A Survey' in S. Grundmann and D. Mazeaud (eds.), n. 44 above, p. 4; M.W. Hesselink, 'The Structure of the New European Private Law' (2002) *Electronic Journal of Comparative Law* 6.4, available at: www.ejcl.org/64/art64-2.html; M.W. Hesselink, 'How many systems of private law are there in Europe? On plural legal sources, multiple identities and the unity of law' in *Centre for Study of European Contract Law Working Paper Series* No. 2012-03, available at: http://ssrn.com/abstract=2046964.

First, at the highest level of their constitutional relevance, principles of the Union's law are regarded as associated, or even coincident, with human rights and fundamental freedoms.

Furthermore, though forming part of the law the Union's law, such principles flow into it from external sources (international law as consolidated in the conventions which bind European States and constitutional traditions which are common to them).

The thought of Ronald M. Dworkin in the field of philosophy and general studies of law offers an illuminating framework in order to understand these two plain assumptions.

First of all, principles of European law are to be identified with fundamental rights which the European citizens are given before the Union, and potentially even against the Union. At the highest constitutional level, which is the field where principles may generally show their most genuine nature, they stand as limits to the legislative and judicial power of the European Union.

From a more general point of view, it is thus evident that the Union's law lacks completeness, in the sense that it is not self-standing: its principles forbid it. However paradoxical it may sound, modern constitutions prevent any legal order from being closed in itself and self-evident, as Ernst-Wolfgang Böckenförde has explained better than anyone else.[58]

According to these theoretical and constitutional explanations of modern legal systems, principles of European law shall be understood as having an anti-positivistic nature and in so far they are opposed to rules. Although principles are recognised by the European Union as norms,[59] they are not settled and shaped in their content by a legislative power, but derived from international law and legal traditions which represent the common core of the Member States' laws.

To conclude, principles are the norms of the Union's law which encapsulate the common core of the laws of the Member States and (with particular regard

---

58 The famous Böckenförde dilemma sounds '*Der freiheitliche, säkularisierte Staat lebt von Voraussetzungen, die er selbst nicht garantieren kann*'. The author further explains: '*Als freiheitlicher Staat kann er einerseits nur bestehen, wenn sich die Freiheit, die er seinen Bürgern gewährt, von innen her, aus der moralischen Substanz des einzelnen und der Homogenität der Gesellschaft, reguliert. Anderseits kann er diese inneren Regulierungskräfte nicht von sich aus, das heißt, mit den Mitteln des Rechtszwanges und autoritativen Gebots zu garantieren versuchen, ohne seine Freiheitlichkeit aufzugeben und – auf säkularisierter Ebene – in jenen Totalitätsanspruch zurückzufallen, aus dem er in den konfessionellen Bürgerkriegen herausgeführt hat*'. For both quotations see W. Böckenförde, *Staat, Gesellschaft, Freiheit. Studien zur Staatstheorie und zum Verfassungsrecht*, Suhrkamp, Frankfurt a.M. 1976, p. 60.

59 This undeniable assumption may be able to include principles also in a positivistic theory of law, depending on what is meant by legal positivism. For a perspective of private law on innumerable (stronger or weaker) versions of legal positivism, see the essays collected in P. Sirena (ed.), *Oltre il 'positivisimo giuridico'. In onore di Angelo Falzea*, Edizioni Scientifiche Italiane, Naples 2011, and esp. F.D. Busnelli, 'In margine alla "grande dicotomia" diritto civile-diritto naturale. Le alterne fortune dei principi generali', ibid., p. 49.

to subsidiarity and proportionality) create the conditions for it to be applied at the European level, especially by the Court of Justice. In contrast, rules are those norms of the Union's law which impose a will of the European legislator, irrespectively of the laws of the Member States, or even against them.

Principles promote the goal of European legal unity by reinforcing what national laws already share in common. Rules do so by cancelling divergences among national laws.

## V. PRINCIPLES IN THE EVOLVING EUROPEAN CONTRACT LAW

### 1. THE PRINCIPLES OF EUROPEAN CONTRACT LAW

According to the previous general assumptions, the Principles of European Contract Law (PECL) and the UNIDROIT Principles of International Commercial Contracts (PICC) are to be taken seriously when they qualify themselves as principles.[60]

Both of them do not properly give, but rather imply a definition of principles. Article 1:101(1) PECL states that they are '*intended to be applied as general rules of contract law in the European Union*'. In the Preamble (*Purpose of Principles*) of the PICC, first paragraph, it is similarly announced that they '*set forth general rules for international commercial contracts*'.[61]

Such provisions apparently stress the generality of the rules set forth by the PECL and the PICC as a criterion to qualify them as principles. However, the decisive reason why they deserve this qualification is that the PECL have been drafted as a written consolidation of a common core of national legal traditions (regarding contracts), as well as the PICC are purported to collect legal practices established in international commerce, i.e. the so-called *lex mercatoria*.

In other words, both the PECL and the PICC aim at reflecting a *ius commune* (*Europaeum*, or even on a larger scale), which as such exists beyond the power of a sovereign legislator.

---

60 Similar considerations apply to the Restatements proposed by the American Law Institute. See P. Frank, 'The American Law Institute 1923–1938' (1998) 26 *HofstraLRev (Hofstra Law Review)* 615.

61 For a survey of the PICC, see V. Heutger, 'The UNIDROIT Principles 2010: Towards a "Global" Law of International Commercial Contracts (17–18 February 2012)' (2012) 20 *ERPL* 889.

## 2. THE DRAFT COMMON FRAME OF REFERENCE

Similar considerations apply to the Draft Common Frame of Reference (DCFR), which explicitly defines its own content as follows: '*Principles, Definitions and Model Rules of European Private Law*'.[62]

It is true that, after dealing with the use of 'principles' by the PECL and the PICC, the Introduction to the DCFR comes to the conclusion that as such they denote '*rules which do not have the force of law*'.[63] But for the reasons already discussed, such an explanation is far from convincing (beside the fact that it evidently blurs the distinction between the two kinds of norms, i.e. principles and rules).

The main reason why the DCFR is thought of as a collection of 'principles' is that it maps the core of private law which is common to Member States. Despite every attempt to deny or to lessen the fact, the DCFR was born and has grown as the blueprint of a European civil code.

This explains as well the decision taken in the *Outline Edition* of 2009 to emphasise as 'underlying' four principles of the DCFR (namely freedom, security, justice and efficiency),[64] because they build the framework where all the others are to be put in and find their teleological explanation.

## 3. THE DIRECTIVES ON EUROPEAN CONTRACT LAW AND THE PROJECT OF A 'COMMON EUROPEAN SALES LAW'

As far as 'hard' law is concerned, principles have found acknowledgement in the Treaty on European Union and in the jurisprudence of the Court of Justice, primarily (but not solely any longer) in the field of human rights and fundamental freedoms.[65]

On the contrary, directives (and regulations) so far enacted to create a European contract law consist of rules, and not of principles, although some of their provisions are clearly based on 'good faith' (take for instance the directive on abusive contract terms),[66] or on 'fair dealing' (take for instance the directive on unfair commercial practices).[67]

---

62 For a series of comments on its provisions, see (2008) 4 *ERCL (European Review of Contract Law)* No. 3, and especially the introductory essay of S. Grundmann, 'The Structure of the DCFR – Which Approach for Today's Contract Law?' (2008) 4 *ERCL* 225. See also U. Breccia, 'Principles, Definitions e Model Rules nel "Comune quadro di riferimento europeo" (Draft Common Frame of Reference)' (2010) *I contratti* 95.

63 DCFR, n. 14 above, p. 9.

64 See section I.1 above.

65 See sections I.1 and IV.2 above.

66 Council Directive 93/13/EEC of 5 April 1993 on unfair terms in consumer contracts.

67 Directive 2005/29/EC of the European Parliament and of the Council of 11 May 2005 concerning unfair business-to-consumer commercial practices in the internal market and

Even if 'good faith' and 'fair dealing' as well have that peculiar vagueness and elasticity making them immediately look like principles, it should be questioned whether they have been actually regarded as such by European legislator.[68] Instead, the enhancement of 'good faith' and 'fair dealing' in the Union's legislation aims at imposing some specific policies, which are pursued on Member States.

In the directive on unfair terms, 'good faith' is used to implement a policy of consumer protection, as well as 'fair dealing' is a legislative tool to pursue protection of competition and market freedom.

This legislative technique is akin to that of principles only with regard to the vagueness and elasticity of the norm, but with towards its settlement the attitude of the legislator is completely different.[69] 'Good faith' and 'fair dealing' have so far been regarded in European legislation not as 'principles', but as 'rules' (or better, as 'general clauses').

A different consideration applies to the project of a common European sales law (CESL).[70]

According to its hierarchical structure, which proceeds from the more general to the more specific, the CESL started by explicitly mentioning and providing its own general principles,[71] which were identified in freedom of contract (Article 1), good faith and fair dealing (Article 2), and cooperation (Article 3).

In Article 2 CESL 'good faith' and 'fair dealing' were not taken into consideration as general clauses or legal standards (as European directives and regulations had done so far), but as genuine (general) principles. They were not expressions of some specific policies pursued by the supranational regulation, but rather marked the switch from the rules enacted by European legislator to the common core of the national laws.

Particularly relevant is the provision about the interpretation of the CESL, which was to be autonomous and '*in accordance with its objectives and the principles underlying it*' (Article 4(1)). The reference to the 'principles underlying it' meant that, in case of uncertainty as to the meaning of the CESL, its provisions

amending Council Directive 84/450/EEC, Directives 97/7/EC, 98/27/EC and 2002/65/EC of the European Parliament and of the Council and Regulation (EC) No. 2006/2004 of the European Parliament and of the Council ('Unfair Commercial Practices Directive').

68 On the question whether 'good faith' might stand as a general principle of European contract law, see the debate between H. Beale, 'General Clauses and Specific Rules in the Principles of European Contract Law: The "Good Faith" Clause' in S. Grundmann and D. Mazeaud (eds.), n. 44 above, p. 205 and O. Lando, 'Is Good Faith an Over-Arching General Clause in the Principles of European Contract Law?' (2007) 15 *ERPL* 841.

69 See section IV above.

70 See section I.1 above.

71 Part I (Introductory provisions), ch. 1 (General principles and application), sec. 1 (General principles), Articles 1–3.

had to be interpreted in accordance with the common core of the laws of the Member States, because it is them which identify the principles of European law.

It is true that Article 4(2) CESL at once added that the interpretation of the CESL in accordance to its objectives and underlying principles should be carried out '*without recourse to the national law that would be applicable in the absence of an agreement to use the CESL or to any other law*'.[72] For several reasons, however, this final restriction did not apply to the common core of the laws of the Member States.[73]

First, such a common core is not 'national law', because it is not enacted by any legislative power and may not be said to be in force in any national legal order. On the contrary, it belongs to the legal traditions which are common to the Member States and therefore forms part of the set of principles of European law.

Secondly, and similarly, such a common core may not be said to be 'applicable in the absence of an agreement to use the CESL'.

As it was designed, the project of the CESL was able to recognise the centrality of principles in European contract law and to balance them more attentively with rules.

This shift of European law is becoming increasingly necessary to the extent that its scope is not yet limited to some specific policies (like consumer protection or competition), however relevant they may be from a social, economic and political point of view. If the European Union intend to create general private law, the evocation of its principles, and therefore of the common laws of the Member States, becomes a vital necessity, as has already been made evident by the DCFR.

## VI. THE BALANCE BETWEEN PRINCIPLES AND RULES

### 1. THE LAW WHICH IS COMMON TO THE MEMBER STATES

The distinction between principles and rules will be finally scrutinised as a question of fine-tuning the level of regulation between national and

[72] The objection has been raised by Prof Simon Whittaker during the SECOLA conference of Messina, where the authors of this chapter has presented and discussed a former version of it.

[73] However, see M. Heidemann, 'European Private Law at the Crossroads: The Proposed European Sales Law' (2012) 20 *ERPL* 1128 et seq., who, while examining the so-called autonomous interpretation method, accuses the users of transnational law to be all 'too tempted on reaching the interface with national law to understand the clauses to be a conflict rule and happily revert back to their own domestic law'.

supranational legislators,[74] and also of shifting power from legislature to judicature (and vice versa).[75] Because of its extreme complexity, the topic can only be superficially sketched in this chapter.

By acknowledging principles, the European legislator promotes legal unity among Member States by enhancing the coordination and also the competition among them and among their laws. In order to achieve the institutional goals of the European Union, it is however to be remarked that the common core of national laws should not be the outcome of a static or passive recognition of what at the first glance looks already to be shared. Such method would lead in fact to the lowest point of possible convergence among the Member States, according to the logic of the *minimum minimorum*. But the aim of promoting legal unity by way of the Union's law should instead impose an obligation to maximise the convergence and therefore to pursue the logic of the *minimum maximorum*. In other words, it is therefore necessary to also include in the common core of the principles of European law implicit and potential consistencies among Member States, with the only impassable limit of the '*not inconsiderable divergences*', set out by the Court of Justice in the *Hoechst* case.[76]

Pursuant to the principle of subsidiarity (Article 5 of the Treaty on European Union), the best way to avoid the risk that national differences, which have been created by centuries of legal positivism, will harm the social and the economic well-being of Europe is to push forward the core of the common tradition of laws. This permits the legislature to opt for solutions which are and have been for centuries under the sharp criticism of scholarship and under the pressure of market, both of them permanently forcing the national laws into the quest for 'better regulation'.[77]

However, a European law consisting of principles alone would be neither possible nor desirable.

---

74 M.E. Storme, 'The Foundations of Private Law in a Multilevel Structure: Balancing, Distribution of Lawmaking Power, and Other Constitutional Issues' (2012) 20 *ERPL* 237; K. Lenaerts and J. Gutiérrez-Fons, 'The Constitutional Allocation of Powers and General Principles of EU Law' (2010) 47 *CMLR (Common Market Law Review)* 1629.

75 S. Grundmann, 'The General Clause or Standard in EC Contract Law Directives – A Survey on Some Important Legal Measures and Aspects in EC Law' in S. Grundmann and D. Mazeaud (eds.), n. 44 above, p. 154; D. Edward, 'Shifting Power from Legislation to Judges and from the Central Level to the National Level' in S. Grundmann and D. Mazeaud (eds.), n. 44 above, p. 79; S. Grundmann and W. Kerber, 'European System of Contract Laws: A Map for Combining the Advantages of Centralised and Decentralised Rule-making' in S. Grundmann and J. Stuyck (eds.), *An Academic Green Paper on European Contract Law*, Kluwer Law International, The Hague 2003, 295.

76 Case 46/87, *Hoechst AG v. Commission* [1989] ECR 2859. See M. Herdegen, 'The Origins and Development of the General Principles of Community Law' in U. Bernitz and J. Nergelius (eds.), n. 5 above, pp. 1, 17–18.

77 Most illuminating is W. Eucken, *Grundsätze der Wirtschaftspolitik*, 6th ed., Mohr, Tübingen 1990, pp. 245 et seq.

## 2. THE RISK OF A DEMOCRATIC DEFICIT AS A RESTRICTION ON LAW-MAKING THROUGH PRINCIPLES

Making law through principles creates a shift of power from parliaments to courts, or, which is the same thing, undermines the legislature in favour of the judicature.[78]

According to the constitutional foundation of modern democracies, in the long run this shift of power cannot but create an unbearable democratic *deficit*, because courts do not have a mandate from the people and do not express their sovereignty.[79]

## 3. THE RISK OF REGULATORY FAILURE AS A RESTRICTION ON LAW-MAKING THROUGH RULES

Coordination and competition among Member States and among their laws do not always maximise the social and economic well-being of Europe, because in some specific and well-recognisable contexts such coordination and competition are exposed to the risk of failing.[80]

In this sense, the principle of subsidiarity is aimed not only at defending national States from a possible subtraction of their sovereignty by the European Union, but also, and perhaps even more so, at tuning the best level of legislation, especially in front of the distinction between principles and rules. The tool of subsidiarity fixes the breaking point beyond which making law through principles shall shift to making law through rules.

At the European level, rules, as opposed to principles, promote legal unity among Member States by cancelling out the national differences among them. However, and as elucidated so many times by scholars studying European integration from an economic point of view, this way of making law hides dangers, too.

---

78 A classical point of reference is the debate between Hans Kelsen and Carl Schmitt about the nature of constitutional justice. For a survey thereof see C. Pinelli, 'The Kelsen/Schmitt Controversy and the Evolving Relations between Constitutional and Internal Law' (2010) 23 *Ratio iuris* 493.

79 J.M. Smits, 'European Private Law and Democracy: A Misunderstood Relationship' in M. Faure and F. Stephen (eds.), *Essays in the Law and Economics of Regulation in Honour of Anthony Ogus*, Intersentia, Antwerp-Oxford 2008, p. 49. See also the European University Institute thesis by M. Bartl, 'Legitimacy and European Private Law', available at: http://papers.ssrn.com/sol3/papers.cfm?abstract_id=2142798.

80 See S. Grundmann, 'The Structure of European Contract Law' (2001) 9 *ERPL* 505.

If the counterbalance of making law through principles is the failure of market, then that of making law through rules is the failure of the European Union itself as a regulator.[81]

Unlike national laws, the Union's law does not have to cope so much with actual criticism from scholarship, which is still mainly national. It also does not have to cope so much with market pressure, because the level of regulation is too high and too far from the players, and tends to be politically irresponsible as well.

## 4. THE PRINCIPLE OF SUBSIDIARITY AS A TOOL FOR ADJUSTING THE LEVEL OF REGULATION

The tool for adjusting the level of regulation between principles and rules at the European level is still that of subsidiarity, which however should be taken even more seriously than in the past, especially by the Court of Justice when controlling the validity of the legislative acts of the Union.

This issue goes far beyond the limits which are necessarily appropriate for this chapter.

---

[81] Fundamental in this respect are the classical studies by James Buchanan on public choice. See particularly J. Buchanan and G. Tullock, *The Calculus of Consent. Logical Foudations of Constitutional Democracy*, Liberty Fund, Indianapolis 1999; J. Buchanan, *The Limits of Liberty. Between Anarchy and the Leviathan*, University of Chicago Press, Chicago 1993; J. Buchanan, *Liberty, Market and State*, New York University Press, New York 1986.

# THE ECJ AND GENERAL PRINCIPLES DERIVED FROM THE *ACQUIS COMMUNAUTAIRE*

Elise Poillot

CONTENTS


I. General Principles as a Remedy to Limits on European Legislature Competences in Contract Law . . . 35
   1. From General Principles Derived from the *Acquis Communautaire* to Structural Principles of Contract Law . . . 35
   2. Select Case Law . . . 37
II. General Principles as a Tool of Court Policy Making in Contract Law . . . 42
   1. Existence of Sectoral Policies . . . 42
   2. Difficulties in Establishing General Policies . . . 43


According to Giuseppe Mazzini, *'[i]n politics, as in any other field, a principle inevitably leads to a system, a series of consequences, a process of applications easy to anticipate for persons with common sense'*.[1] This assertion certainly applies to European contract law. This contribution aims at demonstrating that the ECJ played an important role in such a process. To understand how such a process started, one must get back to the foundations of European Union law.

In the beginning was the EEC. And from the very beginning, the EEC was both a market and a political system. Any political agreement, leading to a legal consensus was aimed at building a market. This economical approach is obvious in the Treaties. Before building a common law a common market had to be built. The goal was to increase trade between Member States. The creation of this common market led to the adoption of common legislation. As a consequence the market preceded the law. In this respect, all the general principles set down in the Treaties are market-oriented. In this respect general principles were predestined to leave the field of what a continental lawyer would call 'public law' to enter the field

---

1 G. Mazzini, *Repubblica e Monarchia*, ch. I.

of private law, more precisely of economic private law. This happened through the channel of the ECJ, which sought to review the conformity of national regulations with EU legislation adopted on the grounds of approximation of laws.

At this point, two very important issues should be clarified. Firstly, for the purpose of this contribution, only principles set or implied by Treaties and by the Charter on Fundamental Rights will be considered general/constitutional principles. Secondly, despite the economic dimension of European law and its market-oriented nature, not all existing general/constitutional principles could play a role in the developing of contract law through the channel of the ECJ. Principles such as subsidiarity and sincere cooperation were not shaped to influence, even indirectly, the field of contract law.

This might not be surprising with respect to the 'subsidiarity principle' which organises the sharing of powers between several levels of authority. As 'a mere institutional principle' it is strictly limited to the allocation of competences. Therefore, its use outside the control by the Court of legitimacy of action of the EU legislature was very unlikely.

Principles of transparency and trust could also not be used in the field of contract law. The former, now acknowledged as a 'constitutional principle' by the Court and the academic world, has very much to do with the formal quality of the EU legislation. It was thus difficult to extend its use outside this scope. However, the transparency principle is a basic principle of EU legislation in the field of contract law (mainly linked with the so-called 'obligation of information').[2]

The principle of trust (*Vertrauensprinzip*) could possibly be used in contract law, as trust certainly is a basic principle in this area. However, its use by the ECJ was limited to relationships existing between EU institutions and EU citizens.

The principle of sincere cooperation (Article 4 EU Treaty), which reminds continental lawyers, and especially French ones, of the good faith principle, is considered a principle notably obliging the parties to collaborate during their contractual relationship. From this point of view, it could of course be used in contract law. However Article 4 of the EU Treaty applies only to relationships between the EU and Member States. That being said, and assuming the fact that the principle of effectiveness derives from it, its influence in the field of contract law cannot be denied.

For the purpose of this contribution, the principle of freedom of movement and its various aspects will not be considered, as its influence on contract law is too indirect. Most of the time, the decisions of the ECJ have led only to setting aside the national legislation at stake. The Court doctrine has not modified the

---

2 See E. Poillot, *Droit européen de la consommation et uniformisation du droit des contrats*, Preface P. de Vareilles-Sommières, LGDJ, 2006, Coll. Bibliothèque de droit privé, t. 463, especially n° 166 ff., 466 ff.

substance of contract law in this field,[3] as was the case when the Court was asked to control the conformity between national law and secondary legislation. For all these reasons, only the principles of non-discrimination proportionality and effectiveness (efficiency) will be dealt with here.

That being said, it should however be clarified that the design of the Court's competence in the frame of the preliminary ruling and the use of the theological method to interpret EU legislation did not make it possible to directly develop general principles in contract law on the grounds of these three constitutional principles. It does not mean that the Court did not intervene in contract law through these principles in an indirect manner, using them to ensure the effectiveness of EU legislation in national legal orders. In this context, the Court clearly used the general principles as a remedy to the limits of the competences allocated to the European legislature (section I). When doing so, the Court undoubtedly established contractual law policies through its jurisprudence (section II).

## I. GENERAL PRINCIPLES AS A REMEDY TO LIMITS ON EUROPEAN LEGISLATURE COMPETENCES IN CONTRACT LAW

As we will see through the chosen examples (section 2), some of the constitutional principles were used to 'fill some gaps' in the EU legislation, especially in the field of remedies. The reason for this lies in the fact that in EU legislation these constitutional or general principles could constitute the legal framework of European contract law. As such they can be described as structural principles (section 1).

### 1. FROM GENERAL PRINCIPLES DERIVED FROM THE *ACQUIS COMMUNAUTAIRE* TO STRUCTURAL PRINCIPLES OF CONTRACT LAW

As contract is an economic tool, it is not difficult to apply to contract law principles that have been shaped to support the building and the functioning of the market. It is then no wonder that principles set by Treaties and the Charter and which were designed to be used in the field of contract law are principles designed to support the building and the functioning of the single market. These principles are proportionality, effectiveness, and to some extent non-discrimination, although there has been a change in the nature of the latter due to the evolution of EU legislation.

---

3 On this issue, see J.W. Rutgers, 'Free Movements and Contract Law' (2008) 4(3) *European Review of Contract Law* 474–486.

Non-discrimination is like a structural principle. It guarantees the exercise of freedom of contract and sets its limits. Non-discrimination is basically an economic principle, as it was initially limited, in the Treaty of Rome, to its economical aspect, i.e. the prohibition on discriminating Member States' legislation in the framework of the common market.[4] After the TFEU and the adoption of the Charter of Fundamental Rights, however, the meaning of non-discrimination as a constitutional principle evolved. Since it is now considered a constitutional principle, discrimination is now that which is founded on sex, ethnicity or race. As a consequence, its content is less and less influenced by market ideology. This is quite a good thing, as the market-oriented nature of other principles should be counterbalanced. Hopefully 'constitutionalisation' of contract law[5] through the Charter will maintain the balance between market ideology and social justice.

Proportionality and effectiveness principles are also market-oriented in the original ideology of the EEC. How they are used depends mostly, however, on the ideological direction given by the Court. Three different approaches can be identified.

The first approach leads to a balancing of the rights through the proportionality principle. From this perspective, proportionality is perfectly appropriate to contract law, as it is a very useful tool to check the economic balance of a contractual relationship. In the example of unfair terms, judicial assessment of the unfairness of a contractual term is based on the control of the balance between the rights and obligations of the parties.

The second approach is the consequence of the omnipresence of the principle of effectiveness in the jurisprudence of the Court. It is of common knowledge that the principle of effectiveness derives from the principle of *effet utile*.[6] Its use in the context of European contract law is the result of the ECJ practice. However, it has been integrated into contract law directives, especially because the decision was made to leave the choice of remedies to Member States.[7] As its effect on contract law is presented in Professor Norbert Reich's contribution, this principle will not be discussed in more detail here. It is however a core principle of European law, and a very interesting emerging principle in the area of contract law.

It can even be considered a post-modern concept not present as such in any civil codes or legislation (in a broad sense) in the field of contract law.

4 On this issue, see, *inter alia*, P. Craig, 'The evolution of the Dingle Market' in C. Barnard and J. Scott (eds.), *The Law of the Single European Market: Unpacking the Premises*, Hart, Oxford 2002, pp. 1–40.

5 On which, C. Mak, 'Constitutional Aspects of a European Civil Code' in A.S. Hartkamp, M.W. Hesselink, E.H. Hondius, C. Mak and C. Edgar du Perron (eds.), *Towards a European Civil Code*, Wolters Kluwer Law and Business, Nijmegen, 2011, pp. 332 ff.

6 See the contribution of N. Reich in this volume, 'The Principle of Effectiveness and EU Contract Law'.

7 See, for example Article 7(2) Directive 93/13/EC and Article 23 Directive 2011/83, even if this was not a regular practice (not integrated in Directive 97/7/EC for example).

It is certainly a promising tool in the area of pre-contractual information and performance of contract, allowing the creation of interesting doctrines filling the gaps left in legislation. Its use would be merely interpretive, i.e. it would permit for example the judge to extend remedies such as resolution of contract where no remedy has been provided.[8]

Effectiveness of contract could also lead to using one remedy rather than another, in a contractual context where several remedies are available. From that perspective, the example of pre-contractual information is very interesting.[9] In France, Luxembourg and Italy, no specific provisions have been adopted in the case of breach of the pre-contractual obligation to inform the other party of the essential elements of the contract. By using the principle of effectiveness, a judge could decide that according to the context the appropriate remedy would be contract resolution (if required by one party) rather than the award of compensation. Another example can be taken from the proposal for a Common European Sales Law where remedies offered for non-conformity of goods are no longer subject to a hierarchy. In this context, the principle of effectiveness would give the opportunity to judges to apply the most appropriate remedy. The Court could also rely on the principle of proportionality to balance the interests at stake and determine whether or not the resolution is adequate for the damage suffered. However, with regard to the competence of the Court, such an activist approach to these principles has not been used yet and remains highly improbable. In fact, the ECJ can only control conformity of national legislation to EU law by interpreting its substance and guide national judges in the interpretation of their own legislation in the light of European law.[10] Though not directly using these structural principles, decisions of the Court have influenced national legislation on specific contracts. Some examples will help demonstrate this.

## 2. SELECT CASE LAW

For the purpose of this study only series of cases directly dealing with 'constitutionalisation' of contract law and effectiveness of remedies will be scrutinised. Non-discrimination plays an important role in the process of 'constitutionalisation' of contract law as its special place within EU law has

---

8 For example, Directive 2011/83/EU provides several obligations of information to be respected by the business. Except for the violation of the information to be provided on the existence of the withdrawal right of the consumers, sanctions are to be determined by the Member States. Relying on the effectiveness principle, the Court could decide that a contract should be terminated, had the business not provided the information on the main characteristics of the goods as required by Article 5(1)(a).

9 See the contribution of N. Reich in this volume, 'The Principle of Effectiveness and EU Contract Law'.

10 See Case C-237/02, *Freiburger Kommunlbauten* [2004] ECR I-3403, and Case C-466/11, *Invitel*, judgment of 26 April 2012, more specifically para. 23.

allowed fundamental rights to meet economics to some extent. Since the *Test-Achat* case[11] has proven to be a very interesting case from that perspective, let us start from here.

The case deals with Directive 2004/113/EC implementing the principle of equal treatment between men and women in the access to supply of goods and services which is said, in the decision, to be a '*fundamental principle of the European Union*' according to the Charter of Fundamental Rights. The preliminary ruling regarded the conformity of a Belgian statute which authorised a discrimination called '*a proportionate distinction drawn on the basis of the gender*' for the purposes of calculating insurance premiums and benefits where sex is a determining factor in the assessment of risk on the basis of relevant and accurate actuarial and statistical data with the principle of equal treatment between men and women.

The Directive itself, in Article 5, provided this derogation to the principle of non-discrimination. This Article permitted Member States to maintain such discrimination with the only obligation being to reconsider the provision after a five-year period. The provision challenged in the case was not only the national provision but also the Article of the Directive itself. The ECJ held that Article 5(2) of the Directive was invalid as it enabled the Member States to maintain without temporal limitation an exemption from the rule of unisex premium and benefits and worked against the achievement of the objective of equal treatment of men and women. The interesting point here, with regard to the use of the constitutional principle of non-discrimination, is that the Court's decision clearly shows the importance of this principle, using a 'constitutional' vocabulary, giving it a full constitutional value. This decision is certainly amongst the first of a forthcoming series that will demonstrate the importance of the principle of non-discrimination in all sectors of contract law.[12] It will definitely have a huge impact on national legislation where this principle has always been regarded as sectoral and confined to areas such as labour or insurance law, as is the case in Luxembourg and France, for example. Besides, it is undoubtedly more than a 'gap-filling decision'. The fact that non-discrimination is considered a constitutional principle gives it a broader dimension. More than affirming the importance of non-discrimination in contract law, this case emphasises the role of fundamental rights in the EU legal system. On the contrary, the 'gap-filling' dimension of the principles of effectiveness and proportionality is certainly their main characteristic.

Surprisingly, in most of the Directives enacted in the field of contract law, remedies were left to the discretion of Member States or were broadly

---

11 Case C-236/09, *Test-Achat* [2011] ECR I-773.

12 This principle has been used in various European projects on contract law, such as the DFCR in Article III.–1:105 which sets forth the *non-discrimination* rule.

determined.[13] Firstly, there is no institutional reason for such a choice.[14] Secondly, Directive 99/44/EC on certain aspects of the sale of consumer goods and associated guarantees almost exclusively deals with remedies!

With regard to the issue of remedies, Directive 93/13/EC on unfair terms in consumer contracts is particularly interesting. According to Article 4(1), an unfair term is non-binding, which is a rather imprecise statement. Respect for the Member States' legal mechanisms certainly explains such imprecision. It leaves Member States the possibility of implementing the provisions of the Directive according to their legal culture. In France, for example, the term is considered to be 'non-written' (non-existent),[15] while in Belgium it is void and in Luxembourg is 'non-written' and void.[16]

If the European legislator determined the remedy for an unfair clause, for some unclear reason he completely ignored the procedural regime for the assessment of unfairness. One reason could be reluctance to violate the so-called principle of Members States' procedural autonomy. As a consequence, several preliminary rulings have been referred to the Court by national judges all facing the same problem: ignorance of one's rights on the part of the consumer. National judges have been asked by a business to find a consumer in breach of his contractual duties in a contractual context involving a possible unfair term, most of the time an arbitration clause or a jurisdictional clause. Usually the consumer had been passive, not defending himself, or if doing so, not raising the issue of the term's unfairness. Faced with the lack of procedural provisions in the Directive, the Courts built the procedural regime of the terms using legal reasoning based on the principle of effectiveness.[17] Having demonstrated to national judges their ability to raise the unfairness of a term on their own motion, the Court eventually reached the conclusion that it was a duty to do so. From the *Océano Grupo* case to the *Invitel* case,[18] the Court constructed a doctrine of procedural effectiveness of unfair terms, which relegated the

---

13 Directives usually contains standard clause providing that Member States will determine the means ensuring the compliance with the Directive's provisions. See for example Article 23(1) of Directive 2011/83/EU on consumer rights stating that '1. Member States shall ensure that adequate and effective means exist to ensure compliance with this Directive'.

14 In her conclusions on the *Invitel* case, Case C-466/11, Advocate General Trstenjak suggests that one of the reason is 'the legal nature of the directive' designed as 'an instrument for the harmonisation of legislation, which under Article 288 TFEU is binding as to the objective to be attained, while it is left largely to national bodies to choose the form and means of doing so' (para. 89).

15 '*Non écrit*'.

16 On the various expressions of the non-binding character of a term, see H. Schulte-Nölke and C. Twigg-Flessner, *EC Consumer Law Compendium, The Consumer Acquis and its transposition in the Member States*, Sellier, Munich 2008, pp. 406 ff.

17 See the contribution of N. Reich in this volume, 'The Principle of Effectiveness and EU Contract Law'.

18 Case C-240/98 to C-224/98, *Océano Grupo* [2000] ECR I-4941; Case C-466/11, *Invitel,* judgment of 26 April 2012.

principle of procedural autonomy to unexpected boundaries. In the *Penzügyi* case[19] the Court even imposed on national judges an obligation to investigate in order to be able to assess the unfairness of the term. To reach this conclusion, the Court always referred to the principle of an effective protection of the consumer justified by the unequal bargaining power of the parties.[20]

In this area, the principle of effectiveness did prove to be a very efficient tool in the hands of the Court to guarantee a high level of protection to consumers.

Compensation is another area of contract law that has been penetrated by the principle of effectiveness. This is very clear in the *Leitner* case.[21] Simone Leitner, an Austrian citizen, went on vacation. She was 'sold' a package holiday and was not very lucky. Salmonella poisoned the food she was given and she spent most of her vacation in bed. Under Austrian law, the non-material damage caused by the loss of her holiday could not be compensated. Therefore, the Austria Court of First Instance refused to award her such compensation. Its decision was challenged and the appellate court, surmising that the interpretation of Article 5 could lead to a different outcome, submitted a preliminary ruling to the ECJ in order to assess the conformity of Austrian legislation that prevented a contractual party from being compensated for non-material damage with the provisions of the Directive on Package Holiday. Simone Leitner was eventually lucky as the Court held that Austrian law was in breach of EU law in this respect. The reasoning of the Court did not expressly refer to the principle of effectiveness but is clearly oriented in that direction. The Court took the view that 'the existence in some Member States but not in others of an obligation to provide compensation for non-material damage would cause significant distortions of competition as non-material damage is a frequent occurrence in that field'. It also highlighted that 'the Directive, and in particular Article 5 thereof, is designed to offer protection to consumers and, in connection with tourist holidays, compensation for non-material damage arising from the loss of enjoyment of the holiday is of particular importance to consumers'.

This case is particularly interesting as the Court implied a general right to non-material compensation in the field of package holidays not only by saying that national legislation that excludes such compensation would not be in conformity with EU law, but also by imposing on all Member States a duty to compensate non-material damage for the loss of the holiday. In doing so,

---

19 Case C-137/08, *VB Penzügyi* [2010] ECR I-10847.

20 On several occasions the Court has held that '[t]he imbalance which exists between the consumer and the seller or supplier may only be corrected by positive action unconnected with the actual parties to the contract'. See case C-240/98 to C-224/98, *Océano Grupo* [2000] ECR I-4941, para. 27; case C-168/05, *Mostaza Claro* [2006] ECR I-10421, para. 26; and case C-40/08, *Asturcom* [2009] ECR I-9579, para. 31.

21 Case C-168/00, *Simone Leitner* [2002] ECR I-2631.

the Court strongly influenced national legislation in this sector through the principle of effectiveness.[22]

Coming to the principle of proportionality, its use seems to be particularly appropriate for controlling the adequacy of a remedy with regard to the legal or contractual context. Two cases support this approach.

In the *Messner* case,[23] a woman bought a computer via a distance contract for €278. More than six months after delivery, the computer display became defective. She informed the seller who refused to repair the defect free of charge. When Mrs Messner realised that she had not been informed of her right of withdrawal, she decided to revoke the contract as that was still possible under German law. The seller claimed she was under the obligation to pay compensation for the use of the computer and asked her to pay €316.

The German court sought a preliminary ruling from the Court as under the second sentence of Article 6(1) and (2) of Directive 97/7, the only charge that might be imposed on the consumer by reason of the exercise of her right of withdrawal is the direct cost of returning the goods. It was held that German law, which requires a consumer to pay fair compensation, was not in breach of EU law in cases where the consumer makes *'use of the goods acquired under a distance contract in a manner incompatible with the principles of civil law, such as those of good faith or unjust enrichment'*. Such a possibility should however be 'in accordance with the purpose of that Directive and, in particular, may not adversely affect the efficiency and effectiveness of the right of withdrawal. It would, for example, be the case if the amount of compensation, such as that referred to in the previous paragraph, were to appear disproportionate in relation to the purchase price of the goods at issue or also if the provision of national law were to place on the consumer the onus of proving that he did not use those goods during the period for withdrawal in a manner which went beyond what was necessary to permit him to make effective use of his right of withdrawal'.

It could surely be argued that in this case, the principle of proportionality plays a minor role in the reasoning of the judge. This is certainly true but what is interesting here is the use made of it in order to balance the rights of consumer and sellers.

The ECJ in the *Putz and Weber* case[24] also took this approach. Defective tiles had been installed and their non-conformity only appeared once they were laid. The issue at stake was the conditions of their replacement. The Court held that if it imposed disproportionate costs on the seller 'it is appropriate to reduce the consumer's right to reimbursement of the costs of removing the goods not

---

22 Regrettably no preliminary ruling related to the obligation of information was ever submitted to the Court. Lack of special remedies in national law makes it a useless tool and an inefficient concept.

23 Case C-489/07, *Pia Messner* [2009] ECR I-7315.

24 Cases C-65/09 and C-87/09, *Gebr. Weber and Ingrid Putz* [2011] ECR I-5257.

in conformity and of installing the replacement goods'.[25] In doing so national judges will 'have to bear in mind, first, the value the goods would have if there were no lack of conformity and the significance of the lack of conformity, and secondly, the Directive's purpose of ensuring a high level of protection for consumers'.[26] Of course, in both cases, and contrary to the cases where the principle of effectiveness had been used, the principle of proportionality was not mentioned as such. However, the *ratio decidendi* of the case, if I may use this expression in this context, is certainly based on that principle.

These cases clearly demonstrate that constitutional principles may be key elements for the Court to fill the legislature's gaps. By doing so, the Court has inevitably established legal policies through its jurisprudence

## II. GENERAL PRINCIPLES AS A TOOL OF COURT POLICY MAKING IN CONTRACT LAW

Abstraction made of the principle of non-discrimination, which, as a fundamental right, rules any kind of contract, the use of constitutional principles by the ECJ led to the existence of sectoral policies (section 1). In the field of contract law, the EU legislator has no general competence. Therefore its actions are only of a sectoral nature. Consequently, the policies of the ECJ are also of a sectoral nature. All the preliminary rulings submitted to the Court refer to a precise question in the framework of a specific directive. In this context, it is very difficult to affirm that general policies have been or could be established (section 2). Difficult does not however mean impossible. It could thus be possible to support the view that some general policies were established.

### 1. EXISTENCE OF SECTORAL POLICIES

These policies can more precisely be described as sectoral and sub-sectoral. The sectoral approach adopted by the EU legislature through the approximation of laws of course limits the scope of Court policies to the areas at stake and theoretically precludes national law from being influenced outside them. In fact, in all the cases mentioned, points of impact are limited to specific areas such as the issue of compensation or remedies. But what is particularly interesting about these sectoral policies is that they differ from one sector to another.

In consumer contracts, the Court policy regarding the procedural regime of unfair terms is undoubtedly 'social'. By obliging the judges to raise *sua sponte* some legal issues, the Court obviously favours the effectiveness of consumer

---

25 As explained in para. 76 of the case.

26 As explained in para. 76 of the case.

protection. This is particularly obvious if a comparison is made with credit[27] and outdoors contracts,[28] two sectors where the Court has held that raising a term by the judge on its own motion was only a possibility. The decisions dealing with compensation of consumers or employees also demonstrate a tendency to favour the weakest party.

On the contrary, when limiting the rights of consumers to reimbursement of the cost of removing the defective goods and of installing the replacement goods under certain circumstances, the Court implements a more market-oriented policy. As for the *Messner* case, the policy underpinning the ruling can be described as a balanced one, taking reasonable care of the interests of all the parties.

These differences in policy orientation are clearly the result of the instrumental function of constitutional principles in the field of contract law. Their 'neutral content' makes them flexible and adaptable to any ideology one wants to promote.

The principle of effectiveness, for example, shows that different conclusions will be reached according to what judges are aiming at. If the target is to protect consumers or employees, the use of effectiveness will allow a social approach to the contract. If the goal is to have the contract performed, then it is more probably a market-oriented policy that will underpin the decision. This flexible nature leads to approaches that can be very different from one case to another.

Of course, this is not very surprising, as the flexible nature of principles allows them to be used in many different ways. Furthermore the 'coexistence between the many sector, and purposive regulatory techniques and traditional market-based solutions of private law administered ex-post by the courts, is not necessarily harmonious'.[29] As a consequence, the use made by the ECJ is not very easily anticipated. However, this unpredictability is acceptable as long as the Court operates through prospective overruling and does not implement policies or develop them so as to make them difficult to coordinate with national legislation. From this perspective, it is certainly satisfying that these policies are still limited to specific sectors.

## 2. DIFFICULTIES IN ESTABLISHING GENERAL POLICIES

As has been demonstrated, it is difficult to say that constitutional principles could lead to the implementation by the ECJ of general policies in contract law, with the exception, of course, of the non-discrimination principle. Whether they

27 Case C-429/05, *Rampion* [2007] ECR I-8017.

28 Case C-227/08, *Eva Martín Martín* [2009] ECR I-11939.

29 H. Muir-Watt and F. Cafaggi, 'Introduction' in H. Muir-Watt and F. Cafaggi (ed.), *The Regulatory Function of European Private Law,* Edward Elgar Publishing, Cheltenham, 2009, specifically p. xxiii.

can be used in any sector of contract law is however not arguable, but the strict limitation of competences of both the legislator and the Court refrains from doing so in an activist manner.

The legislature has not (yet) been given any competence in the field of 'general contract law'. The Court is strictly bound by the question referred and will answer on the basis of the autonomous interpretation principle which limits the influence of the Court's decision to the scope of the legislation at stake. But the more EU legislature adopts legislation in the field of contract law, the more it will be possible for the Court to rely on constitutional principles to establish general policies. From this point of view, the possible promulgation of a regulation for a Common European Sales Law could be the start of this process.

Whether this will happen is another question. In the end, there are still a lot of uncertainties surrounding general principles derived from the *acquis communautaire*.

# THE PRINCIPLE OF EFFECTIVENESS AND EU CONTRACT LAW

Norbert REICH*

CONTENTS

I. A Constitutional Starting Point: Article 47 of the Charter . . . . . . . . . . . . . 46
II. Effectiveness versus Procedural Autonomy . . . . . . . . . . . . . . . . . . . . . . . . . . 49
III. Some Examples Applying the Effectiveness Test in Mandatory EU Contract Law . . . . . . . . . . . . . . . . . . . . . . . . . . . . . . . . . . . . . . . . . . . . . . 53
1. The Classical Case: *Von Colson and Kamann* . . . . . . . . . . . . . . . . . . . . . 53
2. An Open Constitutional Dimension: *Kücükdevici* . . . . . . . . . . . . . . . . 56
3. Effective Protection Against Unfair Terms in Consumer Contracts: *Invitel* . . . . . . . . . . . . . . . . . . . . . . . . . . . . . . . . . . . . . . . . . . . . . 57
4. The Effectiveness Regime in ADR/ODR Instruments: *Alassini* . . . . . 59
5. The Extent of Strict Liability in Sales Law: *Weber/Putz* . . . . . . . . . . . . 61
IV. Some General Conclusions . . . . . . . . . . . . . . . . . . . . . . . . . . . . . . . . . . . . . . . . 63
1. Overview of the Case Studies . . . . . . . . . . . . . . . . . . . . . . . . . . . . . . . . . . 63
2. The Importance of Article 47 Charter and Article 19(1) TEU for EU Contract Law Revisited . . . . . . . . . . . . . . . . . . . . . . . . . . . . . . . . 63
3. 'Full' Effectiveness: Too 'Full', Too 'Empty', or 'Just Right'? The Need for a Balancing Approach . . . . . . . . . . . . . . . . . . . . . . . . . . . 64

---

* n.reich1@gmx.net. The paper continues prior reflections which will not be cited individually, namely: *Individueller und kollektiver Rechtsschutz im EU-Verbraucherrecht – Von der 'Nationalisierung' zur 'Konstitutionalisierung' von Rechtsbehelfen*, Schriftenreihe der Juristischen Studiengesellschaft Hannover, vol. 51, 2012; (with H.-W. MICKLITZ, P. ROTT and K. TONNER) *European Consumer Law*, 2nd ed., Intersentia, Antwerp 2014, §8 (Legal Protection of Individual and Collective Consumer Interests); 'Effective Private Law Remedies in Discrimination Cases' in R. SCHULZE (ed.), *Non-discrimination in European Private Law*, Mohr Siebeck, Tübingen 2011, pp. 57–80; 'The Social, Political and Cultural Dimension of EU Private Law' in R. SCHULZE, *European Private Law – Current Status and Perspectives*, Sellier, Munich 2011, pp. 57–88; 'The interrelation between rights and duties in EU Law: Reflections on the state of liability law in the multilevel governance system of the Union – Is there a need for a more coherent approach in European private law?' (2010) *YEL (Oxford Yearbook of European Law)* 112–163. References to other authors are kept at a minimum. I thank Hans Micklitz, EUI-Florence, for valuable critical remarks on an earlier draft. Responsibility as usual lies with the author.

# I. A CONSTITUTIONAL STARTING POINT: ARTICLE 47 OF THE CHARTER

There has been an intense debate on 'constitutionalisation of private law' in general, perhaps less intense with EU private law in particular, and even less with regard to the impact of EU fundamental rights on national contract law. The discussion has mostly been concerned with substantive provisions, e.g. in labour, non-discrimination, services of general economic interest, and consumer law, provided these provisions had a 'horizontal' scope of application, that is are applicable between private parties – employer–employee, trader–consumer, provider–client. Indeed, the Charter of Fundamental Rights in the EU contains many gateways in this direction, e.g. Articles 21/23 on non-discrimination, Article 30 on protection against unjustified dismissal, Article 36 on services in the general economic interest, and Article 38 on consumer protection, but their impact on contractual relations is still unclear, particularly if contrasted with the freedom to conduct a business in Article 16 and the right to property in Article 17 Charter. Despite the UK, Polish and Czech opt-outs, I am sure that this debate will continue in the future and will keep the CJEU and national courts as well as legal writing quite busy. In this wonderful new world of constitutionally guaranteed EU rights and freedoms, another provision of the Charter is easily forgotten, namely Article 47(1), which says in plain language:

> 'Everyone whose rights and freedoms guaranteed by the law of the Union are violated has the right to an effective remedy before a tribunal in compliance with the conditions laid down in this Article.'

It seems that the importance of this article for private law still remains to be discovered, and of the authors who have referred to it I found only Hans Micklitz's brief remark in the conclusion paper of a EUI conference in 2009 that:[1]

> 'Article 47 will have a key role to play. Since 2000 the CJEU has regularly referred to Article 47, often in tandem with Articles 6 and 13 (ECHR), but it seems that *Alassini*[2] was the first occasion where the CJEU was ready to give Article 47 more weight in strengthening the role and function of ADR mechanisms as a means of access to justice.'

---

1 H.-W. Micklitz, 'The CJEU between the Individual Citizen and the Member States – A Plea for a Judge Made European Law on Remedies' in H.-W. Micklitz and B. de Witte (eds.), *The European Court of Justice and the Autonomy of the Member States*, Intersentia, Antwerp 2012, pp. 349, 373.

2 Case C-317/08, *Rosalba Alassini and others v. Telecom Italia* [2010] ECR I-2213.

A monograph by the former Procureur General of the Hoge Raad Arthur Hartkamp[3] concludes:

> 'Even before this provision [Article 47(1)] entered into force, the CJEU gave it a remarkably broad interpretation by invoking the principle to justify the recognition of a substantive right, namely the right of an individual to hold the Union liable on grounds of unjust enrichment.'

Most cases concerning Article 47 centre on more 'classical' questions of effective protection in or by court proceedings, which could also have arisen under Articles 6/13 ECHR, for example *Unibet*[4] on standing in administrative proceedings, *DEB*[5] on legal aid for legal persons, *Kadi*[6] on protection of persons charged with terror activities, and *Mono Car Styling*[7] with regard to workers' right of action to enforce information owed to them in the event of collective redundancy. More recently, in *Kušinová*[8] the Court wrote concerning the interpretation and application of Directive 93/13 to execution proceedings in the consumer's family home: 'Article 47 of the Charter concerns the right to an effective judicial remedy. Those mandatory requirements are applicable to the implementation of Directive 93/13'. In all cases, the reference to Article 47 is surprisingly short and does not go into any detail or does not concern the substance of the case. The opinions of the AGs in the cases mentioned do not seem to be more exhaustive.

A somewhat closer look at the structure and contents of Article 47 (in relation to Article 19(1) sentence 2 of the TEU) may be useful for our purposes. It requires first that a '*right*' exists under Union law. In contract law this is limited to those EU acts which intend to impose *mandatory provisions* in favour of a specific group of persons; if EU law leaves contractual autonomy more or less untouched, Article 47(1) cannot be invoked. This mandatory nature is usually the case in contract law matters concerning non-discrimination and consumer protection to be discussed here, but not limited to them. It will depend on the applicable EU legislation as interpreted by the CJEU. In addition to their mandatory nature, these provisions should take direct effect under general principles of EU law that must be sufficiently precise and unconditional. Their so-called 'horizontal effects' will be discussed later.

---

3 A. Hartkamp, *European Law and National Private Law*, Kluwer Law International, The Hague 2012, para. 110, insisting on the 'gap-filling function' of the effectiveness principle as codified in article 47 and referring to case C-47/70 P, *Masdar v. EU Commission* [2008] ECR I-9761, para. 50 which finds the claim for unjust enrichment of a private person against the Commission to be based on Article 47.

4 Case C-432/05, *Unibet v. Justiekanslern* [2007] ECR I-2271.

5 Case C-279/09, *DEB Deutsche Energiehandels- und Beratungsgesellschaft mbH v. Bundesrepublik Deutschland* [2010] ECR I-13849.

6 Case C-402/05 and 415/05 P, *Kadi and others v. Council of the EU* [2008] ECR I-6351.

7 Case C-12/08, *Mono Car Styling SA, in liquidation v. Dervis Odemis and others* [2009] ECR I-6653, para. 47.

8 Case C-34/13, *Kušinova v. SMART cap.*, judgment of 10 September 2014, para. 47.

This right must be 'ensured' by an *effective remedy*. In my understanding, the English term is somewhat broader that the German translation '*wirksamer Rechtsbehelf*' and the French term '*recours effectif*'; while the German and French terminology seems to be restricted to access and management of genuine court proceedings, the English term also includes remedies of a pre-trial nature, in particular those related to contract law matters before a case being taken to court. In a purpose-oriented interpretation of EU law as required by Article 52 Charter, I prefer the broad English concept of remedy instead of the narrow German and French understanding. Indeed, there could and would be no effective 'judicial protection' without the prior grant of remedies in the area of private law rights.

These remedies may relate both to substance and/or to procedures: *Substantive remedies* include compensation, restitution, and preclusion of the application of a non-conforming national rule. *Procedural remedies* relate to issues of standing, injunctions, time-limits and evidence rules.[9] However it should be kept in mind that it will not always be easy to differentiate precisely between substantive and procedural remedies, and this is related very much to applicable national law. Obviously they depend on the legislative EU act in question. These remedies must in the end be able to be enforced before a tribunal; but this does not exclude alternative dispute resolution mechanisms (ADR) if they do not preclude access to courts, as the Court states in *Alassini*. The concept of *effectiveness* will be discussed in the next section.

Article 19(1) sentence 2 TEU puts the responsibility for 'providing remedies sufficient to ensure effective legal protection in the fields covered by Union law' on Member States through the status of their courts of law as 'Union courts'. With regard to contract law matters, the general principles limiting the 'horizontal direct effect' of EU law, in particular directives, should be respected. Without going into detail, the most important effect of EU law on national law will be the principle of *consistent interpretation*. In the *DRK* case[10] the Court insisted

> 'that, if the application of interpretative methods recognised by national law enables, in certain circumstances, a provision of domestic law to be construed in such a way as to avoid conflict with another rule of domestic law or the scope of that provision to be restricted to that end by applying it only in so far as it is compatible with the rule concerned, the national court is bound to use those methods in order to achieve the result sought by the directive. In such circumstances, the national court must, when applying the provisions of national law specifically intended to implement the directive, interpret those provisions so far as possible in such a way that they are applied in conformity with the objectives of the directive'.

9 See the seminal paper by W. van Gerven, 'Of Rights, Remedies, and Procedures' (2000) *CMLRev (Common Market Law Review)* 501 with examples on p. 522.

10 Case C-397/01, *Bernhard Pfeifer and others v. Deutsches Rotes Kreuz* [2004] ECR I-8835, paras. 117–118.

These principles have been restated in *Adeneler*.[11] It insisted on the principle of consistent interpretation:

> '[W]here a directive is transposed belatedly, the general obligation owed by national courts to interpret domestic law in conformity with the directive exists only once the period for its transposition has expired'.

However, courts must abstain from taking any measures liable seriously to compromise the attainment of the results prescribed by the directive from the very day it enters into force, whether or not already implemented.[12] The Court also made clear that this obligation 'is limited by general principles of law, particularly those of legal certainty and non-retroactivity, and that obligation cannot serve as the basis for an interpretation of national law *contra legem*'.[13]

The principle of EU law conforming (consistent) interpretation is therefore to be understood as an obligation of the national judge to use the full range of interpretation possibilities – including those of a teleological restriction as in the case at hand – to make sure that national law conforms to EU directives with direct effect, even if this amounts to imposing a burden on a private party. Therefore, the original distinction between denying horizontal effect of directives and imposing an EU-conforming interpretation of national law loses much of its importance, at least in relationships governed by civil and commercial law.

To summarise the approach chosen by the Court, EU law conforming interpretation has been widely accepted in order to ensure the supremacy of Union law without attaining full uniformity.[14] It allows the development of EU-specific rights, which must be protected under the effectiveness criteria of Article 47 Charter to be discussed below.

## II. EFFECTIVENESS VERSUS PROCEDURAL AUTONOMY

The principle of effectiveness as provided in Article 47 Charter and Article 19(1) TEU is seemingly an old acquaintance of EU law. It was, as is well known, first developed in the *Comet/Rewe* cases dating from 1976 and basically requires that national remedies and procedural rules must not render the exercise of Union

11 Case C-212/04, *K. Adeneler and others v. ELG* [2006] ECR I-6057, para. 115.

12 Ibid., para. 121.

13 Ibid., para. 110.

14 For German constitutional law, see the decision of the BVerfG (2. Kammer des 2. Senats) of 26.09.2011, (2012) *EuZW (Europäische Zeitschrift für Wirtschaftsrecht)* 197, insisting on the methodological limits under national law which allow also a 'teleological restriction' of existing provisions.

rights *practically impossible*[15] or – as was later added[16] – *excessively difficult*. Parallel to this, the CJEU developed the principle of '*equivalence*' based on non-discrimination considerations: rights under EU law should not be treated less favourably than those similar to domestic actions.[17] However, these principles only allow a 'minimum', not an adequate, protection, as AG van Gerven had observed;[18] they have a mostly 'negative content', as the intense case law shows. They eliminate restrictions *to* protection, but do not create remedies *for* protection.

The explanation for this limited effect of the effectiveness principle – in contrast to what the wording seems to suggest – is the so-called 'procedural autonomy' of Member States. Its standard formula reads:

> '[I]n the absence of Community rules on this subject, it is for the domestic legal system of each Member State to designate the courts having jurisdiction and to determine the procedural conditions governing actions at law intended to ensure the protection of the rights which citizens have from the direct effect of Community law'.[19]

Later litigation has tried to clarify the scope and limits of the principle of procedural autonomy, which has remained a controversial principle in doctrine in its balancing with the seemingly opposing principles of 'effectiveness' and 'equivalence'. Some authors criticise the Court – in contrast to US federal doctrine – for not respecting the constitutional demarcation of the enforcement of EU law, which is exclusively a matter of Member States, unless the EU has acquired specific competence. In this spirit, the Swedish author Lindholm writes:[20]

> '[I]t appears better to, as is done under the American doctrine, approach the issue of what procedural rules state courts shall apply to Community rights as a constitutional issue focusing on the proper division of powers between union and states.'[21]

---

15 Case 33/76, *Rewe Central Finanz* [1976] ECR 1989, para. 5; case 45/76, *Comet* [1976] ECR 2043, paras. 13–16.

16 Case 199/82, *San Georgio* [1983] ECR 3595, para. 14.

17 Case law on defining equivalence in practice has been quite complex and cannot be adequately discussed here; the Court prefers a broad teleological, not a narrow formal approach, see T. Tridimas, *General Principles of EU Law*, 2$^{nd}$ ed., Oxford University Press, Oxford 2006, p. 418.

18 See n. 9 above, pp. 504/529.

19 See the above mentioned *Rewe Central Finanz* and *Comet* cases, n. 15 above.

20 J. Lindholm, *State Procedure and Unions Rights*, J. Foerlag, Umaea 2007.

21 J. Lindholm, n. 20 above, p. 256.

However, the author does not correctly understand the different starting points of the American and the European doctrines:[22] while in the US there exists a system of clearly separated jurisdictions on a state and a federal level with their own procedures, in the EU there has never been such a separation because the jurisdiction of EU courts is very limited; Member State courts had to take on most of the load of enforcing EU law, and this enforcement should not be frustrated by unjustified restrictions against which the CJEU developed its theories of 'effectiveness' and 'equivalence', at first mostly in administrative matters, but also later in civil law proceedings.

On the other hand, some authors criticise or even deny the existence of such a principle of 'procedural autonomy' or find a more or less contradictory or sometimes only symbolic application by the Court.[23] In my opinion, it seems that this controversy is to some extent rendered superfluous by a closer look at the more recent case law of the CJEU.

There are many cases where the Court went beyond the merely negative approach of the classical *Rewe/Comet* formula and developed a positive *effet utile* or 'full effectiveness' test requiring Member State courts to create or improve remedies of their own, of which I will give some examples later. I have called this a *hybridisation approach* which tries to combine Member State autonomy – whether remedial or procedural[24] – with the imperatives of enforcement of EU granted rights.[25] In short it requires a three-step test:

- the first step is concerned with finding appropriate national remedies in case of violations of rights granted by the EU (whether primary or secondary law); therefore, the applicable Member State law has to be clarified, in the end by the competent national court of law;
- second, this 'national remedy' has to be measured:
  - against the yardstick of the 'negative' EU principles of effectiveness and equivalence; and

22 See my critique: N. Reich, 'Federalism and Effective Legal Protection' in A. Colombi Ciacchi et al. (eds), *Liability in the Third Millennium. Liber Amicorum Gert Brüggemeier*, Nomos, Baden-Baden 2009, p. 381.

23 A. Adinolphi, 'The "Procedural Autonomy" of Member States and the Constraints Stemming from the ECJ's Case Law: Is Judicial Activism Still Necessary' in H.-W. Micklitz and B. de Witte, n. 1 above, pp. 281; M. Bobek, 'Why there is No Principle of "Procedural Autonomy" of the Member States' in H.-W. Micklitz and B. de Witte, n. 1 above, pp. 305; D.-U. Galetta, *Procedural Autonomy of EU Member States: Paradise Lost?*, Springer, Heidelberg 2011, p. 34 referring to the principle of consistent interpretation as a limitation of procedural autonomy, in particular in sex discrimination cases, p. 41.

24 See V. Trstenjak and E. Beysen, 'European Consumer Protection Law: *Curia semper dabit remedium?*' (2011) *CMLRev* 95, 109.

25 N. Reich, '"Horizontal liability" in EC Law – "Hybridisation" of remedies for compensation in case of breaches of EC rights' (2007) *CMLRev* 705.

  - if the result is unsatisfactory from an EU law point of view as interpreted by the *effet utile* principle of the CJEU, it has to be 'upgraded' to meet EU standards;
- this remedy thus found is a 'hybrid' insofar as it takes up elements of national law in the limits of the principle of procedural autonomy, as well as effectiveness both in a negative and in a positive sense. It should be '*sufficient*' to ensure effective protection in the words of Article 19(1)(2) TEU, that is to meet the 'adequacy' standard by AG van Gerven.[26]

The circular relationship between

- remedies under national law ('procedural autonomy');
- the effectiveness principle (Article 47 Charter); and
- their 'upgrading' via the principle of consistent interpretation to 'hybrids' (Article 19(1) TEU) can be demonstrated in the following way:

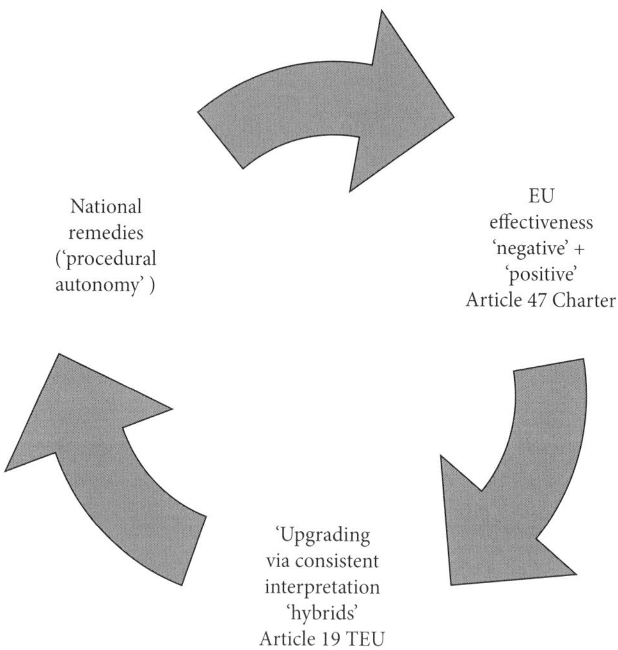


[26] W. van Gerven, n. 9 above, p. 529.

# III. SOME EXAMPLES APPLYING THE EFFECTIVENESS TEST IN MANDATORY EU CONTRACT LAW

## 1. THE CLASSICAL CASE: *VON COLSON AND KAMANN*

*Von Colson*[27] concerned the refusal to employ a woman as a warden in a male prison. This was clearly regarded as a discrimination based on the sex of the candidate which could not be justified under the restrictive regime of justifications of the then applicable Directive 76/206/EEC, now Directive 2006/54/EC.[28] Whether this refusal could be qualified as a contract or a tort case depends on the national law and is not a matter for the CJEU to decide. Under German law, this case came under the principle of *culpa in contrahendo* as a matter of (pre-)contractual liability[29] allowing only compensation of the so-called 'negative interest', that is the damage which would not have occurred had the defendant acted legally. In the specific situation this would have to be limited to the costs of making the (unsuccessful) application, e.g. costs for mailing, transportation for an interview and the like, but not to the 'positive interest' under a contract.

This rather trifling amount of compensation did not suffice in the eyes of the Court, which insisted on the principle of effectiveness in a positive sense regarding the provision of a remedy:[30]

> '[Compensation must] be such as to guarantee real and effective judicial protection, [...] have a real deterrent effect on the employer [and] must in any event be adequate in relation to the damages sustained [...] purely nominal [compensation] e.g. the reimbursement of expenses incurred by them [the candidates] in submitting their application, would not satisfy the requirement of an effective transposition of the directive.'

In this still very important judgment, the Court rejected a merely symbolic compensation as incompatible with the principle of effectiveness in a positive sense, including also the scope of the remedy under contact law (or pre-contractual obligations as under German *culpa* principles). It is not quite clear on what legal principle the Court based its principle of full compensation since the Directive was silent on this point, especially as the Court held at the same time

27 Case 14/83, *Von Colson and Kamann v. Land Nordrhein-Westfalen* [1984] ECR 1891.

28 Recast Directive 2006/54/EC of the EP and the Council of 5 July 2006 on the implementation of the principle of equal opportunities and equal treatment of men and women in matters of employment [2006] *OJ* L204/23.

29 This is different now under the EU conflict law regimes of Article 1(2)(i) of Regulation 593/5008 (Rome I) and Article 12 of Regulation 864/2007 (Rome II).

30 *Von Colson and Kamann v. Land Nordrhein-Westfalen*, n. 27 above, paras. 23–24.

that Mrs von Colson did not have the right to a contract. In this light it would be difficult to explain the claimant's right to full compensation on the basis of a traditional contract theory. In my opinion, the damage which the Court strove to remedy by its ruling was primarily 'moral'. This raises the question of whether EU law should require non-material damages to be awarded more generally for breaches of EU gender-based discrimination prohibitions which I think would be justified, provided a certain threshold of injury is met.[31] The overall context of this case law on compensation as inaugurated by *Von Colson*, even though not phrased in these terms, certainly has a constitutional dimension, which is now well settled under Article 47 as mentioned, in connection with the prohibition on gender-based discrimination in Article 23 of the Charter.

German courts and doctrine after *Von Colson* were at pains to find an adequate remedy under the 'upgraded' law of compensation, which at this time took a very restrictive approach towards compensation of 'non-material harm' (*Schmerzensgeld*). In the end, the legislator had to intervene by developing a system of lump-sum payments not exceeding three months' earnings based on a hypothetical contract of employment entered into, even though this caused some problems in the in cases of multiple complainants where a cap on compensation of six months' salary was imposed by law. This regulation was put before the Court in the later *Draehmpaehl* case[32] where the plaintiff had applied for a job despite the advertisement excluding male candidates; in a parallel case another male candidate had applied for the same job. But what was the damage Mr Draehmpaehl suffered as a result of the discriminatory job advertisement for which he applied without a chance of being seriously considered for selection? The reasoning of the CJEU offers an inherent contradiction:[33]

> 'It is indisputable that such applicants, not having suffered any damage through exclusion from the recruitment procedure, cannot claim that the extent of the damage they have sustained is the same as that sustained by applicants who would have obtained the position if there had been no discrimination in the selection process.'

Indeed, Mr Draehmpaehl did not suffer any damage, because he would not have qualified for the job and probably would not have taken it even if selected, as was clear from the facts; the litigation was more or less a test case to put the German anti-discrimination rules on trial. So why should Mr Draehmpaehl get any compensation? What was his loss caused by the discriminatory advertisement? Should he be compensated in full at all, despite the upper limit in legislation?

---

31 The Court recognises this with regard to compensation for 'lost holiday' in package tours, see case C-168/00, *Simone Leitner v. TUI Deutschland* [2002] ECR I-2631; there is no reason to treat discrimination cases less stringently.

32 Case C-180/95, *Draehmpaehl v. Urania Immobilienservice OHG* [1997] ECR I-2195.

33 Ibid., para 33.

The CJEU to some extent took account of this situation in allowing a limitation of compensation:[34]

> '[The directive] does not preclude provisions of domestic law which prescribe an upper limit of three months' salary for the compensation which may be claimed by an applicant where the employer can prove that, because the applicant engaged had superior qualification, the unsuccessful applicant would not have obtained that vacant position, even if there had been no discrimination in the selection process. In contrast, the directive precludes provisions of domestic law which, unlike other provisions of domestic civil and labour law, prescribe an upper limit of three months' salary for the amount of compensation which may be claimed by an applicant discriminated against on grounds of sex in the making of an appointment where that applicant would have obtained the vacant position if the selection process had been carried out without discrimination.'

This seems to be a compromise solution between, on the one hand, using compensation as a remedy for breaches of the non-discrimination obligation and, on the other, limiting it in cases where no real damage has been caused.[35] But in my opinion this is a 'bad compromise' where the individual claiming compensation has suffered no damage – he or she should not be entitled to any compensation; a cap on compensation can only be applied where there is actually a duty to compensate. With regard to multiple claimants, the Court was quite hostile to the six-month cap imposed by law on the aggregate amount of compensation.

Even if the *Draehmpaehl* case is understood by the Court (and AG Léger) as a logical consequence of *Von Colson*, there seem to be inherent misunderstandings of the non-discrimination law in granting compensation to Mr Draehmpaehl, who had suffered no damage. In my opinion the objective of EU non-discrimination law is to sanction effectively a discriminatory treatment in cases such as that suffered by Mrs von Colson in not being able to get a job as an officer in a male prison, Mrs Kreil[36] in not being admitted to professional training in the German *Bundeswehr* despite her qualifications, Mrs Dekker in being excluded from taking a job at a child centre because of her pregnancy, which obviously can only affect women,[37] or Mrs Coote for not receiving a reference letter for a new job after termination of her former employment contract.[38] These women have all been victims of a 'sufficiently serious breach'

34 Ibid., para 37.

35 U. Magnus and W. Wurmnest, *Casebook Europäisches Haftungs- und Schadensrecht*, Nomos, Baden-Baden 2002, p. 101.

36 Case C-285/98, *Tanja Kreil v. Germany* [2000] ECR I-7403.

37 Case 177/88, *Dekker v. Stichting Vormingscentrum voor Jong Volwassenen (VJV-Centrum) Plus* [1990] ECR I-3941.

38 Case C-185/97, *Coote v. Granada Hospitality* [1998] ECR I-5199; for a discussion of the issues see H.-W. Micklitz, *The Politics of Judicial Co-operation*, Cambridge University Press, Cambridge 2005, pp. 210–213, 269–270.

of the non-discrimination obligation by their potential or former employer, and therefore should be compensated for their injuries, even though they may only concern moral prejudice. This is not the case with Mr Draehmpaehl (and other claimants), who had not sustained any (real or moral) damage by the (admittedly discriminatory) job advertisement.

It arises from this discussion that 'effective remedy' does not mean compensation for anybody who free rides on an injury!

## 2. AN OPEN CONSTITUTIONAL DIMENSION: *KÜCÜKDEVICI*

The question of an effective remedy in discrimination matters clearly came up in the *Kücükdevici* case[39] but not so much regarding compensation or restitution, but as precluding the application of a provision in national contract law shortening the notice periods for young employees which violated the Framework Directive 2000/78/EC[40] forbidding age discrimination. The problem with this remedy was that it stood in contrast to well-established principles that do not allow horizontal direct effect of directives. In the prior *Mangold* case[41] the CJEU had seemingly allowed such an effect based on an alleged 'general principle of age discrimination', but the reasoning remained shaky and controversial.

The question concerned the dismissal periods in a contract for employment, which would increase with age, but beginning only after having reached the age of 25 years. The CJEU, in its judgment of 19 January 2010 – referring to Article 21 (but not Article 47) of the Charter[42] under the principle of '*full effectiveness*', required the national court to disapply the discriminatory provision without the necessity to first refer the case to the Court.[43] The *Bundesarbeitsgericht* (the Federal Labour Court) followed suit and in the judgment of 9 September 2010 simply set aside the contested German provision (§622 (2) para. 2 BGB) which discriminated against young employees with regard to the notice period

39 Case C-555/07, *Seda Kücükdevici v. Swedex GmbH* [2010] ECR I-365, recently confirmed by case C-447/09, *R. Prigge and others v. Lufthansa* [2011] ECR I-8003, para. 38; the broad approach of the Court has been criticised M. Dougan, 'In Defence of *Mangold*?' in A. Arnull et al., *A Constitutional Order of States – Essays in Honour of Alan Dashwood*, Hart, Oxford 2011, pp. 219 et seq.

40 Council Directive 2000/78/EC of 27 November 2000 establishing a general framework for equal treatment in employment and occupation [2000] *OJ* L303/16.

41 Case C-144/04, *Werner Mangold v. Rüdiger Helm* [2005] ECR I-9981; confirmed for German law by the German Constitutional Court, BVerfGE 126, 286 with dissenting opinion by Judge Landau referring to the Lisbon judgment and criticising the *Mangold* judgment of the ECJ, pp. 318, 324. For an assessment of the cooperation between the CJEU and the BVerfG see the paper by H. Sauer, 'Europas Richter Hand in Hand?' (2011) *EuZW* 94.

42 *Werner Mangold v. Rüdiger Helm*, n. 41 above, para. 22.

43 Ibid., para. 54.

for termination of employment by excluding from calculation the employment period accrued before the age of 25.[44] In its stead the court used the general rule contained in §622 (2) para. 1 BGB on the calculation of the length of employment.

## 3. EFFECTIVE PROTECTION AGAINST UNFAIR TERMS IN CONSUMER CONTRACTS: *INVITEL*

The Unfair Terms Directive 93/13/EEC[45] has led to a number of spectacular judgments of the CJEU insisting on the principle of effective protection justified by the unequal bargaining power of the parties, lately highlighted by the recent *Invitel* judgment.[46] This concerns the requirement imposed on national courts to apply *ex officio* certain protective provisions, in particular Article 6. The case law started with *Océano* concerning jurisdiction clauses,[47] was continued in *Claro*[48] and *Asturcom*[49] with arbitration clauses in consumer contracts, and was confirmed and refined in *Pannon:*[50]

> 'The Court is therefore required to ensure the effectiveness of the protection intended to be given by the provisions of the Directive. Consequently, the role thus attributed to the national court by Community law in this area is not limited to a mere power to rule on the possible unfairness of a contractual term, but also consists of the obligation to examine that issue of its own motion, where it has available to it the legal and factual elements necessary for that task, including when it is assessing whether it has territorial jurisdiction.'

---

44 BAG, 2 AZR 714/08, (2011) *ZIP (Zeitschrift für Wirtschaftsrecht)* 444.

45 Council Directive 93/13/EEC of 5 April 1993 on unfair terms in consumer contracts [1993] *OJ* L95/29.

46 Case C-472/10, *Nemzeti Fogyaszróvédelni Hatóság v. Invitel*, judgment of 26.04.2012; the prior opinion AG Trstenjak of 06.12.2011 has been commented by H.-W. Micklitz and N. Reich (2012) *EuZW* 126, the judgment itself by H.-W. Micklitz and N. Reich, 'AGB-Recht und UWG – (endlich) ein Ende des Kästchendenkens nach Pernicova und Invitel' (2012) *EWS (Europäisches Wirtschafts- und Steuerrecht)* 257.

47 Joined cases C-240–244/98, *Océano Grupo ed. v. Quintero and others* [2000] ECR I-4941.

48 Case C-168/05, *E.M.M. Claro v. Centro Movil Milenium* [2006] ECR I-10421.

49 Case C-40/08, *Asturcom v. Christina Rodrigues Nogueria* [2009] ECR I-9579; comment H. Schebasta, 'Does the National Court Know European Law' in H.-W. Micklitz and N. Reich (eds.), *The Impact of the Internal Market on the Private Law of Member Countries*, EUI Working Papers 2009/22, at 47 = (2010) *ERPrL (European Review of Private Law)* 847, insisting that in *Asturcom* which concerned a consumer who 'in total inertia' did not raise any defences against an arbitration proceedings, including the *res iudicata* of the final award against her (para. 34), the CJEU did not apply the effectiveness, but the less stringent equivalence test.

50 Case C-243/08, *Pannon v. Erzsébet Sustikné Győrfi* [2009] ECR I-4713; see also case C-137/08, *VB Penzügyi Lizing v. Ferenc Schneider* [2010] ECR I-10847, para. 106.

The problem with this approach is the apparent conflict with the principle of procedural autonomy of Member States, as established by the *van Schinjdel* case[51] which is usually cited as the clearest recognition of this principle in civil proceedings depending on the initiative of the parties. But it is often overlooked that the Court made an express exception for a court intervention on its own motion based on a *public interest* test. A joint paper by AG Trstenjak and Beysen[52] justified this case law as follows:

> '[A] less stringent application of the concept of procedural autonomy of the Member States can be observed in the case law of the CJEU with regard to the enforcement of consumer rights under the different consumer protection directives.'

The case to be discussed here concerns the effects of an action for an injunction by the Hungarian consumer protection office against the fixed-line telephone network *Invitel* whose general business conditions (GBC) introduced clauses on fees for money order (and additional postal fees) without specifying the calculation of these fees, and were thus charged as being unfair under Article 3 and the (indicative) Annex of the Unfair Terms Directive. Two questions were submitted to the Court, one concerning the fairness of these clauses which will not be discussed in this context, the other more interesting here on the effects of a successful injunction on individual consumer contracts.

Under German law, this problem is seemingly 'solved' by the so-called '*Einredelösung*' of §11 of the Act on Injunctions (*Unterlassungsklagengesetz*): once the judgment prohibiting the use of such a clause has attained force of *res judicata*, the consumer can object to its further use, but only with effects for the future and only with regard to the specific defendant, not with regard to other businesses even if they using the same incriminated clause.[53] In practice this solution has played no role and has not been an effective remedy for the individual consumer who has been the object of an incriminated clause.

*Invitel* offers a much more far-reaching solution under an implicit principle of 'positive effectiveness' of this problem which means that German law will have to be changed: the Court first insists on 'the deterrent nature and dissuasive purpose of the measures to be adopted' under Article 7(2) of the Unfair Terms Directive.[54] It then goes on to say:[55]

---

51 Joined cases C-430–432/93, *Van Schijndel and Van Veen v. Stichting Pensioenfonds* [1995] ECR I-4705, para. 21.

52 V. Trstenjak and E. Beysen, n. 24 above, p. 119.

53 Critique H.-W. Micklitz and N. Reich (2012) *EuZW*, n. 46 above, p. 128 with further references.

54 Case C-472/10, *Nemzeti Fogyaszróvédelni Hatóság v. Invitel*, judgment of 26.04.2012, para. 37

55 Ibid., para 43.

'[W]here the unfair nature of the term included in the GBC of consumer contracts has been recognised in an action for an injunction [...] the national courts are required, of their own motion, and also as regards to the future, to draw all the consequences provided for by national law in order to ensure that consumer who have concluded a contract to which those GBC apply will not be bound by that term'.

It is clear that these consequences must be attached to national law, as suggested in the *hybridisation approach*, but they must take two directions:

- one concerning the individual contract in which the incriminated clause is 'not binding on the consumer' according to Article 6, which as a consequence means that money paid under the unfair clause must be returned to the consumer under the national doctrines of unjust enrichment or restitution; and
- the second concerning future effects of the unfair terms whose continued use must be prohibited under Article 7(1).

National – in my understanding German – law has to be upgraded accordingly. The so-called *Einredelösung* will have to be substituted by the invalidation of the clause (*Unwirksamkeitslösung*) to be applied *ex officio* by the competent national court and not depending on a motion of the consumer.

## 4. THE EFFECTIVENESS REGIME IN ADR/ODR INSTRUMENTS: *ALASSINI*

Before discussing the issue of effective remedies in ADR mechanisms, it is useful to remember the facts of the *Alassini* case:[56] the applicant in the case that lead to a preliminary ruling before the European Court of Justice was Rosalba Alassini, while the defendant was Telecom Italia SpA. The applicant, as a consumer, had a dispute with her telecoms services provider. She asked for compensation for damages suffered as a consequence of the breach of contract and also for a declaration of the fact that she would not have to pay the sum of money claimed by Telecom Italia SpA. Italian legislation imposes an obligation on consumers to carry out out-of-court dispute resolution (before www.co.re.com or another body) before starting a court proceeding, based on Article 34 of the Universal Services Directive 2002/22/EC.[57] Co.re.com had not yet been set up in the region of Campania (where the applicant comes from), and for this reason, the applicant considered that her right to effective judicial protection had been violated. The defendant argued, based on Articles 3 and

[56] Case C-317/08, *Rosalba Alassini and others v. Telecom Italia* [2010] ECR I-2213.

[57] Directive 2002/22/EC of 7 March 2002 of the EP and of the Council on Universal Services in Electronic Communications [ 2002] *OJ* L108/51.

13 of the Italian Dispute Settlement Rules that the fact that co.re.com was not yet established in that region did not violate the applicant's rights. As provided in Article 13 of the Dispute Settlement Rules, she should have tried to start the obligatory out-of-court dispute resolution before the other bodies mentioned in the said article.

The judgment of the Court did not go into the details of the (doubtful!) effectiveness of the Italian procedures, which indeed seem to be quite insufficient. Instead, it established some general rules on ADR/ODR proceedings in contract-related matters, based on Recommendation 98/257/EC[58] containing the seven principles of independence and transparency of ADR mechanisms, an adversarial system, efficiency, legality, freedom of access and freedom of representation. The Court first insisted that, even though recommendations are not formally binding (Article 288(3) TFEU), they still have an importance for applying and interpreting national law based on them,[59] for example in the Italian ODR regulations implementing Article 34 of Direction 2002/22/EC. The Court established some general principles on the establishment and use of ADR proceedings, thereby expressly referring to Article 47 Charter.[60] It also stated the advantages and criteria for these proceedings:[61]

- the result is not binding: the consumer can bring later legal proceedings;
- it does not result in a substantial delay, for the completion is 30 days from the date of the request; if the procedure is not finished after these 30 days, the parties can go to court;
- there is interruption of the prescription of rights during this process;
- before co.re.com there are no fees, and before the other organisations it has not been said that they entail significant costs.

The judgment seems to have set up general principles for ADR/ODR proceedings under the imperative EU law having been taken up in several recent (vertical and sectoral) directives.[62] The Commission's proposal of 20 November 2011 on ADR/ODR instruments – now Directive 2013/11/EC and Regulation (EU) No.

58 Commission Recommendation 98/257/EC of 30 March 1998 on the principles applicable to the bodies responsible for out-of-court settlement of consumer disputes [1998] *OJ* L115/31; Directive 2013/11/EU of the European Parliament and the Council of 21 May 2013 on consumer ADR [2013] *OJ* L165/13; Regulation (EU) No. 524/2013 of the European Parliament and of the Council of 21 May 2013 on Consumer ADR [2013] *OJ* L165/1.

59 See case C-322/88, *Grimaldi (Salvatore) v. Fonds des maladies professionnelles* [1989] ECR 4407.

60 Case C-317/08, *Rosalba Alassini and others v. Telecom Italia* [2010] ECR I-2213, para. 61.

61 Ibid., paras. 54–57.

62 For a discussion see H.-W. Micklitz, 'Brauchen Unternehmen und Verbraucher eine neue Architektur des Verbraucherrechts?' in *Gutachten zum 69. Deutschen Juristentag*, C.H. Beck, Munich 2012, p. 13 insisting that *Alassini* has given a more or less formal recognition to the ADR principles of Recommendation 98/207.

524/2013[63] – aims to establish a horizontal regime which is uniformly applicable all over the EU.

## 5. THE EXTENT OF STRICT LIABILITY IN SALES LAW: *WEBER/PUTZ*

The facts of the litigation in the *Weber*[64] and *Putz*[65] cases decided by the CJEU on 16 June 2011 against the critical opinion of AG Mazak of 18 May 2010 are probably well known and need not be discussed in detail here. These case are a good and at the same time controversial example of the impact of EU law on traditional concepts on remedies in sales law beyond the wording of Directive 99/44/EC. They concern reimbursement of additional costs by the consumer for replacing the defective product and installing a conforming one, e.g. by tearing off and replacing the defective tiles which had been used for floor panelling, or by disconnecting and reconnecting the dishwasher which did not function. The AG rejected this claim under EU law, but the CJEU upheld it as a causal consequence of the seller's obligation to deliver a conforming good. The reasoning of the Court is surprisingly short and based on the rather unspecific provisions in the Directive that repair and replacement should be done within 'a reasonable time', 'free of charge' and 'without significant inconvenience to the consumer', even if the contract did not include installation. This creates a *strict liability regime* of the seller not only for the act of replacing the non-conforming good as such, but also for the emerging follow-up costs even after the transfer of the risk. In order to avoid overcharging the seller, the Court referred to the option for an action on recourse against the previous seller/producer according to Article 4 Directive 99/44/EC.[66] The Court was also asked whether Article 3(3) Directive 99/44/EC was to be read as an 'absolute' or a 'relative' defence of the impossibility of the seller to repair or replace the non-conforming good. The 'dominant opinion' (*herrschende Meinung*) of German law at the time under the implementing provision of §439 BGB understood as an 'absolute proportionality test': if one of the remedies was impossible and the other disproportionate regarding costs, this had the consequence of a total loss of first-stage remedies under sales law. The Court however opted for a 'relative proportionality defence' as corroborated by recital 11: even if one remedy (repair) would be impossible and the other (replacement) result in disproportionate costs for the seller, the consumer would not be at a complete loss of his first-stage remedies; disproportionate costs of replacement (including cost for disconnecting and reconnecting) would only allow the seller to reduce

63 COM(2011) 793 and 794 for Proposals of the EP and the Council on a Directive on consumer ADR and a Regulation on consumer ODR.
64 Case C-65/09, [2011] ECR I-5257.
65 Case C-87/09, [2011] ECR I-5257.
66 Ibid., para. 48.

them 'to an account proportionate to the value the goods would have if there were no lack of conformity and the significance of the lack of conformity'.[67]

The German Federal Court (BGH), in its judgment of 21 December 2011,[68] followed suit under the principle of consistent interpretation, and extended the scope of replacement beyond mere disconnection to reconnection, which had thus far been rejected by its earlier case law. It also followed suit concerning the 'relative proportionality test' under Article 3(3) Directive 44/99/EC, and interpreted §439 BGB restrictively using the method of 'teleological reduction' of German law which it had already applied in its follow-up judgment to *Quelle*.[69] It discussed in detail the different proposals in legal writing for how to implement the proportionality criteria; it found an amount of €600 to be reimbursed to the consumer to be adequate for the value of conforming tiles (€1,200) and the importance of their non-conformity.

I will not discuss the *efficiency* problems of the judgment, particularly concerning its possible negative effects on distance selling. Interestingly, Grundmann,[70] who sides more with the critical economic analysis of EU consumer law being sceptical with mandatory provisions, hails the outcome of the *Weber/Putz* case as the 'recognition of a strict liability system in a chain of contracting conceiving contracts not in isolation but embedded in markets.'

In this context, I am more concerned with the *effectiveness* argument with reference to the consumer protection objective of the Directive, given a broad reach by the Court, but at the same time reduced by a balancing element taking into account the economic situation of the seller, or rather of the specific transaction. Under the 'relative proportionality test', the Court avoids the complete loss of the consumer's first-stage remedies, which would have been the consequence of the 'absolute test', thereby seriously undermining the principle of effective consumer protection under Article 47 Charter read together with Directive 99/44/EC. Under these criteria, the judgment certainly has a certain deterrent effect on the sale of non-conforming goods, especially when they need to be installed, like a dishwasher, or put into place, like the tiles. At the same time, the CJEU used a proportionality argument based on a 'fair balancing' (para. 75) principle that the consumer has to bear some of the risks of this transaction. Such balancing is also possible under a strict liability regime for compensation of costs caused as result of the delivery of a non-conforming good. Thus, the effectiveness argument leads to *specific risk-sharing and risk-distribution* between the seller and the consumer, protecting at the same time the consumer's rights under Directive 99/44/EC without excessively increasing the seller's risks. Effectiveness of consumer protection does not mean that the consumer's transaction is completely risk free – but he should at least not carry all its risks.

---

67 Ibid., para. 74.

68 BGH, VIII ZR 70/08, (2012) *NJW (Neue Juristische Wochenschrift)* 1073 – *Putz/Weber II*.

69 BGH VIII ZR 2008/05, judgment of 26 November 2008, (2009) *NJW* 427 – *Quelle*.

70 S. Grundmann, 'Consumer Sales', in: E. Terryn et al., *Liber amicorum J. Stuyck*, Intersentia, Cambridge 2013, p. 742.

# IV. SOME GENERAL CONCLUSIONS

## 1. OVERVIEW OF THE CASE STUDIES

| CJEU case 'upgrade' | EU rights | National remedies | National procedures | EU 'upgrade' |
|---|---|---|---|---|
| *Von Colson* | No gender-based discrimination – Directive 2007/76 | *Culpa in contrahendo* – token compensation | | Adequate compensation, deterrent effect |
| *Kücükdevici* | No age-based discrimination – Directive 2000/78 | No special dismissal protection for young employees | | Preclusionary effect of Directive 2000/78 read together with Article 21 Charter |
| *Invitel* | No unfair terms – Directive 93/13 | | 'Abstract' injunction of consumer office | Spill-over effect on individual consumer contract |
| *Alassini* | Access to (courts of) law – Recommendation 98/2007 | | Mandatory ODR; procedural principles unclear | Upgrading of recommendation – four ODR (Article 47) principles: not binding, no substantial delay, no prescription, no significant costs |
| *Weber/Putz* | Conformity of product and installation – Directive 1999/44 | Replacement only; earlier BGH case law: only disconnection – §439 BGB: absolute proportionality: if one remedy is disproportionate the other also fails | | Strict liability for disconnecting and reconnecting – 'relative proportionality test' – limited to either repair or replacement – proportionate reduction of recoverable costs |

## 2. THE IMPORTANCE OF ARTICLE 47 CHARTER AND ARTICLE 19(1) TEU FOR EU CONTRACT LAW REVISITED

The case studies should have given an impression of the complex interpretation and balancing problems behind the effectiveness requirement in EU contract law. Even though the Court refers to Article 47 Charter only in the *Alassini* case (lately in *Košenová* without any impact on the judgment), I suggest that the principles on which it is based form the 'hidden agenda' of the Court ever since *Von Colson*. An express reference to Article 47 Charter and Article 19(1) TEU does not attach anything new to the principle of effectiveness, but only makes it conform to the more recent constitutionalisation of EU private law. Effectiveness has, as could be seen, a 'negative' and a 'positive' side, both now enshrined in Article 47: 'negative' insofar as it allows a first test of national law on whether it makes the implementation of personal rights under EU non-discrimination or consumer contract directives 'impossible or excessively difficult'. It is still a forceful and to some extent easy argument which the Court used in *Alassini*. It is supplemented by the equivalence test that prevents Member State law from prescribing lower standards for EU-based claims than for those under national law; *Asturcom* is a good of this concerning the *ex officio* protection of the consumer against an unfair term.

But effectiveness also has a *positive* side, and the case studies should have demonstrated exactly this. It results in what I have called an 'upgrading' of remedies, both in a substantive and in a procedural context. The so-called 'remedial' and 'procedural' autonomy of Member States is put on trial, but not completely abandoned. It results in a *'hybridisation' of remedies* having to be introduced into national law using the classical method of 'directive conforming interpretation', supplemented recently by a 'negative horizontal effect' of directives if they can be based on the Charter of Fundamental Rights, in particular the non-discrimination provisions of Articles 21 and 23. It seems arguable that the principle of consumer protection in Article 38 Charter read together with Articles 12/169 TFEU allows a similar 'preclusionary effect' of horizontal EU directives.[71]

To avoid possible fears of the 'overextension' of the effectiveness principle it should be remembered that it is only relevant in areas where secondary EU law creates or intends to create rights, for example in favour of discriminated persons or consumers. This is always a matter of interpretation and requires in my understanding that the provisions on which these are based are *mandatory* in nature. EU contract law insofar as it exists in B2B or C2C relations at all is usually based on default provisions and therefore does not qualify for the EU effectiveness test.

## 3. 'FULL' EFFECTIVENESS: TOO 'FULL', TOO 'EMPTY', OR 'JUST RIGHT'? THE NEED FOR A BALANCING APPROACH

My last point is concerned with a legal-political question: is the Court not overstepping its mandate to interpret EU law when it goes about reshaping remedies based on national law? This criticism does not so much rely on the effectiveness

[71] This is the interesting argument by O. Mörsdorf, 'Die Auswirkungen des neuen "Grundrechts auf Verbraucherschutz" gem. Art. 38 GrCh auf den nationalen Verbraucherschutz' (2010) *JZ (Juristenzeitung)* 759.

and equivalence principles in the negative sense – they have been recognised as general constitutional principles of EU law ever since, and are, of course, not limited to (mandatory) contract law, but also even more so relate to procedural and administrative issues. The criticism is directed against the *positive 'full effectiveness'* principle which the Court had developed in the cases analysed here and which are at odds with traditional Member State remedial principles. The abrogation of the fault principle for compensation in contract law substituted by strict liability rules, the 'use' (some say 'abuse') of compensation for deterrence purposes, the limitation of procedural autonomy of Member States in proceedings concerning unfair terms, the recognition of ADR instruments as a prerequisite for later proceedings before courts of law under certain qualifying conditions – not much 'autonomy' of Member States seems to be left. Is the CJEU not acting '*ultra vires*', as was argued by the plaintiffs in the *Honeywell* litigation before the German Constitutional Court criticising *Mangold*, but finally rejected by the same BVerfG which confirmed the wide scope and competence the CJEU enjoys in interpreting, and in the end developing, EU law, even to the 'detriment' of cherished principles of Member States' law?[72]

It must also be remembered that even in cases where the CJEU required an 'upgrading' of national remedies and procedures to protect rights granted under EU law, it left a wide margin of discretion to national courts to accomplish the right balancing between conflicting interests. The best example is the *Weber/Putz* case. Even if the extension of the strict seller's liability beyond the mere 'bodily' quality of the goods sold at the time of transfer of risk itself may seem 'revolutionary', the ensuing remedies for the consumer are nonetheless still limited by a proportionality argument taking into account the legitimate interests of the seller and the character of the transaction itself. It is of no surprise that the BGH[73] in its follow-up judgment quite straightforwardly divided the risk between seller and consumer to one half for each.

This chapter has not discussed cases where the Court did not seem to be ready to take a more forward-looking approach to providing remedies in protecting EU rights. The best example – one that is often criticised – concerns the so-called *Heininger* saga[74] where Court had to consider the effects of a consumer's withdrawal from the bank mortgage credit which was entered into at the doorstep and proposed by a project developer. The BGH was very quick to give its answer based on the doctrine that real estate and credit transactions are legally separate from each other.[75] The withdrawal of one (the mortgage) does not affect the other (purchase of real estate). The only consequence of withdrawal from the credit contract is to avoid it. What are the consequences of avoidance?

72 *Honeywell*, n. 41 above.
73 BGH, n. 68 above, 1079.
74 C-481/99, *Heininger v. Bayrische Hypo- und Vereinsbank* [2001] ECR I-9945.
75 BGH, XI ZR 91/99, judgment of 9 April 2002, (2002) *NJW* 1881, 1884 – *Heininger II*.

Does the consumer have to pay back the credit in full and without the privilege of instalments, as the case law of the BGH seemed to suggest? Does he have to pay the contracted interests, including those accruing over time? Does it make any difference that he has not been informed about an eventual right of withdrawal? Could he raise a claim of compensation against the bank for not having been adequately informed under the German theory of '*culpa in contrahendo*'?[76] Or could one even argue, as the Commission did, that the credit and the purchase contract form an economic unit, which must be judged together, even if they are formally separate?

These were the questions that came before the CJEU in the follow-up cases of *Schulte*[77] and *Crailsheimer Volksbank*[78] via references from lower courts that were quite opposed to the restrictive case law of the BGH. In its reasoning, the Court put forward the following legal doctrines:

- starting from a formal approach in following the opinion of AG Léger,[79] it held that the withdrawal by the consumer avoided the credit transaction and that therefore the parties had to re-install the original state of affairs, namely, that the consumer had received the credit without justification and therefore had to pay back the money immediately and in full (*Schulte*, para. 87);
- it was of no relevance for the purpose for which the credit was used; the CJEU indirectly rejected the idea of 'linked contracts' as a principle of EU law, which would however not be precluded under national law (para. 80);
- the consumer had to pay market interest for the credit money used without justification, thus restoring the status quo ante (para. 92);
- however, States have to 'ensure that their legislation protects consumers who have been unable to avoid exposure to such risks (loss of rental income and property value incurred because of not knowing of their right of cancellation under the Directive), by adopting suitable measures to allow them to avoid bearing the consequences of the materialisation of those risks' (para. 101).

In the end this means that the consumer's economic situation is not improved after withdrawal; a claim for compensation will be difficult to prove in practice. The Court did not attach any importance to the effectiveness principle it had

---

76 For a discussion see N. Reich, 'Balancing in Private Law and the Imperatives of the Public Interest: National Experiences and (Missed?) European Opportunities' in R. Brownsword et al. (eds.), *Modern Tendencies in Private Law*, Hart, Oxford 2011, p. 221; H. Unberath and A. Johnston, 'The Double Headed Approach of the CJEU Concerning Consumer Protection' (2007) *CMLRev* 1237, 1261; T. Möllers and P. Grassi, 'Die Europarechtswidrigkeit der Schrottimmobilienrechtsprechung zur Haustürwiderrufs-RiLi 85/577/EWG durch deutsche Gerichte' (2010) *Verbraucher und Recht* 3.

77 Case C-350/03, *Elisabeth Schulte and Wolfgang Schulte v. Deutsche Bausparkasse Badenia AG* [2005] ECR I-9215.

78 Case C-229/04, *Crailsheimer Volksbank eG v. Klaus Conrads and others* [2005] ECR I-9293.

79 Opinion of AG Léger in *Crailsheimer Volksbank* (2 June 2005) paras. 54, 72.

used in other cases.[80] Instead, it relied on the theory of a formal separation of transactions, as confirmed in the Opinion of AG Léger of 29 October 2004 in *Schulte*:[81]

> 'I think a purposive interpretation of the Directive, just like its practical effect, do not permit a requirement that the cancellation of the secured credit agreement should produce an effect, in one way or another, on the validity of the property purchase contract'.

Whether the effectiveness paradigm used here would allow different answers remains an open question; there are no easy answers. It is to some extent caught in between the 'full autonomy' of Member States to protect citizens as they wish under their national rules of remedies and procedures unless there has been express EU legislation (the *Heininger* saga being an example of this because the Doorstep Directive 85/577/EEC left the provision of remedies to national law) – and the seemingly opposing 'full effectiveness' approach relevant whenever there is a deficiency in the available remedies under national or EU law as in the cases studied here. But even under the 'full effectiveness' approach, compromise solutions must and will be sought by the CJEU, often resulting in a *balancing of different interests*.[82] This balancing should not be done so much using formal competence considerations, but rather using substantive proportionality criteria, as has recently been demonstrated in *Weber/Putz*.

---

80 See H.-W. Micklitz, n. 1 above, p. 386.

81 *Schulte*, n. 77 above, para. 95

82 See my paper, n. 76 above; critique also by H. Rösler, *Europäische Gerichtsbarkeit auf dem Gebiet des Zivilrechts*, Mohr Siebeck, Tübingen 2012, p. 156: '*der EuGH (hat) die wirkliche Dimension und dogmatische Komplexität des Problems wohl nicht recht erfasst*'.

# THE PRINCIPLE OF PROPORTIONALITY AND EUROPEAN CONTRACT LAW

Caroline Cauffman

CONTENTS

I. The 'Classic' Content of the 'Principle of Proportionality' in EU Law ... 72
II. Expressions of the Principle of Proportionality in EU Contract Law .... 73
1. The Anti-Discrimination Directives ... 73
2. The Unfair Terms Directive... 74
3. The Consumer Sales Directive ... 75
4. The Consumer Rights Directive... 75
5. The CESL ... 76
6. Expressions of a Single Principle of Proportionality?... 79
III. The Principle of Proportionality as an Autonomous General Principle of EU Contract Law... 81
1. The Principle of Proportionality as an Aid to the Interpretation of EU Contract Law ... 82
a) Overview of Case Law... 82
aa) *Messner*... 82
bb) *Weber*... 85
b) 'Proportionate' Interpretation of the Law versus the Theory of Abuse of Rights ... 90
aa) National Rules on Abuse of Rights... 90
bb) An EU Theory on Abuse of Law? ... 92
cc) The Relationship between 'Proportionate' Interpretation and the Theory of Abuse of Rights... 94
2. A Gap-Filling Function for the Principle of Proportionality?... 95
3. The Principle of Proportionality as a Ground for Judicial Review... 96
IV. Conclusion... 97

The principle of proportionality goes to the root of the law the essence of which is the balancing of competing rights and interests. This insight is not new. The Romans already pictured their goddess of justice, Justitia, as a (blindfolded) woman with a balance. In EU law, proportionality was recognised as a general principle of law in *Internationale Handelsgesellschaft.*[1]

In the relationship between the principle of proportionality and European contract law two dimensions can be distinguished. Firstly, there is the typical EU law dimension. The principle of proportionality serves as an instrument to delineate the respective powers of the EU and the Member States. As such it is used in Article 5(2) and (4) TEU which state that the Union shall act only within the limits of the competences conferred upon it by the Member States in the Treaties to attain the objectives set out therein and that, under the principle of proportionality, the content and form of Union action shall not exceed what is necessary to achieve the objectives of the Treaties. To this dimension also belongs the proportionality test used in the control of the compatibility of national legislation with the EU fundamental freedoms. The principle of proportionality evidently also fulfils these functions when legislation in the field of contract law is concerned. Proportionality in the meaning of Article 5(2) and (4) TEU is discussed whenever the EU plans to adopt legislation harmonising elements of contract law or when the desirability of a more general instrument of EU contract law (an EU code of contract law and the like) is discussed.[2] *Gysbrechts* provides an example of the use of the proportionality test to determine the compatibility of national legislation on contract law with the fundamental freedoms. In this case the Court of Justice held that a Belgian rule on distance contracts, to the extent that it was interpreted as prohibiting the distance seller to require that a consumer provide his payment card number before the expiry of the withdrawal period, went beyond what is necessary to attain the pursued objective of consumer protection and constituted an obstacle to the free movement of goods contrary to Article 35 TFEU (ex-Article 29 EC).[3] This dimension of the relationship between the principle of proportionality and contract law is rather of a public law character. It has to do with the competences, the powers of legislatures at several levels of a multi-level legal system.

However, the function of the principle of proportionality is not limited to determining the respective powers of the EU and the Member States. It also plays a role *within* contract law, in balancing the rights and obligations of the contracting parties. It is this more private law related dimension of the

1 Case 11/70, *Internationale Handelsgesellschaft mbH v. Einfuhr- und Vorratsstelle für Getreide und Futtermittel* [1970] ECR 1125.

2 See e.g. Explanatory Memorandum to the Proposal for a Regulation of the European Parliament and of the Council on a Common European Sales Law, COM(2011) 635 final, p. 10. Criticised by the Bundestag, see Bundestags-Drucksache 17/8000, p. 7.

3 Case C-205/07, *Criminal proceedings v. Lodewijk Gysbrechts and Santurel Inter BVBA* [2008] ECR I-9947.

relationship between the principle of proportionality and contract law this contribution will focus on. However, as will be shown below, the distinction between the public law and the private law dimension of the principle of proportionality is not always easy to make in the context of EU contract law. There is a fine line between using the principle of proportionality as a means to determine the rights and obligations of the contracting parties, and using the principle of proportionality to determine the power of the EU and/or the Member States to determine the rights and obligations of the parties in a way that respects the principle of proportionality. It is precisely because of these delineation issues that EU law usually does not distinguish between public law and private law and that it is important that certain fundamental principles of law apply across the public–private divide.

That the principle of proportionality plays an important role within contract law was recognised by the General Court in *Distilleria F. Palma SpA* where it was stated that:

> '44 [...] the third paragraph of Article 5 EC, which enshrines the principle of proportionality, is intended to regulate all the Community's means of action, whether contractual or non-contractual.
> 45 However, according to the principle pacta sunt servanda, which constitutes a fundamental principle of any legal order [...], the contract concluded between the Commission and Palma is, in principle intangible. Therefore, any obligation on the part of the Commission to accept one of the amendments of the contract proposed by Palma can only arise from the contract itself or the general principles which govern contractual relations, among which is the principle of proportionality'.[4]

The General Court thus not only recognises that the principle of proportionality can play a role in contractual affairs to which the Commission is a party, it also recognises that the principle of proportionality is one of the general principles which govern contractual relations.

When the principle of proportionality is one of the general principles which govern contractual relations, it can be expected that it is an underlying principle of more specific rules of EU contract law. That this is indeed so will be illustrated in section II of this contribution. In section III, it will be investigated whether the principle of proportionality can in addition play a role as an autonomous principle, apart from more specific rules. Finally, some general conclusions about the principle of proportionality in contract law will be formulated. First, however, it needs to be explained what the concept of 'the principle of proportionality' refers to.

---

4 Case T-154/01, *Distilleria F. Palma SpA v. Commission of the European Communities* [2004] ECR II-1493.

# I. THE 'CLASSIC' CONTENT OF THE 'PRINCIPLE OF PROPORTIONALITY' IN EU LAW

The principle of proportionality is inspired by German law, where it comprises three elements: suitability, necessity and proportionality *sensu stricto*. The suitability test requires that the measure is suitable to reach the desired, legitimate end. The necessity test questions whether the measure is necessary to reach the desired aim, whether there was no less restrictive measure that would equally serve the desired aim. The proportionality test *sensu stricto* evaluates the balance between the measure and the restrictions it involves.[5]

Most scholars agree that these three elements also form part of the EU principle of proportionality, although they usually add that the Court of Justice does not always explicitly apply the three criteria of the proportionality test.[6] Understandably, it does not do so where the first or second criterion already fails, so that there is no need to test the second or third criterion before concluding that the measure is disproportionate. However, also in other cases the Court of Justice sometimes deviates from the three-step proportionality test.[7] Moreover, the intensity of the proportionality test depends on the purpose of the measure, the nature and importance of other rights and interests involved and the competence of the Court to test possible discretionary competences of other instances. The proportionality test is the strictest where individual rights are limited. It is strict where administrative sanctions are involved. Where discretionary competences and complicated assessments are involved, the Court will only intervene when manifestly disproportionate choices were made.[8]

The three-stage proportionality test also applies in human rights cases, determining the extent to which governments may limit human rights.[9]

At this point, I will not yet answer the question whether the three-stage proportionality test also applies in matters of European contract law. For the purpose of the next section where European contract law[10] will be 'scanned' for expressions of

---

5 P. Craig and G. de Búrca, *EU Law, Text, Cases, and Materials*, Oxford University Press, Oxford 2011, p. 526.

6 See e.g. W. van Gerven, 'The Effect of Proportionality on the Actions of Member States of the European Community: National Viewpoints from Continental Europe' in E. Elis (ed.), *The Principle of Proportionality in the Laws of Europe*, Hart, Oxford 1999, pp. 37 et seq.; P. Craig and G. de Búrca, n. 5 above, p. 526.

7 P. Craig and G. de Búrca, n. 5 above, p. 526.

8 W. van Gerven and S. Lierman, 'Algemeen Deel. Veertig jaar later. Privaat- en publiekrecht in een meergelaagd kader van regelgeving, rechtsvorming en regeltoepassing', in *Beginselen van Belgisch Privaatrecht*, Kluwer, Mechelen 2010, pp. 536 et seq.

9 See e.g. D. Ehlers, 'General Principles' in D. Ehlers (ed.), *European Fundamental Rights and Freedoms*, de Gruyter, Berlin 2007, n° 48, p. 53.

10 This contribution will only focus on 'private' contracts; for the application of the principle of proportionality in the field of public procurement, see K. Wauters and J. Jan Ghysels, 'Le principe de proportionnalité et l'attribution de contrats publics' in *Liber Amicorum Francis Haumont*, forthcoming.

the principle of proportionality, a more open and flexible notion of proportionality as a balancing of interests will be used. Only afterwards will it be investigated whether the results of this scanning exercise respond to the three-step test.

## II. EXPRESSIONS OF THE PRINCIPLE OF PROPORTIONALITY IN EU CONTRACT LAW

### 1. THE ANTI-DISCRIMINATION DIRECTIVES

In the field of anti-discrimination law, the EU has adopted a number of directives ordering the Member States to adopt national legislatures which offers individual protection against certain types of discrimination not only by governmental institutions but also by other individuals. These directives are relevant for contract law as some of them protect against discrimination in labour contracts[11] and/or against discrimination in the field of access to and supply of goods and services to the public, which includes concluding contracts relating to goods and services which are offered to the public in general.[12]

The anti-discrimination directives use the principle of proportionality to determine when certain types of unequal treatment by subjects of public or private law constitute direct or indirect discrimination. In particular they provide, or better allow the national legislators to provide, that certain types of unequal treatment shall not constitute direct or indirect discrimination when they are objectively and reasonably justified by a legitimate aim, and if the means of achieving that aim are appropriate and necessary.[13] This formulation reflects the traditional ground for justification of limitations of human rights. We recognise clearly two of the three elements that are considered characteristic of the principle of proportionality in EU law: suitability (appropriateness) and necessity. Although proportionality is not explicitly mentioned it is generally accepted that a proportionality test is included in the requirement of an objective and reasonable justification by a legitimate aim: the measure needs to be proportionate to the aim pursued.[14]

---

11 Council Directive 2000/43/EC of 29 June 2000 implementing the principle of equal treatment between persons irrespective of racial or ethnic origin [2000] *OJ* L180/22; Council Directive 2000/78/EC of 27 November 2000 establishing a general framework for equal treatment in employment and occupation [2000] *OJ* L303/16; Directive 2006/54/EC of the European Parliament and of the Council of 5 July 2006 on the implementation of the principle of equal opportunities and equal treatment of men and women in matters of employment and occupation (recast) [2006] *OJ* L204/23.

12 Council Directive 2000/43/EC of 29 June 2000 implementing the principle of equal treatment between persons irrespective of racial or ethnic origin [2000] *OJ* L180/22.

13 Articles 2(2)(b) and 6(1) Directive 2000/78/EC; Articles 2(2)(b) and 4 Directive 2000/43/EC; Articles 2(1)(b) and 14(2) Directive 2006/54/EC.

14 O.M. Arnardótti, *Equality and Non-Discrimination Under the European Convention on Human Rights*, Kluwer Law International, The Hague 2003, pp. 42–51.

National legislation implementing the anti-discrimination directives thus limits the contractual freedom of (public as well as private) employers and of subjects of public and private law offering goods and services to the public. The freedom to choose one's contracting partner and to determine autonomously the terms and conditions of the contract finds its limits in the principle of equal treatment. Yet in certain cases the principle of proportionality in turn limits the scope of the duty of equal treatment.

## 2. THE UNFAIR TERMS DIRECTIVE

The idea of balancing the rights and obligations of the parties can also be found in the Unfair Terms Directive. According to Article 3(1) of this directive:

> 'A contractual term which has not been individually negotiated shall be regarded as unfair if, contrary to the requirement of good faith, it causes a significant imbalance in the parties' rights and obligations arising under the contract, to the detriment of the consumer'.

The unfairness of a contractual term is to be assessed, taking into account the nature of the goods or services for which the contract was concluded and by referring, at the time of the conclusion of the contract, to all the circumstances attending the conclusion of the contract and to all the other terms of the contract or of another contract on which it is dependent (Article 4(1)).

The preamble adds:

> 'that the assessment, according to the general criteria chosen, of the unfair character of terms, in particular in sale or supply activities of a public nature providing collective services which take account of solidarity among users, must be supplemented by a means of making an overall evaluation of the different interests involved'.

According to the preamble this constitutes the requirement of good faith. It adds that:

> 'in making an assessment of good faith, particular regard shall be had to the strength of the bargaining positions of the parties, whether the consumer had an inducement to agree to the term and whether the goods or services were sold or supplied to the special order of the consumer; [...] the requirement of good faith may be satisfied by the seller or supplier where he deals fairly and equitably with the other party whose legitimate interests he has to take into account'.

Furthermore, the nature of goods or services should have an influence on assessing the unfairness of contractual terms.

The assessment of the unfair character shall, however, not be made of terms which describe the main subject matter of the contract nor the quality/price ratio of the goods or services supplied, in so far as these terms are in plain intelligible language (Article 4(2)). The main subject matter of the contract and the price/ quality ratio may nevertheless be taken into account in assessing the fairness of other terms.[15]

## 3. THE CONSUMER SALES DIRECTIVE

In the Consumer Sales Directive the impact of the principle of proportionality can be seen in the rules on the primary remedies for non-conformity: the consumer may require the seller to repair the goods or he may require the seller to replace them, in either case free of charge, unless this is impossible or disproportionate. A remedy shall be deemed to be disproportionate if it imposes costs on the seller which, in comparison with the alternative remedy, are unreasonable, taking into account the value the goods would have if there were no lack of conformity, the significance of the lack of conformity, and whether the alternative remedy could be completed without significant inconvenience to the consumer. Any repair or replacement is to be completed within a reasonable time and without any significant inconvenience to the consumer, taking account of the nature of the goods and the purpose for which the consumer required the goods (Article 3(3)). In addition, the secondary remedy to require an appropriate reduction of the price (Article 3(5)) can be seen as an application of the principle of proportionality. Both the rules on primary and those on secondary remedies are mandatory (Article 7).

## 4. THE CONSUMER RIGHTS DIRECTIVE

Article 14(3) Consumer Rights Directive provides that where a consumer exercises his right of withdrawal he shall pay to the trader an amount which is in proportion to what has been provided until the time the consumer has informed the trader of the exercise of the right of withdrawal, in comparison with the full coverage of the contract. The proportionate amount to be paid by the consumer to the trader shall be calculated on the basis of the total price agreed in the contract. If the total price is excessive, the proportionate amount shall be calculated on the basis of the market value of what has been provided.

Article 24 instructs Member States to lay down effective, proportionate and dissuasive sanctions for infringements of the national provisions adopted implementing this Directive and to take all measures necessary to ensure that they are implemented.

15 Preamble of the Unfair Terms Directive.

## 5. THE CESL

The CESL[16] does not explicitly recognise a general principle of proportionality. Article 2(1) CESL, however, establishes a general duty for each party to act in accordance with good faith and fair dealing. Good faith and fair dealing is defined as a standard of conduct characterised by honesty, openness and consideration for the interests of the other party to the transaction or relationship in question (Article 2(b) Proposition for a Regulation on a CESL). In particular, the fact that the interests of the other party need to be considered is in a way the expression of the principle of proportionality as it requires a balancing of interests.

Furthermore, in numerous specific rules of the CESL the influence of the principle of proportionality can be detected. This is for example the case for the rule which allows a party to avoid a contract if, at the time of the conclusion of the contract:

> '(a) that party was dependent on, or had a relationship of trust with, the other party, was in economic distress or had urgent needs, was improvident, ignorant, or inexperienced; and
> (b) the other party knew or could be expected to have known this and, in the light of the circumstances and purpose of the contract, exploited the first party's situation by taking an excessive benefit or unfair advantage'.

It is important to note, however, that the mere disproportion between the rights and obligations of the parties does not suffice to render the contract voidable. Something more is required, namely the unfair exploitation of a weakness of the other party.

The principle of proportionality can also be detected in Articles 74(1) and 75(2) CESL which provide that where the price or any other contract term is to be determined by one party or by a third party and that party's determination is grossly unreasonable, then the price normally charged or term normally used in comparable circumstances at the time of the conclusion of the contract or, if no such price or term is available, a reasonable price or a reasonable term is substituted. In these cases too, there is, apart from the disproportionality, a lack of consent of the disadvantaged party to the precise amount of the price.

---

16 Proposal for a Regulation of the European Parliament and of the Council on a Common European Sales Law, /* COM/2011/0635 final – 2011/0284 (COD) */. In the meantime, this proposal has been withdrawn (Communication from the Commission to the European Parliament, the Council, the European Economic and social committee and the Committee of the Regions, Commission Work Programme 2015 – A New Start /* COM/2014/0910 final */). However, as the CESL built on the DCFR, which was the result of an enormous comparative study aimed at the development of optimal rules of EU private law and it might re-emerge in some amended form in the context of the Commission's activities relating to e-commerce in the Digital Single Market it is still worth discussing the CESL in this contribution.

A further instance where proportionality is at stake is the control of unfair terms in consumer contracts. Article 83 CESL provides that:

> '1. In a contract between a trader and a consumer, a contract term supplied by the trader which has not been individually negotiated within the meaning of Article 7 is unfair for the purposes of this Section if it causes a significant imbalance in the parties' rights and obligations arising under the contract, to the detriment of the consumer, contrary to good faith and fair dealing.
> 2. When assessing the unfairness of a contract term for the purposes of this Section, regard is to be had to:
> (a) whether the trader complied with the duty of transparency set out in Article 82;
> (b) the nature of what is to be provided under the contract;
> (c) the circumstances prevailing during the conclusion of the contract;
> (d) to the other contract terms; and
> (e) to the terms of any other contract on which the contract depends'.

Again, the rule does not aim to set aside all disproportional terms, but only those not individually negotiated. Moreover, the control of unfair terms does not apply to the definition of the main subject matter of the contract or to the appropriateness of the price to be paid in so far as the trader has complied with the duty of transparency (Article 80(2)).

The influence of the principle of transparency is also clear in the rules on change of circumstances.

Under Article 89:

> 'A party must perform its obligations even if performance has become more onerous, whether because the cost of performance has increased or because the value of what is to be received in return has diminished'.

However,

> 'Where performance becomes excessively onerous because of an exceptional change of circumstances, the parties have a duty to enter into negotiations with a view to adapting or terminating the contract'.

Finally, the rules on remedies for non-performance contain numerous references to the principle of proportionality.

- in B2B relationships, the buyer may refuse an offer to cure only if (a) cure cannot be effected promptly and without significant inconvenience to the buyer; (b) the buyer has reason to believe that the seller's future performance cannot be relied on; or (c) delay in performance would amount to a fundamental non-performance (Article 109(4)). This shows that the interests of both parties need to be balanced;

- the buyer's right to performance of the seller's obligations ends where the burden or expense of performance would be disproportionate to the benefit that the buyer would obtain (Article 110(3)(b)). Similarly, the seller may require a buyer who is unwilling to accept performance, to take delivery and to pay for the goods, unless the seller could have made a reasonable substitute transaction without significant effort or expense (Article 132);
- where, in a consumer sales contract, the trader is required to remedy a lack of conformity pursuant to Article 110(2) the consumer may choose between repair and replacement unless the option chosen would be unlawful or impossible or, compared to the other option available, would impose costs on the seller that would be disproportionate taking into account: (a) the value the goods would have if there were no lack of conformity; (b) the significance of the lack of conformity; and (c) whether the alternative remedy could be completed without significant inconvenience to the consumer (Article 111(1));
- a party's right to withhold performance extends to the whole or part of the performance to the extent justified by the non-performance. Where a party's obligations are to be performed in separate parts or are otherwise divisible, the other party may withhold performance only in relation to that part which has not been performed, unless the non-performance is such as to justify withholding the other party's performance as a whole (Articles 113(3) and 133(3));
- where the seller's obligations under the contract are to be performed in separate parts or are otherwise divisible, then if there is a ground for termination of a part to which a part of the price can be apportioned, the buyer may terminate only in relation to that part, unless the buyer cannot be expected to accept performance of the other parts or the non-performance is such as to justify termination of the contract as a whole. Where the seller's obligations under the contract are not divisible or a part of the price cannot be apportioned, the buyer may terminate only if the non-performance is such as to justify termination of the contract as a whole (Article 117). Similarly, where the buyer's obligations under the contract are to be performed in separate parts or are otherwise divisible, then if there is a ground for termination of a part which corresponds to a divisible part of the seller's obligations, the seller may terminate only in relation to that part. However, this does not apply if the non-performance is fundamental in relation to the contract as a whole. Where the buyer's obligations under the contract are not to be performed in separate parts, the seller may terminate only if the non-performance is fundamental in relation to the contract as a whole (Article 137);
- a buyer who accepts a performance not conforming to the contract may reduce the price. The reduction is to be proportionate to the decrease in the value of what was received in performance at the time performance was made compared to the value of what would have been received by a conforming performance (Article 120(1));

- the principle of proportionality also inspired the rules on restitution in case of avoidance or termination. Where the return of the received is possible but would cause unreasonable effort or expense, the recipient may choose to pay the monetary value, provided that this would not harm the other party's proprietary interests (Article 173(1)). In addition, any obligation to return or to pay may be modified to the extent that its performance would be grossly inequitable, taking into account in particular whether the party did not cause, or lacked knowledge of, the ground for avoidance or termination (Article 176).

## 6. EXPRESSIONS OF A SINGLE PRINCIPLE OF PROPORTIONALITY?

In the provisions mentioned above the third element of the classic definition of the principle of proportionality, namely proportionality *sensu stricto*, can be clearly detected. The two other criteria, suitability and necessity, are often not explicitly mentioned. Do they not form an essential part of the principle of proportionality in private law?

It seems that a distinction is to be made in relation to the public–private divide. Firstly, the mandatory rules of contract law constitute a limitation by the European (and in case of implementation of directives the national) legislature of the contracting parties contractual freedom. In comparing human rights cases and EU law cases on the limitation of individual rights, it appears logical that the EU acts imposing mandatory rules of contract law need to comply with the three elements of the proportionality test (as it is generally accepted in EU law).

In the Unfair Terms Directive, for example, the seller's freedom of contract is limited only where he made a disproportionate use of it, causing by means of not individually negotiated terms a significant imbalance between his rights and obligations and those of the consumer. The sanction of non-bindingness is suitable to protect the consumer against unfair terms. It also seems necessary – or at least there seems to be no less severe measure that is able to offer equal protection.[17] The non-bindingness requirement in the directive is moreover limited to the unfair clause itself: it does not extend to the remainder of the contract. Furthermore, the so-called core provision terms describing the main subject matter of the contract and the quality/price ratio of the goods or services supplied are only subject to the unfair terms control if these terms are not in plain intelligible language (Article 4(2)). It is important to note that the Unfair Terms

17 Allowing the reduction of the unfair term to an acceptable one will probably not have an equal discouraging effect, see A.S. Hartkamp and C.H. Sieburgh, *Mr. C Asser's Handleiding voor de beoefening van het Nederlands burgerlijk recht*, 6-III, *Verbintenissenrecht, Algemene leer der overeenkomsten*, Kluwer, Deventer 2010, n° 645.

Directive thus only affects 'hidden' disproportionality, which the consumer was probably not aware of. Disproportionality affecting the main subject matter that was clearly expressed in the contract, and to which the consumer can be expected to have fully and consciously agreed, remain unaffected. Where the principle of freedom of contract fully plays its role, it prevails over the principle of proportionality.

In certain cases the suitability and necessity of the choices made by the EU is less clear. Whether the two-stage system of remedies for non-conformity in a consumer sales contract is suitable and necessary to guarantee a high level of consumer protection is for example disputable. It could be argued that the consumer would be better protected if the right of termination was immediately available. This is however a matter where policy choices are made, where there is room for discretion, and in such cases the principle of proportionality is to be applied less strictly.

Where the directives provide that Member States need to lay down effective, proportionate and dissuasive sanctions, it seems that a strict three-stage test of proportionality applies, comparable to the EU cases on administrative sanctions.

From the perspective of the protection of individual rights, a less strict application of the principle of proportionality seems required where the EU would only lay down non-mandatory rules. In particular, it seems that the necessity criterion might be unnecessary and the suitability criterion should be applied loosely. Only a 'manifest' unsuitability seems to be problematic.

Until this point we have been discussing whether when laying down rules of EU contract law the EU respected the principle of proportionality in limiting the rights of the contracting parties and/or weighing the rights and interest of the contracting parties.

A different (though not always easy to distinguish) question is whether the three-step proportionality test also applies to decisions on the lawfulness of the behaviour of the contracting parties where the law provides that the contracting parties need to take 'proportionality' into account when deciding whether to conclude a contract or not and/or when exercising their contractual rights. As mentioned above, this is indeed the case where the anti-discrimination directives provide that certain types of unequal treatment in relation to certain types of contracts shall not constitute direct or indirect discrimination when they are objectively and reasonably justified by a legitimate aim, and if the means of achieving that aim are appropriate and necessary; proportionality *sensu stricto* being implied in the requirement of an objective and reasonable justification by a legitimate aim.[18]

In other cases, the concept of proportionality clearly seems to be limited to the element of proportionality *sensu stricto*. This is for example the case where Article 14(3) Consumer Rights Directive provides how the proportionate

[18] Cf. above.

amount to be paid by the consumer who exercises his right of withdrawal is to be determined.

In a third type of case, the aim pursued by the parties involved and the suitability of the measures used to pursue it may be an element that is to be taken into account when determining the proportionality of the respective rights and interests. This seems to be the case for the unfairness test under the Unfair Terms Directive.

The interim conclusion thus seems to indeed be that where European contract law refers to proportionality, it always refers to a balancing exercise of rights and interests or benefits and detriments, but that it does not always include a test of the suitability and necessity of an act for the pursuit of a legitimate aim. However, this does not seem to be typical of contract law. As is clear from the name of the principle, the essence of the principle of proportionality is its third element: proportionality *sensu stricto*. The criteria of necessity and suitability are implied in the principle of proportionality when the object of the proportionality test is an act that is the result of a decision to take action or not to do so and a decision on the type of action to be taken. Where an instrument of European contract law would introduce or implicitly contain a general duty of good faith or proportionality, contract-related acts which are carried out without being suitable for a legitimate aim or while there is an option available for the person carrying out the act that is equally efficient for that person but less intrusive of the rights and interests of another will most likely be contrary to that general duty of good faith/proportionality. Whether the principle of proportionality can currently be regarded as an autonomous general principle of EU contract law is investigated in the next section.

## III. THE PRINCIPLE OF PROPORTIONALITY AS AN AUTONOMOUS GENERAL PRINCIPLE OF EU CONTRACT LAW

Since *Internationale Handelsgesellschaft*, the principle of proportionality has been recognised as a general principle of EU law. In *Distilleria F. Palma SpA* the General Court recognised the principle of proportionality as a general principle of contract law (cf. above). It is widely recognised that general principles of EU law fulfil a triple function. Firstly, general principles serve as an aid to interpretation of both EU law and national law falling within the scope of EU law, which must be interpreted in light of the general principles. Secondly, they fulfil a gap-filling function, enabling the European Court of Justice to fill normative gaps left either by the authors of the Treaties or by the EU legislature. Finally, they may be relied upon as grounds for judicial review. EU legislation in breach of a general principle is to be held void and national law falling within the scope of EU law that contravenes a general principle must be set aside.[19] Does the principle of proportionality fulfil all these functions within European contract law?

## 1. THE PRINCIPLE OF PROPORTIONALITY AS AN AID TO THE INTERPRETATION OF EU CONTRACT LAW

### a) *Overview of Case Law*

Cases where the Court of Justice when interpreting EU law on preliminary referrals made by national courts in some way balances the interests of the parties involved are numerous. I will focus on two cases where the Court more explicitly referred to the requirement of proportionality.

#### aa) *Messner*

On 2 December 2005, Ms Messner bought from a professional seller a second-hand laptop computer on the internet at a price of €278.00. In August 2006 the computer display became defective. Ms Messner informed the seller of that screen defect on 4 August 2006. The defendant refused to repair the defect free of charge. Ms Messner thereupon revoked the contract and sought reimbursement of €278.00 before the *Amtsgericht* Lahr. By way of counterclaim the seller submitted that Ms Messner was obliged to pay him compensation for value inasmuch as she had been using the laptop computer for approximately eight months. For a comparable laptop computer, he argued, the average market rental price for three months would be €118.80, with the result that the compensation for the period during which Ms Messner had been using the computer at issue came to €316.80. The *Amtsgericht* Lahr then decided to stay the proceedings and to refer the following question to the Court for a preliminary ruling:

> 'Is Article 6(2) in conjunction with the second sentence of Article 6(1) of Directive 97/7 [...] to be interpreted as precluding a provision of national law which provides that, in the case of a revocation by a consumer within the revocation period, a seller may claim compensation for the value of the use of the consumer goods delivered?'[20]

---

19 K. Lenaerts and J.A. Guttiérrez-Fons, 'The constitutional allocation of powers and general principles of EU law' (2010) 47 *CMLR (Common Market Law Review)* 1669 referring to *inter alia* T. Tridimas, *The General Principles of EU Law*, Oxford University Press, Oxford 2006; X. Groussot, *General Principles of Community Law*, European Law Publishing, Groningen 2006.

20 Case C-489/07, *Pia Messner v. Firma Stefan Krüger* [2009] ECR I-7315, para. 16.

The Court of Justice pointed out that under the second sentence of Article 6(1) and Article 6(2) of the Distance Selling Directive, the only charge that may be imposed on the consumer by reason of the exercise of his right of withdrawal is the direct cost of returning the goods. This prohibition of imposing charges other than those resulting directly from the return of the goods serves to prevent consumers from being dissuaded from exercising their rights out of fear of adverse financial consequences. Furthermore, the right of withdrawal is designed to protect the consumer in the particular situation of mail-order sales, in which he 'is not actually able to see the product or ascertain the nature of the service provided before concluding the contract'.[21] The right of withdrawal is therefore intended to offset the disadvantage for the consumer resulting from a distance contract by granting him an appropriate period for reflection during which he can examine and test the goods acquired. According to the Court a general requirement to pay compensation for the value of the use of consumer goods acquired under a distance contract is incompatible with those objectives.[22]

However, the power of the directive does not intend to grant the consumer rights beyond what is necessary to allow him effective exercise of his right of withdrawal. In particular, the prohibition laid down in the second sentence of Article 6(1) and Article 6(2) do not preclude, in principle, a legal provision of a Member State which requires a consumer to pay a fair compensation if he has made use of the goods acquired under a distance contract in a manner incompatible with the principles of civil law, such as those of good faith or unjust enrichment. Therefore, it follows from the last part of recital 14 in the preamble to Directive 97/7 that the Member States are to determine the other conditions and arrangements following exercise of the right of withdrawal. That power must, however, be exercised in accordance with the purpose of that directive and, in particular, may not adversely affect the efficiency and effectiveness of the right of withdrawal. Such would, for example, be the case if the amount of compensation, such as that referred to in the previous paragraph, were to appear disproportionate in relation to the purchase price of the goods at issue or also if the provision of national law were to place on the consumer the onus of proving that he did not use those goods during the period for withdrawal in a manner which went beyond what was necessary to permit him to make effective use of his right of withdrawal.[23]

According to the Court of Justice, it is in the light of those principles that the national court must resolve the actual case before it, taking due account of all the elements of that case and, in particular, of the nature of the goods at issue and the length of the period at the end of which, as a result of the seller's failure to meet his obligation to provide information, the consumer exercised his right of withdrawal. In sum, the Court held that:

---

21 Recital 14.

22 Case C-489/07, *Pia Messner v. Firma Stefan Krüger* [2009] ECR I-7315, paras. 18–22.

23 Ibid., paras. 25–28.

'the provisions of the second sentence of Article 6(1) and Article 6(2) of Directive 97/7 must be interpreted as precluding a provision of national law which provides in general that, in the case of withdrawal by a consumer within the withdrawal period, a seller may claim compensation for the value of the use of the consumer goods acquired under a distance contract. However, those provisions do not prevent the consumer from being required to pay compensation for the use of the goods in the case where he has made use of those goods in a manner incompatible with the principles of civil law, such as those of good faith or unjust enrichment, on condition that the purpose of that directive and, in particular, the efficiency and effectiveness of the right of withdrawal are not adversely affected, this being a matter for the national court to determine'.[24]

In this case the function of the principle of proportionality as a means to determine the extent of the consumer's rights and obligations is intertwined with its public law function to delineate the powers of the EU and the Member States. What is at stake is the interpretation of an EU measure in the field of consumer law. According to Article 5(4) TEU:

'Under the principle of proportionality, the content and form of Union action shall not exceed what is necessary to achieve the objectives of the Treaties'.

If the interpretation of secondary EU law is open to more than one interpretation, preference is to be given to the interpretation rendering the provisions of secondary EU law consistent with primary EU law.[25] It follows that the Distance Selling Directive is open to more than one interpretation. Preference is to be given to the interpretation in accordance with the principle of proportionality as a general principle of law and its application in Article 5(4) TEU. The Court seems to have combined this 'legalising' interpretation with a teleological interpretation, choosing the interpretation which best serves the purpose for which the provision was made.[26]

The Court's interpretation of the Distance Selling Directive in *Messner* seems to satisfy the three criteria of the proportionality test. Although this is not made explicit in the Court's judgment, the harmonised right of the consumer to not have to pay charges other than those resulting directly from the return of the goods when exercising his right of withdrawal is suitable to achieve the desired aim of allowing the consumer to exercise his right of withdrawal which is granted to the consumer in the context of a measure

24 Ibid., para. 29.

25 Case 218/82, *Commission of the European Communities v. Council of the European Communities* [1983] ECR 4063, para. 15; cases 201/85 and 202/85, *Marthe Klensch and others v. Secrétaire d'État à l'Agriculture et à la Viticulture* [1986] ECR 3477, para. 21; case C-135/93, *Kingdom of Spain v. Commission of the European Communities* [1995] ECR I-1651, para. 37.

26 H.G. Schermers and D.F. Waelbroeck, *Judicial Protection in the European Union*, 6th ed., Kluwer Law International, The Hague 2001, pp. 19–20.

directed at the attainment of the aims of the internal market. However, the right is limited to what is necessary to achieve that aim. When the consumer exceeds the limits of what is necessary to allow the consumer to effectively exercise his right of withdrawal, in particular by having used the goods acquired under a distance contract in a manner incompatible with the principles of civil law, such as those of good faith or unjust enrichment, he may be subjected to a legal provision of a Member State which requires him to pay fair compensation. Here the principle of proportionality in its strict sense kicks in: the compensation the consumer is to pay needs to be fair, which implies that it must not be disproportionate. The Court of Justice goes on to explain that the power of the Member States to determine the other conditions and arrangements following exercise of the right of withdrawal is not absolute, but must be exercised in accordance with the purpose of that directive and, in particular, may not adversely affect the efficiency and effectiveness of the right of withdrawal. The Court of Justice refers explicitly to the principle of proportionality where it explains that the Member States would, for example, exceed their powers if the amount of compensation were to appear *disproportionate* in relation to the purchase price of the goods at issue, or if the provision of national law were to place on the consumer the onus of proving that he did not use those goods during the period for withdrawal in a manner which went beyond what was necessary to permit him to make effective use of his right of withdrawal. Although the explicit reference to proportionality is only made by way of example, it is clear that the Court intends in any case to prevent excessive, unreasonable claims.

It is to be noticed that the reasonableness or proportionality is to be judged taking into account both the purpose of the rules in question and all the circumstances of the case. The consumer is not entitled to use his rights in a way unreasonable or disproportionate given the purpose for which they were given. The remedies the national legislator may foresee for such unreasonable use of rights may not in themselves be unreasonable or disproportionate, taking into account the way in which the rights were used, nor undermine the aim for which the consumer's rights were introduced.

#### bb) *Weber*

Mr Wittmer concluded a consumer sale in respect of polished tiles at a price of €1,382.27. After about two thirds of the tiles had been laid down in his house, Mr Wittmer noticed that there was shading on the tiles which was visible to the naked eye. Mr Wittmer submitted a complaint to his seller, Mr Weber. After having consulted the manufacturer of the tiles, Mr Weber rejected the complaint. In an independent procedure for taking evidence instituted by Mr Wittmer, the appointed expert concluded that the shadings were unremovable fine micro-brushmarks, meaning that the only remedy possible was complete replacement of the tiles. Mr Wittmer claimed for replacement of the tiles and compensation for the removal of the defective tiles. The German BGB made a preliminary referral to the Court of Justice on

> 'whether the first and second subparagraphs of Article 3(3) of the Directive must be interpreted as precluding the seller from being able, under national law, to refuse to replace goods not in conformity on the ground that replacement would impose costs on him, because of the obligation to remove the goods from where they have been installed and to install the replacement goods there, that are disproportionate with regard to the value that the goods would have if there were no lack of conformity and to the significance of the lack of conformity'.[27]

One would expect a system inspired by the general principle of proportionality to answer this question in the negative. In order to reach such a negative answer, Weber, as well as the Austrian and German governments, argued that the aim of the Directive could not be to require the seller to bear economically unreasonable costs in the event that there is only one primary remedy, replacement, available. Although there is nothing in the wording of Article 3(3) to shed light on that situation, in such a case, in accordance with the scheme of that Article, recourse should be had *a fortiori* to the criteria laid down in the second subparagraph of Article 3(3), the list in which is not exhaustive. Furthermore, if a comparison with the cost of the alternative remedy is indeed impossible, a possible disproportionality can however be examined with the aid of the other criteria enumerated in that subparagraph. In any event, in view of the purpose of that provision, which is to protect the seller from economically unreasonable disadvantages, that provision should be given an interpretation also ensuring protection if there is no alternative remedy available.

The Court of Justice chose a more sophisticated approach. It pointed out that, although the first subparagraph of Article 3(3) is, in principle, formulated in a manner which is sufficiently broad to cover cases of absolute lack of proportionality,[28] the second subparagraph of Article 3(3) defines the term 'disproportionate' exclusively in relation to the other remedy, thus limiting it to cases of relative lack of proportionality. This follows from the wording of Article 3(3) and from recital 11. If only one of the two primary remedies is possible, the seller may therefore not refuse the only remedy allowing the goods to be brought into conformity with the contract. According to the Court of Justice, that choice derives from the fact that the Directive favours, in the interest of both parties to the contract, the performance thereof by means of

---

27 Case C-65/09, *Weber GmbH v. Jürgen Wittmer* [2011] ECR I-5257, para. 63.

28 Absolute disproportionality refers to disproportionality with regard to the value that the goods would have if there were no lack of conformity and to the significance of the lack of conformity.

repair or replacement, rather than cancellation of the contract or reduction in the selling price. That choice is explained, in addition, by the fact that generally those two last alternative remedies do not ensure the same level of protection for consumers as the bringing into conformity of the goods. This leads the Court of Justice to the conclusion that the second subparagraph of Article 3(3) of the Directive precludes national legislation from granting the seller the right to refuse the only possible remedy because of its absolute lack of proportionality. Nevertheless, the Court adds, the second subparagraph of Article 3(3) nevertheless allows effective protection of the legitimate financial interests of the seller, in addition to the protection provided for in Articles 4 and 5 of the Directive. In particular in Weber, where replacement of the defective goods, the only possible remedy, involved disproportionate costs because of the need to remove the goods not in conformity from where they were installed and to install the replacement goods, Article 3(3) of the Directive does not preclude the consumer's right to reimbursement of the cost of removing the defective goods and installing the replacement goods from being limited, where necessary, to an amount proportionate to the value the goods would have if there were no lack of conformity and the significance of the lack of conformity. Such limitation leaves intact the consumer's right to seek replacement of goods not in conformity. According to the Court, this is in conformity with Article 3 which aims to establish a fair balance between the interests of the consumer and the seller, by guaranteeing the weak party to the contract, the consumer, complete and effective protection from faulty performance by the seller of his contractual obligations, while enabling account to be taken of economic considerations advanced by the seller. The Court further specifies that:

> '[i]n considering whether, in the case in the main proceedings, it is appropriate to reduce the consumer's right to reimbursement of the costs of removing the goods not in conformity and of installing the replacement goods, the referring court will therefore have to bear in mind, first, the value the goods would have if there were no lack of conformity and the significance of the lack of conformity, and secondly, the Directive's purpose of ensuring a high level of protection for consumers. The possibility of making such a reduction cannot therefore result in the consumer's right to reimbursement of those costs being effectively rendered devoid of substance, in the event that he had installed in good faith the defective goods, in a manner consistent with their nature and purpose, before the defect became apparent'.[29]

Finally, the Court adds, in the event that the right to reimbursement of those costs is reduced, the consumer should be able to request, instead of replacement of the goods not in conformity, an appropriate price reduction or rescission of the contract, pursuant to the last indent of Article 3(5) of the Directive, since the

---

[29] Case 65/09, *Weber GmbH v. Jürgen Wittmer* [2011] ECR I-5257, para. 76.

fact that a consumer cannot have the defective goods brought into conformity without having to bear part of these costs constitutes significant inconvenience for the consumer.[30]

The Court's reasoning thus aims to reconcile the wording of Article 3 Consumer Sales Directive with the need to protect the seller's interests. But is it also compatible with the principle of proportionality? The prohibition for national legislators to grant the seller the right to refuse where repair is impossible, the only remaining primary remedy of replacement because it is 'absolutely' disproportionate, is *suitable* to achieve the aim of the Directive to favour, in the interest of both parties, performance of the contract rather than cancellation or price reduction. It is *necessary* because the latter remedies do not ensure the same level of protection to the consumer than the former.

Is it *proportionate* in the strict sense? Without any counterbalancing measure to protect the legitimate interests of the seller, the proportionality could be at peril. According to the Court, the Directive does however allow effective protection of the legitimate financial interests of the seller, in addition to the protection provided for in Articles 4 and 5 of the Directive. Where replacement, as the only possible remedy, involves disproportionate costs because of the need to remove the non-conforming goods from where they were installed and to install the replacement goods, the seller's duty to replace the non-conforming goods can be mitigated by limiting the consumer's right to reimbursement of the cost of removing the defective goods and installing the replacement goods, where necessary, to an amount proportionate to the value the goods would have if there were no lack of conformity and significance to the lack of conformity. This saves the prohibition on national legislators granting the seller the right to refuse replacement where repair is impossible, although this is 'absolutely' disproportionate, from failing the proportionality test on the ground that it would cause disproportionate inconvenience to the seller.

However, the protection of the legitimate financial interests of the seller must in turn not have disproportionate consequences for the buyer. The Court of Justice recognises this, stating that the possibility of making such a reduction cannot result in the consumer's right to reimbursement of those costs being effectively rendered void of substance, in the event that he had installed the defective good in good faith, in a manner consistent with their nature and purpose, before the defect became apparent. When this would mean that the reduction of the removal and reinstallation costs is only possible in the event that the consumer had not installed the defective goods in good faith, in a manner consistent with their nature and purpose, before the defect became apparent, this seems justified. In such a case it would indeed be disproportionate to require the seller to bear all the costs of the removal of the non-conforming goods and the reinstallation of conforming goods.

30 Ibid., para. 77.

If the possibility of making the reduction also exists in the event the consumer installed the defective goods in good faith, in a manner consistent with their nature and purpose, before the defect became apparent provided it does not render the consumer's right to reimbursement of those costs being effectively rendered void of substance, the question arises when the consumer's right to reimbursement will be considered void of substance.

When it is foreseeable for the seller that the goods will be installed by the consumer and the installation and removal of the goods may entail costs which far exceed the value of the goods sold, it seems questionable whether or not the limitation of the seller's liability is justified for the removal and reinstallation of the goods to an amount proportionate not only to the significance of the non-conformity but also to the value of the goods sold and where the goods turn out to be non-conforming after they have been installed in good faith by the consumer. The Court took care to make clear that it constitutes significant inconvenience for the consumer when reduction of the right to reimbursement of the costs of removing the non-conforming goods and reinstalling conforming goods have the consequence that the consumer cannot have the defective goods brought into conformity without having to bear part of these costs. He should be able to request, instead of replacement of the goods not in conformity, an appropriate price reduction or rescission of the contract, pursuant to the last indent of Article 3(5) of the Directive.

In my opinion, it is nevertheless not certain that this will always lead to a solution that sufficiently takes into account the interests of the consumer. Price reduction and restitution following termination are inherently limited to the purchase price, which can be significantly lower than the cost of removal and reinstallation or the inconvenience resulting from leaving the defective goods installed.

In order to reach a proportionate answer to the question of whether the costs of removal of non-conforming goods and the installation of replacement goods are to be borne by the seller, in the event that the consumer claims the only available primary remedy of replacement after having installed the defective goods in good faith, in a manner consistent with their nature and purpose, before the defect became apparent, I would suggest a different approach. In my opinion the costs of removal and reinstallation do not need to be balanced against the value of the goods in the absence of the non-conformity, but against the interest of the consumer in obtaining replacement of the non-conforming goods including removal of the defective goods and installation of the replacing goods, depending on the seriousness of the defect and on the removal and reinstallation costs. If, given the seriousness of the defect, the consumer cannot be expected to keep the defective goods installed, the low value of the goods compared to the costs of the removal of the defective goods and the reinstallation of conforming goods does not seem to justify the limitation of the seller's obligation where the defective goods were installed in good faith in accordance with the nature of the good before the defect became apparent. Where the seller takes the risk of selling low-quality goods which are intended to be installed, knowing that the removal of the goods once installed will result in significant costs, he should not be able to invoke the price of the goods to limit his liability.

*b) 'Proportionate' Interpretation of the Law versus the Theory of Abuse of Rights*

When reading *Weber*, the question comes to mind whether a disproportional use of the remedies offered in the Consumer Sales Directive by the consumer could also be remedied by national rules on abuse of rights or even by a European theory of abuse of rights.

aa) National Rules on Abuse of Rights

Many national legal systems contain rules limiting an excessive use of contractual rights. In Belgium, France and Germany, these rules are known as the theory of abuse of rights. They have mainly been developed by case law and legal scholarship relating them to the provisions of the respective civil codes dealing with good faith. In Belgium for example, the *Cour de cassation* held in a decision of 1983 that an abuse of rights constitutes an infringement of the duty to perform contracts in good faith laid down in Article 1134(3) CC.[31] This means that as soon as one of the criteria for abuse of rights is satisfied, there is an infringement of Article 1134(3) CC. In other words, abuse of contractual rights is sufficient to conclude to an infringement of Article 1134(3) CC. In a decision of 1990 the Court made clear that abuse of contractual rights is also a necessary condition for the application of Article 1134 CC.[32] The theory of abuse of rights was previously recognised in the field of property law. According to this theory, there is abuse of law where a subject of law exercises a right in a way manifestly exceeding the boundaries of the normal use of that right by a reasonable and careful person. This is, for example, the case when a right is exercised in a way entailing a disproportionate burden for another party compared to the benefit pursued by the right holder.

The Dutch equivalent is Article 6:248(2) Dutch Civil Code which lays down the so-called limitative function of reasonableness and fairness: a rule which applies between the parties as a result of a contract is inapplicable to the

---

31 Cass. 19 September 1983, *Arr. Cass.* 1983–84, 52, *Pas.* 1984, I, 55, *JT* 1985, 56, note S. Dufrène, *RCJB* 1986, 282, note J.-L. Fagnart, *RW* 1983–84, 1480.

32 Cass. 17 May 1990, *Arr. Cass.* 1989–90, 1188, *Bull.* 1990, 1061, *JT* 1990, 442, *Pas.* 1990, I, 1061, *RCJB* 1990, 595, note J. Heenen, *RW* 1990–91, 1085, *Res Jur. Imm.* 1991, 121, *T. Not.* 1990, 402, note, *TBH* 1991, 207, note S. Cnudde. Compare in France: P. Stoffel-Munck, *L'abus dans le contrat, essai d'une théorie*, LGDJ, Paris 2000, pp. 66 et seq.

extent that in the given circumstances this would be irreconcilable with the requirements of reasonableness and fairness. It must be noted, however, that in the Netherlands abuse of rights is a not a necessary condition for the application of the limitative function of reasonableness and fairness.[33] A similar situation exists in Germany and in Greece.[34]

In a series of cases on the use of rights following from the Second Directive 77/91 on Company Law,[35] the Greek courts made a number of preliminary referrals to the Court of Justice on the question whether the use of these rights could be limited on the basis of the national rules on abuse of law. While the Court in *Pafitis* seemed to reject the limitation of rights individuals possess on the basis of EU law by national rules of abuse of law, stating that such rules must not detract from the full effect and uniform application of Community law in the Member States,[36] it recognised the ability of national courts to prevent the abusive exercise of EU rights by individuals in later cases. In particular, in *Kefalas*, the Court decided

> 'that Community law does not preclude national courts from applying a provision of national law in order to assess whether a right arising from a provision of Community law is being exercised abusively'.[37]

The Court supported this judgment referring to earlier case law according to which Community law cannot be relied on for abusive or fraudulent ends.[38] However, it repeated its statement that the application of such a national rule must

33 A.-K. Lenaerts, 'The General Principle of the Prohibition of Abuse of Rights: A Critical Position on Its Role in a Codified European Contract Law' (2010) *ERPL (European Review of Private Law)* 1127 with further references.

34 §242 BGB. Compare Article 281 Greek Civil Code which provides that the exercise of a right is prohibited where it manifestly exceeds the bounds of good faith or morality or the economic or social purpose of that right.

35 Second Council Directive 77/91/EEC of 13 December 1976 on coordination of safeguards which, for the protection of the interests of members and others, are required by Member States of companies within the meaning of the second paragraph of Article 58 of the Treaty, in respect of the formation of public limited liability companies and the maintenance and alteration of their capital, with a view to making such safeguards equivalent [1977] *OJ* L26/1.

36 Case C-441/93, *Panagis Pafitis and others v. Trapeza Kentrikis Ellados A.E. and others* [1996] ECR I-1347, para. 68.

37 Case C-367/96, *Alexandros Kefalas and others v. Elliniko Dimosio (Greek State) and Organismos Oikonomikis Anasygkrotisis Epicheiriseon AE (OAE)* [1998] ECR I-2843, operative part.

38 The Court referred in particular, regarding freedom to supply services, to case 33/74, *van Binsbergen v. Bedrijfsvereniging Metaalnijverheid* [1974] ECR 1299, para. 13, and case C-23/93, *TV 10 v. Commissariaat voor de Media* [1994] ECR I-4795, para. 21; regarding the free movement of goods, case 229/83, *Leclerc and others v. 'Au Blé Vert' and others* [1985] ECR 1, para. 27; regarding freedom of movement for workers, case 39/86, *Lair v. Universität Hannover* [1988] ECR 3161, para. 43; regarding the common agricultural policy, case C-8/92, *General Milk Products v. Hauptzollamt Hamburg-Jonas* [1993] ECR I-779, para. 21; and regarding social security, case C-206/94, *Brennet v. Paletta* [1996] ECR I-2357, para. 24.

### cc) The Relationship between 'Proportionate' Interpretation and the Theory of Abuse of Rights

There is a fine line between 'proportionate' interpretation of legal rules and the recognition of the theory of abuse of rights as a limitation of an excessive use of rights.[44] In the former case, a legal rule conferring a right on a person is interpreted in such a way that the right is limited by the principle of proportionality, that it does not exist in cases where it would lead to disproportionate results. In the latter case, it is recognised that a right may not be abused, that a right which according to the wording of a rule is available may not be used in such a way that it would lead to disproportionate results. In theory, the former case deals with the existence of a right, the latter with the use thereof. The distinction caused quite some controversy amongst French scholars writing at the beginning of the twentieth century; a first group pleading for the recognition of the theory of abuse of rights,[45] a second group arguing that there is no such thing as abuse of a right, because the right ends where abuse begins.[46] As such, the distinction was rather academic; what actually mattered was the determination of the criteria that limited the existence/use of a right and the consequences of exceeding the boundaries of (the legitimate use of) the right. Proportionality has been proposed as a useful criterion for determining the limits of (the legitimate use) of rights. In Belgium this criterion has been accepted by the *Cour de cassation*;[47] in France it is suggested *de lege ferenda* by eminent lawyers.[48]

In EU law, the distinction is further complicated by the fact that the Court of Justice has the sole competence to interpret EU law, and not to apply the law to the facts of a case. This may be a reason why the Court may be more willing to approach the problem of disproportionate consequences of a legal rule via the route of interpretation. In fact, *Weber* shows that the Court when interpreting rules of EU contract law is willing to go into quite some detail in explaining how a certain rule is to be interpreted taking into account the principle of proportionality in a case with specific characteristics such as that in the course of which the preliminary referral is made. From a constitutional perspective, this is probably to be preferred over a wide use of national provisions on abuse of law to prevent the excessive exercise of EU contractual rights. Allowing national

---

44 Compare S. Vogenauer, n. 42 above, pp. 558–560.

45 Main author: L. Josserand, *De l'abus des droits*, Rousseau, Paris 1905; L. Josserand, *De l'esprit des droits et de leur relativité: théorie dite de l'abus des droits*, 2nd ed., Dalloz, Paris 1939.

46 Main author: M. Planiol, *Traité élémentaire de droit civil*, II, LGDJ, Paris 1909, n° 871, p. 286.

47 In property law: Cass. 10 September 1971, *Pas.* 1972, I, 8, *Arr. Cass.* 1972, 31, with the opinion of Procureur-Général Ganshof Van Der Meersch, *RCJB* 1976, note P. Van Ommesaghe. In contract law: Cass. 19 September 1983, *Arr. Cass.* 1983, 52, *Bull.* 1984, 55, *JT* 1985, 56, note S. Dufrène, *JTT* 1984, 57, *Pas.* 1984, I, 55, *RCJB* 1986, 282, note J. Fagnart, *RW* 1983–84, 1480, *TBH* 1984, 276, note W. Rauws, *TSR* 1983, 486.

48 G. Cornu, *Introduction au droit*, 13th ed., Montchrestien, Paris 2007, n° 151 *in fine*.

rules on abuse of rights to set aside rules of EU origin is indeed difficult to reconcile with the principle of the primacy of EU law over national law.[49] Yet the Court of Justice has accepted the application of such national rules in the Greek company law cases mentioned above and the General Court seemed to apply a general concept of abuse of rights as a part of the wider general principle of good faith in *Citymo* (cf. *supra*). Recourse to national rules on abuse of rights or the general principle of good faith thus seems to be a possibility, albeit one that comes only after the stage of the interpretation of the legal rule in question, to be used for combating remaining unfairness without altering the scope of the rule in question or compromising the objectives pursued by it.[50]

## 2. A GAP-FILLING FUNCTION FOR THE PRINCIPLE OF PROPORTIONALITY?

Only fragmentary parts of contract law are harmonised. What falls outside the scope of the harmonised rules is subject to the national contract law of the Member States. This reduces the risk of gaps in European contract law; they will be quite easily supplemented by means of rules of national law. This was certainly the case where EU (consumer) contract law consisted only of minimum harmonisation directives. As far as the minimum level of protection required by the directive was respected, these directives did not oppose the application of additional rules of national law. The risk of gaps may increase with the growing number of maximum harmonisation directives where they prohibit Member States to keep in place or adopt additional rules within the harmonised field. Although these directives generally provide that they do not affect the general rules of contract law, the distinction between the general rules of contract law that may remain applicable and those that are excluded is not always clear. It is not certain whether when confronted with gaps in the maximally harmonised rules leading to disproportionate unfairness, the court will allow the general rules of contract law to fill them in, or whether it will itself supplement them

---

49 Case 106/77, *Simmenthal (II)* [1978] ECR 629; D. Anagnostopoulou, 'Do Francovich and the Principle of Proportionality Weaken Simmenthal (II) and Confirm Abuse of Rights?' (2001) *CMLR* 772; A.-K. Lenaerts, n. 33 above, p. 1131; V. Karayannis, 'L'abus de droits découlant de l'ordre juridique communautaire. A propos de l'arrêt C-367/96 Alexandros Kefalas e.a./Elliniko Dimosio (Etat hellénique)' (1999) *CDE (Cahiers de droit européen)* 532; D. Triantaffylou, 'Abuse of Rights versus Primacy?' (1999) *CMLR* 159; D. Triantaffylou, 'L'interdiction des abus de droit en tant que principe général du droit communautaire' (2002) *CDE* 622; Y. van Gerven, 'Wetsontduiking en rechtsmisbruik in het gemeenschapsrecht' in *Liber Amicorum Walter van Gerven*, Kluwer, Deurne 2000, p. 354. *Contra*: F. Ranieri, 'Verbot des Rechtsmissbrauchs und Europäisches Gemeinschaftsprivatrecht' (2001) *ZEuP (Zeitschrift für Europäisches Privatrecht)* 170.

50 Compare *Alexandros Kefalas and others v. Elliniko Dimosio (Greek State) and Organismos Oikonomikis Anasygkrotisis Epicheiriseon AE (OAE)*, n. 37 above, paras. 20 and 22.

based on general principles of EU (contract) law such as the principle of proportionality. The need to fill in gaps based on the general principles of EU (contract) law will further increase in case the EU were to move on to introducing contract law regulations covering entire contracts. Indeed, it is more consistent with the legal nature of a directly effective regulation that does not need to be implemented in national law, to fill in gaps by means of the principles underlying it and the principles of EU law in general than to have recourse to national law. This can be illustrated by reference to Article 4(2) CESL which provides that:

> 'Issues within the scope of the Common European Sales Law but not expressly settled by it are to be settled in accordance with the objectives and the principles underlying it and all its provisions, without recourse to the national law that would be applicable in the absence of an agreement to use the Common European Sales Law or to any other law'.

The principle of proportionality could for example fill the gap of the absence of a general written rule prohibiting abuse of contractual rights of EU origin. As mentioned in the previous paragraph, the General Court however seems to have equated the theory of abuse of rights in relation to the exercise of contractual freedom with the general principle of good faith. Nevertheless, this does not necessarily render the principle of proportionality superfluous in this field. The principle of proportionality could be used as a criterion to test good faith in the sense that behaviour in conflict with the principle of proportionality could be presumed to be contrary to good faith.

## 3. THE PRINCIPLE OF PROPORTIONALITY AS A GROUND FOR JUDICIAL REVIEW

A third characteristic of general principles of EU law is that they may be relied upon as grounds for judicial review. EU legislation in breach of a general principle is to be held void and national law falling within the scope of EU law that contravenes a general principle must be set aside. When the principle of proportionality is used in the context of judicial review of EU or national legislation on contract law, it will usually relate to the relative competences of the EU and the Member States. Nevertheless, the principle of proportionality could also be used as a ground for judicial review when the substantive rules of mandatory EU contract law in particular do not respect the principle of proportionality when balancing the interests of the parties or when determining the penalties for non-compliance with mandatory rules. The strictness of the proportionality test will however depend *inter alia* on the impact of the rules on the rights, interests and freedoms of the parties and the nature of the limited rights, interests and freedoms. Where a complicated balancing of interests is involved, the Court will probably be reluctant to interfere. However, in the unlikely case that an EU legislative measure on contract law would provide for manifestly disproportionate contractual rights or remedies the Court could probably declare the measure void for infringement of the general principle of proportionality which governs contractual relations. In similar circumstances, national measures falling within the scope of EU law could probably be set aside. Certain contract law directives, such as the Consumer Rights Directive explicitly provide that Member States need to provide effective, proportional and dissuasive sanctions.[51] When the Member States in such cases would provide disproportionate sanctions the national law will clearly contravene EU law. In such a case, it will however be a specific legislative application of the principle of proportionality that will be infringed, and not the general principle of proportionality as such.

## IV. CONCLUSION

It is generally accepted that the principle of proportionality in EU law comprises three elements: suitability, necessity and proportionality *sensu stricto*.

In the provisions for EU contract law to express the principle of proportionality, the third element of the classic definition of the principle of proportionality, namely proportionality *sensu stricto*, can be clearly detected. The two other criteria, suitability and necessity, are often not explicitly mentioned.

Nevertheless, it seems that the EU needs to respect the three elements of the principle of proportionality when laying down mandatory rules limiting the rights of the contracting parties and/or weighing the rights and interest of the contracting parties. How strict each of the criteria is to be interpreted depends on the content and purpose of the mandatory rule in question, for example whether it imposes penalties for infringement of certain mandatory rules, or balances the rights of the contracting parties in case of non-performance of a contract. From the perspective of the protection of individual rights, a less strict application of the principle of proportionality seems to be required where the EU would only lay down non-mandatory rules. In particular, it seems that the necessity criterion might be superfluous and the suitability criterion should be applied loosely. Only a 'manifest' unsuitability seems to be problematic.

A different (though not always easy to distinguish) question is whether the three-step proportionality test also applies where the law provides that the contracting parties need to take 'proportionality' into account. Some provisions of EU contract law refer only to the third element of the principle of proportionality, namely proportionality *sensu stricto*. The answer seems to depend on the object of the proportionality test. The essence of the principle

[51] Article 24 Consumer Rights Directive.

of proportionality is its third element: proportionality *sensu stricto*. When proportionality is only to be taken into account to determine the amount of, for example, compensation, only the third element of the proportionality test needs to be taken into account. The criteria of necessity and suitability are however implied in the principle of proportionality when the object of the proportionality test is an act that is the result of a decision to take action or not and when it is a decision on the type of action to be taken.

The European legislation does not contain a general duty to take the principle of proportionality into account when deciding to conclude a contract or not and to exercise contractual rights. However, it follows from the General Court's decision in *Distilleria F. Palma* that the principle of proportionality forms part of European contract law as an unwritten autonomous principle, which is to be taken into account throughout European contract law, even where it is not expressed in more specific provisions. As such, the general principle of proportionality plays a role in the interpretation of rules of EU contract law. The Court of Justice interprets rules of EU contract law in such a way that the right a person derives from such a rule is limited by the principle of proportionality, i.e. that it does not exist in cases where it would lead to disproportionate results.

The principle of proportionality can also be used to fill in gaps in EU contract law. Where EU (consumer) contract law consisted only of minimum harmonisation directives, gaps could relatively easily be supplemented by national rules of contract law. The risk of gaps may increase with the growing number of maximum harmonisation directives where they prohibit Member States to keep in place or adopt additional rules within the harmonised field. The need to fill in gaps based on the general principles of EU (contract) law would further increase if the EU were to introduce contract law regulations covering entire contracts. The principle of proportionality could fill the gap of the absence of a general written rule prohibiting abuse of contractual rights of EU origin. In *Citymo*, the General Court seems to have equated the theory of abuse in relation to the exercise of contractual freedom with the general principle of good faith, which could be thought to render the use of the principle of proportionality superfluous in this field. However, the principle of proportionality could be used as a criterion to test good faith in the sense that behaviour in conflict with the principle of proportionality could be presumed to be contrary to good faith.

Finally, when the principle of proportionality is used in the context of judicial review of EU or national legislation on contract law, it will usually relate to the relative competences of the EU and the Member States. Nevertheless, the principle of proportionality could also be used as a ground for judicial review when the substantive rules of mandatory EU contract law in particular do not respect the principle of proportionality when balancing the interests of the parties or when determining the penalties for non-compliance with mandatory rules.

# 'GENERAL PRINCIPLES' AND 'UNDERLYING PRINCIPLES' IN THE PROPOSED COMMON EUROPEAN SALES LAW AND THEIR ROLE IN ITS INTERPRETATION

Simon WHITTAKER

CONTENTS

I. The Evolution of 'Principles' in the DCFR .......................... 100
II. Two Types of 'Principles' in the CESL? .............................. 105
1. General Principles of the CESL ............................... 106
2. 'Underlying Principles' and the Interpretation of the CESL ....... 112
III. Conclusion ................................................... 120

European lawyers have frequent and important recourse to the language of principle in their exposition and development of the law (EU or national) and this has been fully reflected in the discussions on European contract law. In this chapter, I will note the differing use of principles in the course of settling the Draft Common Frame of Reference (DCFR)[1] and then look in more detail at the role of principles in the proposed Common European Sales Law (CESL),[2] which

1 STUDY GROUP on a European Civil Code, Research Group on EC Private Law (*Acquis* Group), *Principles, Definitions and Model Rules of European Private Law, Draft Common Frame of Reference* (DCFR), full edition, Sellier, Munich 2009 and Oxford University Press, Oxford 2010, in 6 volumes, Introduction (by C. VON BAR, H. BEALE, E. CLIVE and H. SCHULTE-NÖLKE). An earlier version of this work was presented to the Commission in December 2007 and published by Sellier in early 2008 with the same title except as an 'Interim Outline Edition'. I shall abbreviate these works as 'DCFR 2009' and 'DCFR 2008' respectively.

2 Proposal for a Regulation of the European Parliament and of the Council on a Common European Sales Law, COM(2011) 635 final ('the Proposal'). This Proposal is prefaced with an Explanatory Memorandum from the Commission and contains two annexes: Annex 1 contains the Common European Sales Law ('CESL') and Annex II contains a 'Standard Information Notice' for use in consumer contracts.

distinguishes between 'general principles' and 'underlying principles'. As will be seen, 'principles' have a very important role in the CESL, not least as regards to its interpretation and the settling of issues within its scope but unsettled by its provisions.

## I. THE EVOLUTION OF 'PRINCIPLES' IN THE DCFR

The identification of 'common' or 'fundamental principles' was a central element in the Commission's communications on the development of European contract law in the first decade of the present century and their idea of constructing a Common Frame of Reference (CFR) for European contract law.[3] At this stage, the Commission saw freedom of contract as the proper starting-point for constructing the model rules. In the Commission's view, 'contractual freedom should be the guiding principle; restrictions should only be foreseen where this could be justified with good reasons.'[4] This concern for principle was reflected in the task entrusted to the authors of the DCFR by the Commission, who were asked to construct 'principles, definitions and model rules' of European private law.[5] The changing way in which the authors of the DCFR interpreted this aspect of their remit is worth noting given that it casts some light on the treatment of principles proposed in the CESL.

In the first version of the DCFR published in 2008, the authors of its *Introduction* interpreted the phrase 'fundamental principles' used by the Commission 'to denote essentially abstract basic values'.[6] Accordingly, principles of this sort did not form part of the text of this version of the DCFR, although some possible future candidates were suggested by its *Introduction*, including 'justice, freedom, protection of human rights, promotion of the internal market, legal certainty, rationality'.[7] In the view of the *Introduction*, though:

---

3 See e.g. Communication from the Commission to the European Parliament and the Council – A more coherent European Contract Law, An Action Plan, COM(2003) 68 final ('Action plan'), para. 4.1.1. There is, of course, another usage found in the naming of the *Principles of European Contract Law* (PECL), which were termed 'principles' rather than 'rules' so as to draw attention to the fact that they do not have the force of law: see DCFR 2009, n. 1 above, vol. I, Introduction, para. 10. The following paragraphs of the text draw on S. Whittaker, 'A Framework of Principle for European Contract Law?' (2009) 125 *LQR (Law Quarterly Review)* 616.

4 Action plan, n. 3 above, para. 62.

5 DCFR 2008, n. 1 above, Introduction, para. 9, p. 8 (which notes that this formed part of the Commission's contract with the drafters of the DCFR).

6 DCFR 2008, n. 1 above, Introduction, para. 11, p. 9.

7 Ibid., para. 22, p. 13.

> 'such fundamental principles do not advance matters much at a practical level because of their high level of abstraction. Abstract principles tend to contradict one another. They always have to be weighed up against one another more exactly because only then are optimal outcomes assured. That task, in turn, can only be accomplished with the help of well-formulated model rules.'[8]

The claim, therefore, appears to have been that the DCFR should in its model rules express a balance between very broad and (sometimes) competing principles of this sort rather than merely to state them. There was, however, considerable criticism of this approach to 'principles'. One of the key issues for this purpose was the position of 'good faith and fair dealing', for this version of the DCFR saw 'good faith and fair dealing' as something which is the subject matter of *rules* ('rules on good faith and fair dealing'), rather than as a principle or general proposition applying throughout the instrument. It also appears to set good faith and fair dealing on a par with '*other* applicable *mandatory* rules' as being *qualifications on* or even exceptions to the principle of freedom of contract expressed in the first part of the article.[9]

The treatment of 'principles' in the second published version of the DCFR published first in 2009 was much more elaborate.[10]

First, the authors of the *Introduction* considered the suggestion made by the *Association Henri Capitant des amis de la culture juridique française* and the *Société de législation comparée* that the CFR should include 'Guiding principles of European contract law'.[11] These 'guiding principles' were described by this French project as supplementary to the revised version of the Principles of European Contract Law (PECL): its system of 'rules aimed at governing the formation and performance of contract' can 'usefully [be] completed by general rules which would preside over the elaboration of each of the specific rules' in the PECL.[12] The 'guiding principles' were built 'around three pillars: freedom of contract, contractual fairness and contractual certainty'.[13] It was

---

8 Ibid., para. 11, p. 9.

9 H. Eidenmüller, F. Faust, H.C. Grigoleit, N. Jansen, G. Wagner and R. Zimmermann, 'The Common Frame of Reference for European Private Law – Policy Choices and Codification Problems' (2008) 28 *OJLS (Oxford Journal of Legal Studies)* 659, 669–694; S. Whittaker, 'The Draft Common Frame of Reference: An Assessment, a report commissioned by the UK Ministry of Justice', November 2008, available at: http://webarchive.nationalarchives.gov.uk/20110201125714/www.justice.gov.uk/publications/eu-contract-law-common-frame-reference.htm, pp. 52–62.

10 DCFR 2009, n. 1 above, Introduction, paras. 10–22, Principles, pp. 60–99.

11 *Principes directeurs du droit européen du contrat: Projet de cadre commun de référence, Principes contractuels communs*, Soc. Législation Comparée, Paris 2008. The majority of this work was published in English as B. Fauvarque-Cosson and D. Mazeaud (eds.), *European Contract Law, Materials for a Common Frame of Reference: Terminology, Guiding Principles, Model Rules*, Sellier, Munich 2008.

12 B. Fauvarque-Cosson and D. Mazeaud (eds.), n. 11 above, p. 421.

13 '*[L]a liberté contractuelle, la loyauté contractuelle et la sécurité contractuelle*': B. Fauvarque-Cosson and D. Mazeaud (eds.), n. 11 above, p. 421. The French text is found in *Projet de cadre commun de reference, Principes contractuels communs,* n. 11 above, pp. 20 et seq.

then explained (in the context of the PECL) how they relate to substantive legal principles and rules. So, for example, 'Contractual Fairness' generates a '[g]eneral duty of good faith and fair dealing' which requires that '[e]ach party is bound to act in conformity with the requirements of good faith and fair dealing from the negotiation of the contract until all of its provisions have been given effect.'[14] However, the *Introduction* to the 2009 DCFR did not choose to follow this pattern, first, because the *principes directeurs* (which they translate as 'governing principles') are limited to contract law, whereas the DCFR extends to many further elements of private law; and, secondly, because:

> 'it does not seem appropriate to incorporate the governing principles as a block of actual model rules at the beginning of the DCFR. They function at a different level. They are a distillation from the model rules and have a more descriptive function. They sometimes overlap and often conflict with each other. Almost all of the sub-principles, it is true, have direct counterparts in Articles of the DCFR but those Articles appear in, and are adapted to, particular contexts where they may be subject to qualifications and exceptions. It would weaken the DCFR to extract them and put them in one group at the beginning: it would clearly be undesirable to duplicate them.'[15]

Instead, principles of such a general nature should be expounded upon in a separate section of their own work, entitled *Principles*, rather than be expressed in a series of propositions.[16] This new section grouped the 'underlying principles' of their own work under the general headings of 'freedom, security, justice and efficiency'.[17] Within 'overriding principles of a high political nature' they placed 'the protection of human rights, the promotion of solidarity and social responsibility, the preservation of cultural and linguistic diversity, the protection and promotion of welfare and the promotion of the internal market.' But '[f]reedom, security, justice and efficiency also have a role to play as overriding principles. They have a double role: the two categories [of underlying and overriding principles] overlap.'[18] As regards the 'underlying principles', their explicit role was set by Article I.-1:102(1) DCFR which provided that '[t]hese rules are to be interpreted and developed autonomously and in accordance with their objectives and the principles underlying them'.

The *Principles* section of the 2009 DCFR[19] consists of an essay of some forty pages which seeks to tie the themes of 'freedom, security, justice and efficiency' to the rules found in the DCFR itself. So, for example, as regards contract,

---

14 B. Fauvarque-Cosson and D. Mazeaud (eds.), n. 11 above, Article 0-301, Guiding Principles of European Contract Law, p. 572.
15 DCFR 2009, n. 1 above, Introduction, para. 13.
16 Ibid.
17 Ibid., para. 15.
18 Ibid., para. 16.
19 Abbreviated as 'Principles'.

'freedom of contract' is posited as the 'starting-point' but successive paragraphs explain when and how the DCFR derogates from this principle: in relation to third parties, contracts harmful to society in general, where a party's consent is defective, restrictions on choice of one's contracting partner, the withholding of relevant information, the control of unfair contract terms and the correction of unequal bargaining power.[20]

This is an extremely truncated overview of the DCFR's essay on *Principles*, but it may serve to show that the DCFR's introductory discussion of principles posits ideas or propositions at a very high level of generality, which are then illustrated by reference to the particular model rules found in the main body of the DCFR. The principles can be seen as basic values or underlying ideals, which sometimes overlap and which sometimes compete.[21] However, what is not explained by the DCFR is precisely the nature of their function given the possible roles foreseen for the Common Frame of Reference (CFR). At the time, the nature and purpose of the CFR had not been set: it might be a 'toolbox' for the European legislator (and possibly also for the Court of Justice) or it might provide the core element of an 'optional instrument'. Nonetheless, it remains difficult to see why the positing of 'freedom, justice, certainty and efficiency' would help in any of these endeavours except in terms of political orientation, that is, setting the project within the wider set of values espoused by the EU and, very generally, national European laws. In my view, principles of this sort would give little genuine help in the resolution of particular problems, whether of interpretation or of the filling of gaps in the DCFR's regulation by judicial development. As was said of their discussion in the 2008 DCFR, 'such a conglomeration of disparate factors is hardly helpful for the interpretation of the DCFR's individual rules.'[22]

Secondly, the 2009 *Introduction* put aside the sense of 'principles' to refer to 'rules which are of a more general nature, such as those on freedom of contract or good faith,' though it considered that '[i]n this sense the DCFR's model rules could be said to include principles.'[23] So, freedom of contract[24] and the binding force of contractual obligation[25] were both clearly stated in the rules of the 2009 DCFR. By contrast, the position of good faith and fair dealing was more complicated and, to an extent, contested.[26] So, the DCFR 2008 provided that 'parties are free to make a contract or other juridical act and to determine its contents, *subject to the rules on good faith and fair dealing* and any other

20 DCFR 2009, n. 1 above, Principles, paras. 3–11.
21 Ibid., para. 62.
22 H. Eidenmüller et al., n. 9 above, p. 672.
23 DCFR 2009, n. 1 above, Introduction, para. 10.
24 Article II.-1:102(1) DCFR 2009 Party autonomy: 'Parties are free to make a contract or other juridical act and to determine its contents, subject to any applicable mandatory rules'.
25 Article II.-1:103(1) DCFR 2009: '[a] valid contract is binding on the parties'.
26 S. Whittaker, n. 3 above, pp. 641–644.

applicable mandatory rules.'[27] Some considered that this provision placed 'party autonomy [...] from the outset [...] under a general proviso of *good faith* and *fair dealing*,'[28] but a more restrictive reading would limit its qualification of party autonomy to those circumstances where particular model rules on good faith would so require.[29] On the other hand, 'the need to promote good faith and fair dealing' was stated as a consideration to which regard should be had in the 'interpretation and development' of *all* the DCFR's rules (together with 'uniformity of application' and 'legal certainty').[30] And even if good faith and fair dealing was merely enshrined in particular rules, these rules covered very many aspects of the 'life of contracts', notably as regards negotiation contrary to good faith and fair dealing,[31] liability for fraudulent non-disclosure,[32] judicial adaptation of a contract in cases of unfair exploitation,[33] and the control of unfair terms[34] and a very broad 'duty to act in accordance with good faith and fair dealing in performing an obligation, in exercising a right to performance, in pursuing or defending a remedy for non-performance, or in exercising a right to terminate an obligation or contractual relationship.'[35] And these particular rules could themselves be seen as reflecting an underlying general principle, under the traditional civil law approach to interpreting a 'codification.'[36]

The treatment of 'good faith and fair dealing' changed significantly in the revised version of the DCFR of 2009. So, while Book I still requires regard to be had to 'good faith and fair dealing' in the interpretation and development of the rules,[37] this supplements an injunction that 'these rules are to be interpreted

---

27 Article II.-1:102(1) DCFR 2008.

28 H. Eidenmüller et al., n. 9 above, p. 674, pp. 678–680 observing that '[t]he DCFR's proviso of good faith [...] extends to all types of contracts and to all provisions contained in them and would, therefore, even countenance extensive judicial scrutiny of the price fixed by the parties in their contract.'

29 S. Whittaker, DCFR Assessment, n. 9 above, pp. 145–148.

30 Article I.-1:102(3) DCFR 2008.

31 Article II.-3:301 DCFR 2009 negotiation contrary to good faith and fair dealing.

32 Article II.-7:205(1) and (3) DCFR 2009 (the latter of which specifies factors to which regard is to be had for this purpose).

33 Article II.-7:207(2): 'Upon the request of the party entitled to avoidance, a court may if it is appropriate adapt the contract in order to bring it into accordance with what might have been agreed had the requirements of good faith and fair dealing been observed.' The DCFR does not, however, use good faith and fair dealing to define when unfair exploitation has taken place.

34 This is true of all three direct tests of control applicable to individual contracts (C2C), commercial contracts (B2B) and consumer contracts (B2C): Articles II.-9:403–II.-9:405 DCFR 2008. Moreover, under Article III.-3:105(2) DCFR 2008 'a term excluding or restricting a remedy for non-performance of an obligation, even if valid and otherwise effective [...] may nevertheless not be invoked if it would be contrary to good faith and fair dealing to do so.'

35 Article III.-1:103(1) DCFR 2008.

36 S. Whittaker, DCFR Assessment, n. 9 above, pp. 147–148.

37 Article I.-1:102(3) DCFR 2009.

[...] in accordance with their objectives and the principles underlying them'.[38] Secondly, Book I contains a new definition of 'good faith and fair dealing', its position as third article of 'General Provisions' giving it both prominence and an apparently general significance.[39] Thirdly, the DCFR 2009 no longer qualifies party autonomy in the making of contracts by reference to 'the rules on good faith and fair dealing', though the parties' freedom remains 'subject to any applicable mandatory rules'.[40] On the other hand, all the uses of 'good faith and fair dealing' found in the DCFR 2008 were retained in the DCFR 2009.[41] In the result, it remained unclear whether there is a general legal principle of good faith and fair dealing in the DCFR. For 'good faith and fair dealing' remains explicitly as an element for the interpretation and development of all the model rules, and yet otherwise appears in the text as an element within particular model rules, even though a very widespread and an important one. This at first suggests a contrast between good faith and fair dealing as a legal concept (which is used specially) and good faith and fair dealing as a legal value or 'underlying principle' (which has the potential to apply generally). However, this position is then blurred by the way in which the DCFR is likely to be viewed by many continental civil lawyers, who would see the various examples of good faith and fair dealing in the model rules as illustrative of a pervasive, general and legal principle in the code as a whole. Indeed, in my view, many would see such an interpretation as necessary in order to achieve the consistency and coherence which is essential to a civil law codification and which lay at the roots of the CFR project.

## II. TWO TYPES OF 'PRINCIPLES' IN THE CESL?

In turning to the proposed CESL, we find that it contains two different types of principle: 'general principles' and 'underlying principles'. So, Articles 1 to 3 CESL set 'freedom of contract', 'good faith and fair dealing' and 'co-operation' as general principles and Article 4(1) on interpretation provides that '[t]he Common European Sales Law is to be interpreted autonomously and in accordance with its objectives and the *principles underlying it*.'[42] This does not mean, of course, that wider principles of EU law are not relevant to the Proposed Regulation – indeed, the Commission's introductory Memorandum refers to the 'subsidiarity principle' and the 'proportionality principle' (both of which it sees as satisfied).[43]

38 Article I.-1:102(1) DCFR 2009.
39 Article I.-1:103 DCFR 2009.
40 Article II.-1:102(1) DCFR 2009.
41 A further example was added as regards new rules for dealing with a unilateral mistake in a contract invalid for failing in a requirement of form: Article II.-1:106 DCFR 2009.
42 Emphasis added.
43 Proposal, Memorandum, pp. 9–10.

More generally, of course, the various principles (such as legal certainty or effectiveness) would remain relevant to the CESL owing to its being contained in an EU Regulation.[44]

What then does the CESL Proposal see as the role or roles of the two sorts of principles to which it refers? And to what extent do they relate to each other?

## 1. GENERAL PRINCIPLES OF THE CESL

The provisions in the CESL on this are worth setting out in full:

> '*Article 1*
> *Freedom of contract*
> 1. Parties are free to conclude a contract and to determine its contents, subject to any applicable mandatory rules.
> 2. Parties may exclude the application of any of the provisions of the Common European Sales Law, or derogate from or vary their effects, unless otherwise stated in those provisions.
>
> *Article 2*
> *Good faith and fair dealing*
> 1. Each party has a duty to act in accordance with good faith and fair dealing.
> 2. Breach of this duty may preclude the party in breach from exercising or relying on a right, remedy or defence which that party would otherwise have, or may make the party liable for any loss thereby caused to the other party.
> 3. The parties may not exclude the application of this Article or derogate from or vary its effects.
>
> *Article 3*
> *Co-operation*
> The parties are obliged to co-operate with each other to the extent that this can be expected for the performance of their contractual obligations.'

Here I would like to consider the role these propositions are intended to play *as* principles and for this purpose the Commission's memorandum and the Proposal's recitals help to a degree. So, the Memorandum explains that:

> '*Part I "Introductory provisions"* sets out the general principles of contract law which all parties need to observe in their dealings, such as good faith and fair dealing. The principle of freedom of contract also assures parties that, unless rules are explicitly designated as mandatory, for example rules of consumer protection, they can deviate from the rules of the Common European Sales Law.'[45]

44 Below, pp. 112–113.
45 Ibid., p. 13.

This explanation, however, serves only to highlight the apparent difference in role as between Article 1 CESL's provision on freedom of contract and Articles 2 and 3's provisions on good faith and fair dealing and cooperation. For, according to the Commission, Article 1's declaration is to 'assure [...] parties that, unless rules are explicitly designated as mandatory, for example rules of consumer protection, they can deviate from the rules of the Common European Sales Law.' The provision is therefore an affirmation of the general position for the information of *parties* to a contract. However, recital 30 seems to have a rather different understanding of the role of Article 1, stating that:

> 'Freedom of contract should be the guiding principle underlying the Common European Sales Law. Party autonomy should be restricted only where and to the extent that this is indispensable, in particular for reasons of consumer protection. Where such a necessity exists, the mandatory nature of the rules in question should be clearly indicated.'

There appear to be two concerns here. The first (set out in Article 1(1)) is that freedom of contract or party autonomy (which the recital sees as synonymous) form the important starting-point from which the Proposal derogates only where this is 'indispensable' as a matter of policy (giving, for example, consumer protection). From this point of view, Article 1's designation of freedom of contract as a 'general principle' seeks to make an important statement of the political orientation of the Proposal. However, the proviso to Article 1(1) and (2) itself goes further than this and at a technical level frames the later treatment of derogations from freedom of contract by reference to 'any applicable mandatory rules', a phrase which is used widely to designate rules incapable of exclusion or derogation (frequently but by no means exclusively as regards rules protecting consumers).[46] Article 1(2) then explains the significance of this by providing generally that:

> 'Parties may exclude the application of any of the provisions of the Common European Sales Law, or derogate from or vary their effects, unless otherwise stated in those provisions.'

In this way, Article 1 sets an important particular rule of interpretation of the CESL.[47] However, the interpretative role of 'freedom of contract/party autonomy' appears to go further than this as recital 20 describes freedom of contract as a 'guiding principle *underlying* the Common European Sales Law.'

46 Cf. Proposal, Article 2(v) 'mandatory rule'. For example, the rules providing remedies for fraud, threats and unfair exploitation are mandatory for all the contracts within the scope of the CESL: Article 56(1) CESL.

47 As will be seen, this causes some difficulty in relation to Article 4's provisions on interpretation.

Accordingly, freedom of contract is intended to be used as a general element in the interpretation of CESL, for, as has been seen, the expression 'principle underlying the Common European Sales Law' is used in Article 4(1) CESL's provision on interpretation. Apparently, therefore, this also means that an explicitly stated 'general principle' may also be an 'underlying principle' for the purposes of Article 4(1).

In my view, though, the treatment of 'good faith and fair dealing' and 'co-operation' combines elements of political orientation as well as technical significance. 'Good faith and fair dealing' is defined by the Proposal as:

> 'a standard of conduct characterised by honesty, openness and consideration for the interests of the other party to the transaction or relationship in question.'[48]

The CESL then designates its own provisions on a 'duty to act in accordance with good faith and fair dealing' as mandatory, by providing that 'the parties may not exclude the application of this Article or derogate from or vary its effects.'[49]

In my view, this treatment of good faith and fair dealing in CESL has an important political significance. First, its position immediately following Article 1's declaration of freedom of contract seeks to balance this 'liberal' starting-point by reference to a general proposition of the same status which imposes a duty on each party to a contract to consider the interests of the other whether in the making or the performance of the contract. To a degree, therefore, the inclusion of 'good faith and fair dealing' as a general principle seeks to align the CESL with those who argue not merely that freedom of contract should be qualified where necessary as a matter of policy (which both positive EU law and the vast majority of European lawyers would accept), but that parties to contracts should not be allowed simply to identify and further their own interests in their mutual dealings.[50] Indeed, this idea is then emphasised by Article 3's provision imposing on the parties to a contract a mutual obligation to cooperate in the performance of their contractual obligations. So, good faith and fair dealing does not merely form an example of a mandatory rule, creating

---

48 Article 2(b) Proposal.

49 Article 2(3) CESL.

50 See, notably, M. Hesselink, 'The CFR and Social Justice' in A. Somma (ed.), *The Politics of the Draft Common Frame of Reference*, Kluwer, The Hague 2009, p. 102 who saw the omission of a general duty of good faith from the DCFR when compared to the inclusion of such a duty in *PECL* as being a striking example of the DCFR being 'more liberal' than the PECL. More generally, Hesselink considered that '[g]eneral clauses can play an important role in promoting social justice in contract law, especially in adding to and in counterbalancing the binding force of contract. Although there may be no logical or necessary link between good faith and social justice, there certainly is a historical one': ibid., p. 111. See also O. Lando, 'The Structure and the Legal Values of the Common Frame of Reference (CFR)' (2007) *European Review of Contract Law* 245, 251 et seq.

an exception to freedom of contract; rather, Articles 1 to 3 CESL give expression to the tension between the importance of party autonomy and the need to regulate the behaviour of market actors, the 'moralisation' or even 'socialisation' of contract law.

Secondly, the principle of good faith and fair dealing retains an important role in the interpretation of other provisions of the CESL. While Article 4 CESL makes no direct mention of good faith and fair dealing for the purposes of interpretation (unlike its predecessor in the DCFR),[51] recital 31 explains that:

> 'The principle of good faith and fair dealing should provide guidance on the way parties have to cooperate. As some rules constitute specific manifestations of the general principle of good faith and fair dealing, they should take precedent [sc. precedence] over the general principle. The general principle should therefore not be used as a tool to amend the specific rights and obligations of parties as set out in the specific rules.'

The first sentence of this recital therefore ties Articles 2 and 3 CESL together, good faith and fair dealing explaining how the parties are to cooperate, but its significance is clearly much wider: Article 2(1)'s duty to act in accordance with good faith and fair dealing sets a general norm or standard by which to assess the behaviour of the parties and therefore must be relevant to the interpretation of specific rules governing their behaviour. On the other hand, the second sentence of recital 31 seeks to subordinate the general principle of good faith and fair dealing to those specific rules which involve or concern good faith and fair dealing: the special rule prevails over the general principle, reflecting Article 4(3) CESL's general statement to similar effect as regards general and special rules.[52] So, for example, the control provided by Article 86 CESL for standard terms in contracts between traders rests on a standard of gross deviation from good commercial practice, contrary to good faith and fair dealing;[53] in this situation, therefore, a court should not simply hold that a standard term in such a contract was unfair as contrary to the general duty to act in accordance with good faith and fair dealing in Article 2(1) CESL without reference to the further requirements specially made by Article 86. What is not entirely clear, though, is whether the specific rules envisaged by recital 31 are only those which use the *phrase* 'good faith and fair dealing' or whether they extend to all rules in the CESL which may be seen as reflecting this principle even where the phrase is not used by the text. This is significant, as a number of rules in the DCFR were seen by its authors as reflecting 'good faith and fair dealing' even while not using

51 Article I.-I:102(3) DCFR 2009.

52 'Where there is a general rule and a special rule applying to a particular situation within the scope of the general rule, the special rule prevails in any case of conflict.'

53 Article 86 CESL.

this phrase.[54] Similarly, recital 31's recognition that some provisions in the CESL would be manifestations of the principle of good faith and fair dealing does suggest that, as with freedom of contract, its status as a 'general principle' would not prevent it from counting as an 'underlying principle' for the purposes of the interpretation of the CESL.

Thirdly, however, Article 2(2) CESL foresees its principle as having a direct normative impact on the behaviour of parties to a contract, providing that breach of the duty to act in accordance with good faith and fair dealing 'may preclude the party in breach from exercising or relying on a right, remedy or defence which that party would otherwise have, or may make the party liable for any loss thereby caused to the other party.' Here, there is a certain ambiguity in the language used: what is the significance of use of the word 'may'? It could be thought to give to a court a discretion as to whether or not in the circumstances these various consequences should follow a finding of a breach of the duty. So, depending on the circumstances, a court could decide whether to preclude the exercise of a right or to impose a liability – or, possibly, do neither. Another and, in my view, much more likely reading of Article 2(2) would instead see it as explaining that, depending on the type of case involved, these various consequences could follow once breach of the duty is established. So, for example, where a party to a contract purported to exercise its right to terminate a contract for fundamental non-performance under Article 114 CESL contrary to good faith and fair dealing, Article 2(2) CESL would enable a court to deny that party's reliance on the exercise of that right.[55] In any event, Article 2(2) makes clear that 'good faith and fair dealing' is *not* merely a value *underlying* or *expressed in* the various rules set out in the CESL: the duty contained in Article 2 can affect any issue falling within the scope of the instrument.

Fourthly, however, there is a further, potentially highly significant combination of the roles of the principle of good faith and fair dealing in legal

---

54 So, the Comments to Article III.-1:103 DCFR (full version, 2010, n. 1 above, vol. I, p. 677) on good faith and fair dealing in performing an obligation observe that: 'Particular applications of the requirement of good faith and fair dealing appear in many specific provisions [...] Good faith and fair dealing could also be said to underpin the debtor's rights to cure a defective performance; the debtor's right to refuse to make specific performance of a contractual obligation if this would involve unreasonable effort and expense; and the requirement that a creditor should limit as far as possible any loss which will be suffered as a result of a non-performance of the obligation by the debtor, thereby reducing the amount of damages'. These examples are now found in the CESL at Article 109 (on cure by the seller); Articles 110 and 111 (qualifications on buyer's right to performance by seller); and Articles 162 and 163 (loss attributable to creditor and reduction of loss).

55 There may be thought to be a restriction on the consequences of breach of the duty of good faith and fair dealing, owing to its expression as a *duty* rather than an *obligation*, though Article 3 expresses the requirement of cooperation as an *obligation* rather than a *duty*. However, unlike the DCFR, where 'obligation' and 'duty' were kept clearly distinct, the CESL appears to adopt a different and looser approach. So, for example, Article 2(y) Proposal defines 'obligation' as 'a *duty* to perform which one party to a legal relationship owes to another'.

interpretation and in direct normative impact, for in some national laws good faith has played an important role in the development of new legal doctrines by the courts, a role most conspicuously seen in the use of §242 BGB in the hands of German courts over the last century.[56] As will be seen, this possible use by the courts (and ultimately by the Court of Justice) is closely related to Article 4(2) CESL's requirement that the courts must settle issues within the scope of the instrument but not expressly settled by it.[57]

Finally, fifthly, the explicit positing of a principle of good faith can be seen as a declaration of cultural identity. For, those national private laws of European States with roots in Roman law all contain reference to good faith following (though generalising) from its presence in the ancient texts.[58] True, the uses to which good faith or its linguistically equivalent concepts across continental Europe have been put have differed considerably, but many civil lawyers have come to see it as a distinctive feature of their tradition. For this purpose, the fact that the English common law does not recognise the existence of a legal principle of good faith in contract[59] is not seen as an obstacle. Some welcome the difference so as to distinguish the proper, social approach to European contract law in contrast what they see as the over-liberal approach of the English common law; whereas others prefer to see various elements in English law as equivalent to good faith, whether in historical equity or modern 'reasonableness'.[60]

Before moving on to the role of 'underlying principles,' we should note the changing status of the proposition that 'unless otherwise stated in this instrument, a contract, statement or any other act which is governed by it need not be made in or evidenced by a particular form.'[61] The Feasibility Study, which preceded the Proposal, treated this provision as one of its three 'general principles'[62] together

56 See for an overview S. Whittaker and R. Zimmermann, 'Good faith in European contract law: surveying the legal landscape' in R. Zimmermann and S. Whittaker (eds.), *Good Faith in European Contract Law*, Cambridge University Press, Cambridge 2000, pp. 7, 18–32.

57 See below, pp. 115–119.

58 For the historical development, see M. Schermaier, 'Bona fides in Roman contract law' in R. Zimmermann and S. Whittaker (eds.), n. 56 above, ch. 2; J. Gordley, 'Good faith in contract law in the medieval ius commune', ibid., ch. 3.

59 S. Whittaker and R. Zimmermann, n. 56 above, pp. 44–48 and see, more recently, S. Whittaker in H. Beale (gen. ed.), *Chitty on Contracts*, 31st ed., Sweet & Maxwell, London 2012, paras. 1-039 et seq.

60 For example M. Hesselink, 'Good Faith' in A.S. Hartkamp et al. (eds.), *Towards a European Civil Code*, 4th ed., Kluwer Law International, Alphen aan den Rijn 2011, p. 309 referring to the role of English equity.

61 Article 6 CESL.

62 Commission Expert Group on European Contract Law, Feasibility Study for a future instrument in European Contract Law (3 May 2011) published as Annex IV to EU Commission, A European contract law for consumers and businesses: Publication of the results of the feasibility study carried out by the Expert Group on European contract law for stakeholders' and legal practitioners' feedback ('Feasibility Study'), available at: http://ec.europa.eu/justice/contract/files/feasibility_study_final.pdf, Article 9.

with freedom of contract and 'good faith and fair dealing.'[63] However, while identically worded, the CESL no longer classes this proposition as a 'general principle' and places it instead in the following section entitled 'Application' (sc. of the CESL), which contains a variety of rules, some more general (notably, Article 4's provision on interpretation) and some more specific, as in the case of the definitions of 'reasonableness', 'not individually negotiated contract terms', and rules on the computation of time.[64] Why did the Commission decide to demote the rule 'no form required' from the status of a general principle? There is no answer available from what the Commission has published, but perhaps it was felt that the special formal requirements which the Proposal itself makes as regards to the agreement of the consumer to use the CESL contained in Articles 8 and 9 of the Proposal and the 'Standard Information Notice' in Annex II should not be seen as an exception to a 'general principle'.

In summary, therefore, while Articles 1 to 3 each have their own technical significances, they also have an important declaratory role, setting out the political and social values which the CESL espouses and making a clear statement of cultural identity by placing it firmly in the tradition of continental civil law. Moreover, Articles 1 and 2 have important implications for the interpretation of the CESL, both as regards to the rules it actually contains and as regards the rules that may subsequently be developed by the courts.

## 2. 'UNDERLYING PRINCIPLES' AND THE INTERPRETATION OF THE CESL

In this final section, I will briefly consider the significance of 'underlying principles' in the interpretation of the CESL. Article 4 of the CESL can be traced through the Feasibility Study,[65] the DCFR[66] and PECL[67] to Article 7 of the Vienna Convention on the International Sale of Goods (CISG).[68] I will note certain textual differences between these predecessors to Article 4 CESL and, in doing so, consider the role of 'underlying principles' under Article 4. The main provisions are as follows:

---

63 In the Feasibility Study, Article 89, 'co-operation' appeared as the first obligation of parties to a sales contract rather than as a general principle, a treatment drawn from Article III.-I:104 DCFR 2009.

64 Articles 5, 7 and 11 CESL.

65 Article 1: Interpretation and development.

66 Article I.-1:102: Interpretation and development.

67 Article I.-1:106.

68 UN Convention on Contracts for the International Sale of Goods of 11 April 1980 (CISG).

| Article 7 CISG | Article I.-1:102 DCFR | Article 4 CESL |
|---|---|---|
| (1) In the interpretation of this Convention, regard is to be had to its international character and to the need to promote uniformity in its application and the observance of good faith in international trade.<br>(2) Questions concerning matters governed by this Convention which are not expressly settled by it are to be settled in conformity with the general principles on which it is based or, in the absence of such principles, in conformity with the law applicable by virtue of the rules of private international law. | (1) These rules are to be interpreted and developed autonomously and in accordance with their objectives and the principles underlying them.<br>(2) They are to be read in the light of any applicable instruments guaranteeing human rights and fundamental freedoms and any applicable constitutional laws.<br>(3) In their interpretation and development regard should be had to the need to promote:<br>(a) uniformity of application;<br>(b) good faith and fair dealing; and<br>(c) legal certainty.<br>(4) Issues within the scope of the rules but not expressly settled by them are so far as possible to be settled in accordance with the principles underlying them.<br>(5) Where there is a general rule and a special rule applying to a particular situation within the scope of the general rule, the special rule prevails in any case of conflict. | (1) The Common European Sales Law is to be interpreted autonomously and in accordance with its objectives and the principles underlying it.<br>(2) Issues within the scope of the [CESL] but not expressly settled by it are to be settled in accordance with the objectives and the principles underlying it and all its provisions, without recourse to the national law that would be applicable in the absence of an agreement to use the [CESL] or to any other law.<br>(3) Where there is a general rule and a special rule applying to a particular situation within the scope of the general rule, the special rule prevails in any case of conflict. |

First, as will be seen, the CESL declares that its provisions must be interpreted autonomously, that is to say, they must be given an EU law meaning distinct from the meanings under applicable national law and for this purpose both its objectives and 'underlying principles' are specified as relevant. This setting of an autonomous interpretation could be thought of as unnecessary given the legal nature of EU regulations, as can the reference to the objectives of the CESL, given that this represents the approach to interpretation of the ECJ in respect of all EU secondary legislation.[69] Certainly, the Court of Justice has made clear the importance of autonomous interpretations and the use of EU legislation's objectives in their construction, even if in somewhat less absolute terms than those of Article 4 CESL, for according to its standard formula:

69 So S. Vogenauer, 'Drafting and Interpretation of a European Contract Law Instrument' in G. Dannemann and S. Vogenauer (eds.), *The Common European Sales Law in Context: Interactions with English and German Law*, Oxford University Press, Oxford 2013, ch. 3, p. 108.

> 'the need for uniform application of Community law and the principle of equality require that the terms of a provision of Community law which makes no express reference to the law of Member States for the purpose of determining its meaning and scope must *normally* be given an autonomous and uniform interpretation throughout the Community; that interpretation must take into account the context of the provision and the purpose of the legislation in question.'[70]

However, this general statement is stated as setting out the normal position and, on occasion, the Court of Justice has held that the definition of a concept used by a directive setting out uniform law can be left to national law subject to this not impairing the effectiveness of the directive.[71] Article 4 CESL rules out such a position of compromise. On the other hand, it is surely right that the proposed Regulation (including the CESL) would fall, following EU law's general approaches, to the interpretation of its secondary legislation, and, as Vogenauer observes, for this purpose the proper 'interpretative context comprises – despite the emphasis on autonomous interpretation – the entire body of EU law, in particular the other measures in the area of contract law.'[72]

We should note, though, a difficulty in referring to the 'objectives' of CESL for this purpose. For the objectives set out in the recitals to the Proposal explain the purposes of the CESL as a whole, that is, fundamentally, why it is created

---

70 Case C-87/98, *Linster* [2000] ECR I-6917, para. 43 (emphasis added); case 327/82, *Ekro* [1984] ECR 107, para. 11. The Court of Justice has added that the EU legislator's choice of the form of a regulation rather than that of a directive as initially proposed 'shows the importance which the EU legislator attaches to the direct applicability of the regulation's provisions and their uniform application': case C-443/03, *Götz Leffler v. Berlin Chemie AG* [2005] ECR I-9611, para. 46; case C-14/08, *Roda Golf* [2009] ECR I-5439, para. 49.

71 See e.g. case C-203/99, *Veedfald v. Århus Amtskommune* [2001] ECR 1–3569, para. 27 in relation to 'damage' in Article 9 of Directive 1985/374/EEC concerning liability for defective products, a particularly striking example given that the ECJ later held that this Directive requires 'complete harmonisation' within its scope: case C-52/00, *Commission v. France* [2002] ECR I-3827, para. 24; case C-154/00, *Commission v. Greece* [2002] ECR I-3879, para. 20; case C-183/00, *Gonzàlez Sanchez v. Medicina Asturiana SA* [2002] ECR I-3901, paras. 25–31.

72 S. Vogenauer, n. 69 above, p. 113. Cf. U. Magnus, 'Interpretation and gap-filling in the CISG and in the CESL' (2012) 11 *Journal of International Trade Law* 266, 273–274 who argues that the inclusion of a special provision (Article 4(1) CESL) governing its interpretation indicates that the proposed Regulation (including both the *chapeau* and the CESL) is to be interpreted differently from other EU laws and so be interpreted in accordance with an international point of reference rather than from an EU-specific perspective, in keeping with the approach set out in Article 7 CISG. However, even if, as I think right, the CJEU were to keep to its own general EU interpretative approach, this would leave open the question whether it could and should properly take into account the interpretation given to provisions in CISG in its interpretation of provisions in CESL whose text follows that earlier instrument. As Magnus observes, there are good practical reasons in terms of predictability of interpretation ('legal certainty') for the CJEU taking on established interpretations of CISG (ibid., pp. 274–275); on the other hand, the CISG is restricted to international *commercial* contracts, whereas the CESL would be available for consumer contracts and commercial contracts only where one of the parties is a SME and this difference could argue for a different interpretative approach as a matter of legal policy.

and the reasons for its availability both in terms of the persons who may choose it and the contracts within its scope, but the recitals to the Proposal do not give us any sense of the objectives of particular provisions within the CESL. Here, there is something of a contrast with the DCFR, whose comments on Article I.-1:102 explain that '[t]he objectives and underlying principles can be derived not only from the introductory remarks preceding these model rules but also from the later articles *and the comments themselves.*' In the case of the CESL, the Commission has not as yet provided either notes or comments on its provisions of a similar kind to those provided by the DCFR, although comments are in the course of being drafted.[73] An official commentary could be invaluable in identifying the objectives of particular provisions within the CESL.

Secondly, there is a noticeable omission from Article 4 CESL when compared to the phrase found in Article I.-1:102 DCFR (and the Feasibility Study) its rules are 'to be interpreted *and developed* autonomously'.[74] The Comments to the DCFR explained that its provision:

> 'has a static and a dynamic aspect. The first envisages foreseeable situations which may occur today: the second, unforeseeable situations which may occur in the future. The words "are to be [...] developed" are important. They are addressed primarily to the courts and are intended to make it clear that judges can develop the principles and rules incrementally.'[75]

Is the omission from the CESL of the idea of judicial development significant? At one level, it could be thought to reflect a sense in the European Commission that the Court of Justice should not be required explicitly to develop the law in the way which the authors of the DCFR earlier foresaw, as this might suggest a degree of European judicial creativity which would give rise to constitutional concerns concerning the proper role of courts.[76] On the other hand, the CESL's lack of distinction between 'interpretation' and 'development' could show merely that the formal distinction found in German scholarship between the two is not to be used in its interpretation.[77] However, as we shall see, Article 4(2) in fact gives enough of a basis for such creativity on the part of European judges without any such an explicit reference.

It is here that Article 4(2) CESL's reference to 'principles underlying' the CESL becomes most significant. Article 4(2) provides that:

---

73 See V. Reding (Vice-President of the Commission and European Justice Commissioner), 'The Common European Sales Law – a useful tool for business', speech delivered 17.12.2012, available at: http://europa.eu/rapid/press-release_SPEECH-12-962_en.htm?locale=en.#PR_metaPressRelease_bottom.

74 Feasibility Study, n. 62 above, Article 1(1).

75 DCFR, n. 1 above, vol. I, p. 87.

76 Below, pp. 118–120.

77 S. Vogenauer, n. 69 above, p. 48.

> 'Issues within the scope of the [CESL] but not expressly settled by it are to be settled in accordance with the objectives and the principles underlying it and all its provisions, without recourse to the national law that would be applicable in the absence of an agreement to use the [CESL] or to any other law.'

This is an immensely important provision and contrasts with the position under Article 7 CISG and Article I.-1:102 DCFR in that it imposes on courts an absolute duty to settle 'issues within the scope of the CESL but not expressly settled by it.' So, by contrast, the CISG accepts that sometimes there may be 'an absence' of 'general principles on which CISG is based' so as to allow the court to settle such issues and holds that these are to be governed by the law otherwise applicable under private international law. Similarly, while the DCFR provides that 'issues within the scope of the rules but not expressly settled by them' are to be settled in accordance with the principles underlying them', this is subject to the proviso 'so far as possible'. By contrast, Article 4(2) CESL emphatically declares that there must be *no* recourse to national law to settle 'issues within the scope of the CESL but not expressly settled by it'. This raises at least two questions. How is a court (and ultimately the Court of Justice) to draw the line between issues not settled by the CESL and yet within its scope? And how is it to identify the 'objectives and principles underlying' the CESL?

As regards the scope of the instrument, we are not concerned here with the relatively straightforward issues of scope set out in the *chapeau* of the Proposal, that is, the restrictions on the parties, the cross-border character and the subject-matter of the contracts for which the CESL is available,[78] but rather with the range of regulation of the CESL in terms of the substantive issues arising from the contracts within its scope. As I have argued elsewhere, this is by no means likely to be straightforward: first, because recital 27 of the Regulation excludes certain issues from the scope of the CESL in a very unclear way (most notably, 'tort') and, secondly, because the line between definition of the scope of an EU legal instrument and limitations or restrictions within the instrument itself is sometimes difficult to draw.[79] For this purpose the CESL itself is long and complex enough to generate a number of issues not settled by its provisions but not quite long enough to settle all of them itself.

Secondly, how is a court to identify 'principles underlying' the CESL for this purpose? From what has been said earlier, the Proposal appears to treat at least freedom of contract and the duty to act in accordance with good faith and

---

78 Articles 4–7 Proposal.

79 S. WHITTAKER, 'The Proposed "Common European Sales Law": Legal Framework and the Agreement of the Parties' (2012) *Modern Law Review* 578, 585–587; S. WHITTAKER, 'Identifying Legal Costs of the Operation of the Common European Sales Law: Legal Framework, Scope of the Uniform Law and National Judicial Evaluations' (2013) 50 *Common Market Law Review* 85, 95–101.

fair dealing as 'principles underlying' the CESL as well as 'general principles'.[80] Perhaps the Court of Justice could develop its own nascent case law on 'general principles of civil law' to help here as well.[81] Although Article 4(2) CESL's stern prohibition on 'recourse [...] to any other law' may at first sight rule them out given their ostensible source in European national laws (being supposedly common to all), it is surely more likely that the Court of Justice would see them as part of EU law and therefore see them as an entirely proper aid for the interpretation of an EU legislative instrument. More generally, the idea of 'underlying principles' seeks to appeal to the way in which at least some national laws treat the interpretation and development of their own civil law codifications. So, just to take the oldest,[82] while Article 5 of the French Civil Code forbids French judges from deciding cases by way of 'general and regulatory proposition' (*disposition générale et règlementaire*), Article 4 of the same Code declares it a 'denial of justice' for courts to 'refuse to decide, on the pretext of the silence, obscurity or insufficiency of legislation'. And, as is well known, Article 5 has not prevented the *Cour de cassation* from recognising various very general doctrines – sometimes referred to as *principes* – which are not present in the Civil Code or are present only by way of particular examples.[83] Nor is the idea of determining the reason for a particular rule and applying it more widely by analogy or reasoning from examples to a general proposition alien to English law, although there it is found in relation to the common law, not in relation to statutes whose 'exceptional' intervention is not the proper object of reasoning

80 Above, pp. 112–113.

81 S. Whittaker, 'The Interpretation of Concepts in European Private Law' in K. Boele-Woelki and W. Grosheide (eds.), *The Future of European Contract Law, Essays in Honour of Ewoud Hondius*, Kluwer Law International, Alphen aan den Rijn 2007, p. 333; S. Weatherill, 'The "principles of civil law" as a basis for interpreting the legislative acquis' (2010) 6 *European Review of Contract Law* 74; M. Hesselink, 'The General Principles of Civil Law: their Nature, Role and Legitimacy' in D. Leczykiewicz and S. Weatherill, *The Involvement of EU Law in Private Law Relationships*, Hart, Oxford 2013, ch. 7. For example, case C-412/06, *Hamilton v. Volksbank Filder eG* [2008] ECR I-2383, para. 42; case C-489/07, *Messner v. Krüger* [2009] ECR I-7315, para. 26; case C-215/08, *E. Friz GmbH v. Carsten von der Heyden* [2010] ECR I-2947, paras. 48 and 49.

82 Cf. the position of some German scholars that the notion of a 'general principle' of law or of the civil law is necessarily 'underlying' rather than stated in the law. So, according to Metzger, 'a general principle of law is a legal standard that is derived from legal rules by way of inductive generalisation': A. Metzger, 'Abuse of Law in EU Private Law: A (Re-)Construction from Fragments' in R. de la Feria and S. Vogenauer (eds.), *Prohibition of Abuse of Law, A General Principle of EU Law?*, Hart, Oxford 2011, ch. 16, p. 236. Metzger identifies the function of these principles as to serve as 'criteria for interpreting existing rules, they may be applied for gap-filling or other *praeter legem* adjudication and, most controversially, they my serve as a yardstick for the correction of existing rules by overruling or by *contra legem* interpretation': ibid., p. 238.

83 C. Jauffrey-Spinosi, 'Théorie et pratique de la clause générale en droit français et dans les autres systèmes juridques romanistes' in S. Grundmann and D. Mazeaud, *General Clauses and Standards in European Contract Law*, Kluwer, The Hague 2006, pp. 23, 30–31. A striking example is the recognition of *enrichissment sans cause*.

by analogy.[84] Finally, the use of two or more particular provisions to form a principle together with reasoning by analogy has been said to found the proper basis of the discovery of general principles under Article 7(2) CISG,[85] from which Article 4(2) CESL is clearly (if indirectly) drawn. Is Article 4(2)'s injunction merely happily in line with this common approach to legal reasoning?

Here, I think that there are two points to be made. First, whatever may have been the case as regards the DCFR, the CESL is *not* a codification of the civil law or even most of the civil law.[86] Rather, it constitutes a system of rules governing most (but not all) general contract law, and making particular provisions for the three categories of contract within its scope: sale of goods, supply of digital content and contracts for related services. While it therefore shares (or should share) the characteristics of 'coherence and consistency' seen in national civil law codifications (and set as desirable by the earlier Commission documents foreseeing the reform of European contract law),[87] it does not purport to be complete; the Proposal acknowledges that some substantive issues fall outside the scope of the CESL, even though they do concern general contract law and were for this reason included with the PECL.[88]

Secondly, as my allusions to French law and to English law suggest, the extent to which and the manner in which courts within national laws develop and change the law and, indeed, make law is conditioned by their wider historical and constitutional context. In the case of English law, the doctrine of precedent

---

84 B. Nicholas, 'The Pre-contractual Obligation to Disclose Information, English Report' in D. Tallon and D. Harris (eds.), *Contract Law Today*, Clarendon, Oxford 1989, ch. 4, p. 178 referring to 'the English lawyer's attitude to statutory provision as being (with a few large-scale exceptions, such as the 1925 properly legislation, and with the increasing important exceptions of those areas of law which have been largely created by statute) *isolated irruptions in to the body of the Common Law*' (emphasis added). This means, for example, that an English court would not see statutory examples of fairness or reasonableness in contract law as establishing a *general principle* of fairness or reasonableness: each legislative use is special to its context and typically defined or explained for its particular purpose. However, this is not to say that an English lawyer never uses the language of principle in interpreting (native UK) legislation. This could be done by a court identifying a general proposition within a particular piece of legislation, especially where this legislation sets up a coherent and exclusive body of regulation of the area of law in question and, as S. Vogenauer, n. 69 above, pp. 103–104, the legislature itself may set out principles of particular pieces of legislation (e.g. the 'overriding objective' in the Civil Procedure Rules Part I, describing itself as a code). Moreover, sometimes a *common law* principle (such as freedom of contract) can be used for the purposes of interpretation, balanced against the provisions of the Act itself.

85 P. Schlechtriem, *Commentary on the UN Convention on the International Sale of Goods (CISG)*, 2nd ed. in translation by G. Thomas, Oxford University Press, Oxford 1998, commentary on Article 7, paras. 29–30, 34.

86 S. Vogenauer, n. 69 above, p. 85 (the scope of the proposed CESL 'will be too limited to resemble that of a full-blown code in the continental post-enlightenment tradition').

87 EC Commission, *European Contract Law and the revision of the acquis: the way forward*, COM(2004) 651 final, pp. 5–6.

88 This is notably true of the law of representation/agency found in ch. 3 PECL, but excluded from the scope of the CESL (Proposal, recital 28).

recognises the legitimacy of judicial law-making (accepting that previous judicial decisions can bind subsequent courts), but it also constrains it; English judges are very much aware of the importance of the line between appropriate and necessary incremental development of the common law and inappropriate and undemocratic intrusion into the legislative function of Parliament.[89] Moreover, English judges' sense of their own constitutional position in relation to Parliament applies equally to their approach to the interpretation of statutes, where traditionally they accept an interpretative role, but deny the legitimacy of filling supposed 'gaps' in statutes.[90] By contrast, while French jurists remain divided as to whether or not *la jurisprudence* is a formal source of law, they accept its practical importance in the exposition of the law even though no French court is *bound* to follow a decision of a court higher in the hierarchy; and French courts have sometimes been very creative in the development of their rather civil code.[91] In the case of German civil law, German legal writers see 'gap-filling', i.e. the (further) 'judicial development of law' (*richterliche Rechtsfortbildung*), as distinct from 'interpretation' of legislation, but overall German courts are much more relaxed about 'gap-filling' than are English courts and have sometimes been very creative in their treatment of civil code provisions, whether this is properly called interpretation or gap-filling.[92]

In this respect, in my view the Court of Justice of the EU is in a very different constitutional position from national supreme courts. It is not that it cannot make law – such a proposition would be wholly unrealistic given its activism from the 1960s in a number of areas. Rather, the Court's development of EU law should be (and generally is) undertaken in a way which is sensitive to its own role within the framework of the Treaties and to the complex relationship between EU law and secondary legislation (and the competences on which the latter is enacted) and the national laws of which it forms a part and to which it is more widely related. Given this constitutional perspective, in my view, Article 4 of the CESL requires the Court of Justice to take on a role which is significantly new: it is not merely required to interpret the provisions contained in CESL that 'settle issues'; it is also required to construct legal propositions for issues which are

89 S. Whittaker, 'Precedent in English Law: A View from the Citadel' (2006) *European Review of Private Law* 705.

90 Z. Bankowski and D.N. MacCormick, 'Statutory Interpretation in the United Kingdom' in D.N. MacCormick and R.S. Summers, *Interpreting Statutes, A Comparative Study*, Aldershot, Dartmouth 1991, ch. 10, p. 362, referring to *Magor & St. Mellos R.D.C. v. Newport Corporation* [1952] AC 189, 191.

91 J. Bell, 'Sources of Law' in J. Bell, S. Boyron and S. Whittaker, *Principles of French Law*, 2nd ed., Oxford University Press, Oxford 2008, pp. 25–32 noting (p. 30) the exception as regards decisions of the Assemblé plénière of the Cour de cassation which bind the lower court in the case in question. Striking examples of the creativity of French judges in the 'development' of civil law can be seen as regards extra-contractual 'liability for the deeds of things' under Article 1384 al. 1 C. civ., and in contract *obligations d'information*, *obligations de sécurité* and the *exception d'inexécution*.

92 S. Vogenauer, n. 69 above, p. 116.

*not* settled by CESL: the Court is required to fill 'gaps' and so to make law. The Proposal therefore does not merely mark a practical shift in competence from the Member States to the EU, but also seeks to enact legislation, which overtly delegates to the Court of Justice a degree of law-making power.

The reason for all this is not hard to find, for if the CESL were to subject the Court's power to settle unsettled legal issues to a proviso of possibility (as with the DCFR),[93] this would allow non-uniform elements into the uniform law which it intends to provide and on which its stated economic purposes depend. It is the development of the internal market that requires the Court of Justice to construct law to fill in any legislative 'gaps' in the scheme set out by the CESL.

## III. CONCLUSION

'Principles' have featured very prominently in the debate surrounding the development of European contract law, but this terminology has referred to a number of different types of general proposition. Sometimes it refers to established principles of EU law (such as the principles of legal certainty, effectiveness or proportionality); sometimes it refers to principles common to the civil laws of Europe (as understood by the Court of Justice); sometimes it refers to 'general principles' stated in a legislative text (as in the case of freedom of contract, good faith and fair dealing, and cooperation in Articles 1–3 CESL) and sometimes to principles 'underlying' rules set out in a legislative text (as foreseen by Article 4 CESL). In each case, we clearly need to appreciate exactly what type of principle is being discussed at any one time so as to assess both its legal status and its legal function or functions.

In the case of the three stated principles in the CESL of freedom of contract, good faith and fair dealing, and cooperation we can identify three main roles: they have an important political role setting out the need for a balance to be taken between a liberal non-interventionist view of contract and a more 'social' view; they have an important legal cultural role, setting the CESL firmly within the European continental civil law tradition; and they may have a direct normative role, sometimes requiring a court to decide in a way which the rules set out in the main body of the CESL would not otherwise require. Moreover, even though they are stated in the text, it is clear that the Proposal sees its 'general principles' as 'underlying principles' for the purposes of the interpretation of its substantive rules and for the settling of issues within the scope of the CESL but not otherwise settled by it. The list of 'underlying principles' within the CESL more generally is much more open to discussion and their identification and explanation will form one of the most important tasks for legal scholarship if the Proposal is enacted in its present or in a similar form.

---

93 Above, p. 115.

In all this, though, the Proposal for the CESL clearly envisages a significantly creative role for courts and, therefore, ultimately the Court of Justice of the EU. Unlike the CISG, the DCFR and even the Feasibility Study, the CESL does not allow the possibility for a court to say that an issue which it sees as within the scope of the CESL cannot be settled by reference to the CESL, rules and principles taken together: recourse to otherwise applicable national law is ruled out in an absolute way. As I have said, the reason for this is the perceived need for parties who have chosen the CESL to govern their contract to be able to look only to the CESL for the regulation of their relations (subject to the important proviso that the issue falls within its scope). As the recitals to the Proposal explain, 'to overcome [existing] contract-law-related barriers, parties should have the possibility to agree that their contracts should be governed by a single uniform set of contract law rules with the same meaning and interpretation in all Member States, a Common Sales Law.'[94] In my view, though, against the economic benefits intended to be generated by such a uniform law must be placed the clear cost in constitutional terms of requiring the Court of Justice to take an overtly creative role in its future interpretation.

94 Proposal, recital 8. The 'contract-law-related barriers' are set out in recitals 2–7.

# CONTRACTUAL AUTONOMY AND EUROPEAN PRIVATE LAW

## Freedom of Contract and its Limits in the Economic Constitution

Salvatore PATTI

CONTENTS

I. Freedom of Contract as a Principle of European Private Law ......... 123
II. Limits of the Freedom of Contract in the Tradition of the European Civil Codes ......... 124
III. New Limits of the Freedom of Contract......... 126
IV. 'Aims' to be Realised by Means of Private Law and the Increase of Mandatory Rules ......... 128
V. New Techniques of Distribution and New Rules of Concluding the Contract......... 129
VI. Sufficient Information as a Condition of the Freedom of Contract..... 131
VII. 'Petrification' of the Law or a New Conception of the Freedom of Contract......... 132

## I. FREEDOM OF CONTRACT AS A PRINCIPLE OF EUROPEAN PRIVATE LAW

Freedom of contract is a concept that characterises the legal systems of the European continent as well as those of the common law and is often expressly foreseen in the civil codes, anchored in the constitutions or otherwise established in the law in action.

Having a look at the different experiences, the meaning attributed to the freedom of contract is not however always consistent and its limits in particular are different. For example, under the common law the duties of good faith in particular during the phase of negotiating are very weak, especially as regards what we call unjustified rescission and the liability that follows from it.

Moreover, in many scientific contributions, private or contractual autonomy and freedom of contract are mentioned without any distinction. Some authors define contractual autonomy as the basis of the freedom of contract; others consider autonomy and freedom to be synonyms. A terminological strictness can be found in the German literature, where for example a distinction is made between *Parteiautonomie*, referring to the parties' freedom to choose the law that will govern the contract, and *Vertrags-* or *Privatautonomie* to indicate the freedom to conclude a contract or not, choose the other contracting party and establish the content of the contract.

With regard to the title of the conference, 'Principles and Specific Rules in European Contract Law', organised by the Society of European Contract (SECOLA), I first of all consider it appropriate to place the freedom of contract among the principles, although in many legal systems this principle is regulated by specific rules, for example, in Article 1322 of the Italian Civil Code. It also needs to be pointed out, however surprising it may seem, that the conceptual definition of principle is not at all certain, especially the difference between principle and general clause. In Italy, for example, no distinction is generally made between the principle of good faith and the general clause of good faith.

This aspect cannot be dealt with in detail now, as the distinction between principles, general clauses and undefined legal concepts has been and is the subject of longer studies and involves important aspects of practical relevance: consider, for example, the debate on the competence of the European Court of Justice with regard to the interpretation of the general clauses.[1]

## II. LIMITS OF THE FREEDOM OF CONTRACT IN THE TRADITION OF THE EUROPEAN CIVIL CODES

The principle of the freedom of contract characterises the contract law of the European legal systems and has a unifying role within them, a role that emerges when contract law is confronted with the discipline of civil liability, recently described as 'an extremely heterogeneous subject'.[2]

It can be said that the unifying role of the freedom of contract has developed not only with regard to its contents, but also with reference to its limits. In fact,

1 S. Patti, 'L'interpretazione delle clausole generali' (2013) *Riv. dir. civ.* 263 et seq., in particular pp. 290 et seq.

2 G. Hager, 'Haftung für vorsätzlich verursachte Vermögensschäden (Economic Torts) im englischen Recht' in H. Kronke et al. (eds.), *Grenzen überwinden – Prinzipien bewahren, Festschrift für Bernd von Hoffmann zum 70. Geburtstag am 28. Dezember 2011*, Gieseking, Bielefeld 2011, pp. 791 et seq.

in the tradition of the European civil codes the freedom of contract has been interpreted in a wider sense, especially in connection with the will theory of the legal transaction.[3] The parties have been considered free to determine the content of the contract, provided that their will had been formed 'freely', namely in the absence of mistakes, fraud or duress. Each contracting party has been considered fully responsible for the evaluation of the economic undertaking and the subjective equivalence of the performances has been deemed sufficient to render the concluded agreement untouchable and (basically) final: *pacta sunt servanda*.

As each party had responsibility for evaluating the economic convenience of the contract, the existence of information duties, which would not arise even in the light of the duty of good faith during the phase of negotiating, was excluded. The Italian Civil Code of 1942 is a good example of this. It has inserted the provision of good faith during the phase of negotiating (Article 1337) but only the duty to notify the other party of any eventual reason for invalidity which a party has (or should have) knowledge of (Article 1338) has been expressly required.

This picture has, as is well known, changed radically in recent decades. The formal parity of the contracting parties did not seem to be sufficient to justify expressions of contractual power, which are a result of situations defined as 'private authority' and cannot be considered legitimate expressions of freedom of contract.[4]

Contract law of European origin has thus established a system of protection for the weaker contracting party – in the first place the consumer – which has deeply affected the concept of the freedom of contract. Besides the limits which can be defined as external ones, namely that they are only appropriate to ensure the compliance with general interests laid down in few mandatory rules, in public order and in morality, as well as to ensure the formation of a contractual will being free of defects, other limits have been added, which are much more incisive and tend to ensure the fairness of the contract, especially through a control of content, and the formation of a will which is 'aware' of the characteristics of the objects under the contract and even of their actual utility.

The new aims of protection have led to the valorisation of principles or general clauses already existing in the European legal systems, first of all the good faith and the solidarity, but they have also led to a profound change in the normative pattern. The discipline of the contract established by the codes was characterised by a reduced number of mandatory rules, as the idea prevailed according to which the freedom of contract has its effect mainly by giving the possibility to modify at one's discretion the models of regulation offered

---

3 See, among others, S. Pugliatti, 'Autonomia privata', in *Enc. dir.*, IV, Milan, 1959, pp. 367 et seq.

4 C. Bianca, *Le autorità private*, Naples, 1977, pp. 62 et seq.

by mandatory rules. Instead, the new contract law with its European imprint has an increasing number of mandatory rules in order to achieve its aims of protection.

Many of them even concern the pre-contractual phase, which in that way contains a series of duties whose non-fulfilment leads to a liability similar to the one traditionally foreseen for the non-fulfilment of contractual duties.

## III. NEW LIMITS OF THE FREEDOM OF CONTRACT

What is the foundation of the freedom of contract in the European context and what are its limits today?

As noted, among others by Stefan Grundmann, this is 'one of the fundamental questions of national contract and private law'.[5] The European states and the European Union are based on the market freedom which represents the premise of the freedom of contract, which for its part has its normative foundation in some of the constitutions of the Member States, in provisions of the national codes, in the EC Treaty and the contract law of European origin. The autonomy of individuals, namely the protagonists of the market, is encouraged and protected as long as it does not collide with the boundaries and barriers set by the States and the European law.

Therefore, besides the traditional limits of the freedom of contract, those established by the economic constitution have been added, namely by the entirety of the rules of European origin which had the function of harmonising the contract law of the European legal systems also and above all in order to protect the consumer, with the consequence – for certain aspects and at least with regard to a traditional view – of determining a reduction of the freedom of contract.

Not only, however, has the number of the mandatory rules increased, but there has also been a new kind of rules imposed, which are not based on a model found in the European civil codes and which – in my opinion – lead to a new meaning of the freedom of contract. I hereby refer to the information rules, which, together with the traditional mandatory rules, generally have the common characteristic that they cannot be derogated by the contracting parties. However, they neither contribute to determining the content of the contract nor do they seek to complement it or to prohibit certain exercises of contractual autonomy; instead, they ensure the actual autonomy of both contracting parties and, most of all, put them in a position of equality when it comes to the decision-making, since they provide the contracting party with the necessary information

---

5 S. Grundmann, W. Kerber and S. Weatherill, *Party Autonomy and the Role of Information in the Internal Market – An Overview, in Party Autonomy and the Role of Information in the Internal Market*, de Gruyter, Berlin/New York 2001, pp. 1 et seq.

he is missing in whole or in part in order to enable him to take a fully informed decision.

The limits of the freedom of contract can still be considered exceptions, but the experience of recent decades makes it possible to identify an evolution, which is primarily characterised by the importance attributed to the principle of good faith and in particular to the information duties. For a long time in Italy, as well as in other countries, good faith has been forgotten or considered to be a sort of elegant adornment in the decisions of the courts. However, the topic of the general conditions of contract brought out the good faith because the role of the main instrument has been attributed to it in some national legal systems (in the first place the German one) and then in the European Directive on unfair terms, and this has allowed a new kind of control, the so-called control of content.

Moreover, the modern discipline of the general conditions in contracts also needs to be seen under a different aspect, since it has established the awareness of the fact that some contractual clauses regulated by the codes and therefore legitimate – such as the penalty clause or the jurisdiction clause – should be considered suspicious or certainly unfair and, thus, ineffective in the event they are included in standard contracts, as they are a result of the difference of power of the contracting parties.

Once such awareness was established, the traditional conception of the freedom of contract contained in the codes has collapsed. The declaration of intent – even without any defects – has no longer been considered sufficient to sustain a contractual regulation unbalanced in favour of one of the contracting parties, which had *de facto* imposed the content of the contract. It has thus been primarily passed on to the control of content of the contract, inconceivable at the time of the formation of the codes and even revolutionary with respect to the traditional conception of the freedom of contract, and secondly, as we will see, it has been passed on to a great use of mandatory rules.

Within this briefly described context, good faith has played, among other things, an important role as an instrument of 'closure', allowing the judge to strike the evasion of the rules of protection, but most of all it helped to impose a new vision of the contract and the contractual autonomy. In a free market, autonomy cannot mean the possibility of reaping unjustified profits from the economic transaction, disrespecting legitimate interests and the other contracting party's 'normal' expectations.

## IV. 'AIMS' TO BE REALISED BY MEANS OF PRIVATE LAW AND THE INCREASE OF MANDATORY RULES

Once the conception of the freedom of contract has changed in favour of a greater contractual justice, the interventions of a protective kind have increased and their nature has increasingly moved away from the one of the traditional instruments of protection. Still, they can – as mentioned – be traced back to two types, which represent different categories of limits of the freedom of contract, whereas in the second case one can even doubt whether it is a limit.

The first type of intervention could be considered today as having a 'traditional' imprint and for certain aspects it finds a model in some rules in the Italian Civil Code of 1942. I refer, above all, to Article 1339. In some sectors the legislator has intervened by means of mandatory rules in order to limit the occurrences of the freedom of contract that should otherwise have been considered legitimate. For example, for some contracts – e.g. the lease – the price cannot be determined freely by the contracting parties, and the dogma of the subjective equivalence of the performances is thereby broken.

But, technically speaking, the laws implementing the European directives on contracts represent a more incisive and pragmatic evolution. Such laws do not just guarantee a certain performance by setting the limit of the equivalent but, in order to realise the set goals, they have an impact on the freedom of using terms considered to be legitimate by the same legislator, namely the freedom of establishing the rule of the relationship.

The autonomy of the parties is limited since the modern rules of private law, often sectorial, have a *determined aim* to be achieved, for example protection of the consumer, while private law traditionally did not include such aims.

Thus, for example, in the Directive on Unfair Terms the possibility of inserting penalty clauses or jurisdiction clauses into the contract is limited. Therefore, clauses traditionally considered legitimate are excluded from the tools of the contracting party.

Moreover, other directives, as is known, have introduced instruments of protection of the buyer which have an impact on the ancient principle according to which, once the contract is concluded, it binds the parties for good or, as the Italian Civil Code establishes with an emphatic formula, 'has the force of law between the parties' (Article 1372(1)). The rules giving the buyer the option to 'rethink' the convenience of the contract – and therefore to 'back off' *after* its conclusion, in the case of sales outside of the business premises, so-called door-to-door sales or distance sales – can be found in this context. In these assumptions, the evaluation of the convenience of the contract that the European codes implicitly imposed on the contracting party prior to the conclusion shifts to a later phase, although it is limited to a few days.

The rules that require these forms of protection are mandatory. This therefore increases the weight of the mandatory law (*zwingendes Vertragsrecht*) and correspondingly the freedom of contract has new limits.

Are those limits admissible or at least justified?

A German academic has recently expressed himself contrariwise[6] and his thesis can be summarised as follows. The freedom of contract is guaranteed by the law of the European Union according to the two traditional components of the freedom to conclude the contract (and to choose the contracting party) and the freedom to define its content. Therefore, a burden of pleading and a burden of proof, borne by the European legislator, as to the existence of special reasons justifying the limitation of the contractual autonomy would be created. Since, for example, the Directive on Distance Contracts – in the recitals (*Erwägungsgründe*) – does not provide any justification for the mandatory nature of the rules therein contained, the invalidity of the waiver – by the buyer – regarding the protection measures contained therein is not justified. A similar observation is made with regard to the project of the Directive on Consumer Rights, which in Article 43 states that consumers may not waive the rights which they have due to this directive. I will shortly return to this thesis.

Information duties by means of mandatory rules were foreseen. They tend to put the contracting party, for example, that acquires a good or a service, in the position of knowing completely and in detail the economic and legal characteristics of the transaction to be performed and then make a fully informed choice.

By means of the information duties one therefore tends to eliminate the knowledge gap which (often) exists between the contracting parties. Information asymmetries have always existed and the private law of the European codes has imposed the burden on each contracting party to obtain the information necessary for a well-considered evaluation of the convenience of the contract. However, the knowledge gap is often enormous in the modern economy – consider for example the financial sector – and a contracting party without the necessary knowledge cannot make a rational choice about whether to conclude the contract and about the 'justice' of the clauses therein contained.

## V. NEW TECHNIQUES OF DISTRIBUTION AND NEW RULES OF CONCLUDING THE CONTRACT

New techniques regarding the distribution of products have determined specific needs of protection, which are met by means of new legal instruments.

6 G. Wagner, 'Zwingendes Vertragsrecht' in H. Eidenmüller et al., *Die Revision des Verbraucher-Acquis*, Tübingen 2011, pp. 3 et seq.

This mainly refers to the sales outside of the business premises, in particular door-to-door sales and sales through the internet. These types of sales are often put together already due to the fact the specific protection foreseen by European law is more or less identical and consists in granting the buyer a period of time – the so-called cooling-off period – which runs from the time of the conclusion of the contract, within which one can go back and dissolve the already concluded contract.

In fact, however, the two cases have different characteristics, as in the case of a door-to-door sale the buyer is subject to the seller's intervention in his private life and is pushed to purchase a good that he often did not think of buying, whereas in the case of sales through the internet the process that leads to the decision to buy is similar to the one for a sale inside business premises, as it is the buyer who – in need of the good – takes the initiative and looks for the product. Thus, in this case specific needs for protection arise due to the fact that the buyer only has the possibility of seeing the product on the computer screen, but is not able, for example, to try it.

Regarding the cases briefly described above, the limit on the freedom of contract derives from the fact that the rules providing the right of withdrawal in favour of the buyer cannot be derogated: therefore, the buyer cannot renounce them.

The reason for the mandatory nature of the rules providing the right of withdrawal can be seen in the need to prevent the waiver of the buyer being foreseen in the general conditions of the seller, thereby emptying the protection of its effectiveness.

On the other hand one can observe that the need to ensure the withdrawal is mainly required in cases of door-to-door sales, not coincidentally also referred to as 'aggressive sales', as the buyer is subject to the initiative of the seller. This need occurs a lot less in cases of sales through the internet, since the initiative of the purchase comes from the buyer, who then has the same opportunity to reflect and evaluate as in the case of sales inside the business premises of the seller. Above all, it can be observed that only in a few cases of a sale through the internet does the buyer have a considerable interest to evaluate the convenience of the purchase after having signed the contract and received the good – for example when there is the need to try a piece of clothing – while in many cases the possibility of changing his decision seems to be the result of a whim, or an insufficient consideration prior to the purchase, which creates costs for the seller which will be added to the price of the product, with a resulting damage for other buyers.

Therefore, the appropriateness of regulating the matter by mandatory rules is doubtful and more room for the freedom of contract is preferred. In particular, it is suggested that the autonomy of individuals might allow the option of providing a dual regulation of negotiations, with or without the right of withdrawal, with the product being priced in the latter case.

The proposal also seems worth considering because the standard contracts of the seller through the internet are, however, subject to the control of content which is provided by the Directives on Unfair Terms.

## VI. SUFFICIENT INFORMATION AS A CONDITION OF THE FREEDOM OF CONTRACT

Slightly different considerations arise with regard to pre-contractual information duties, which together with the right of withdrawal are the most interesting innovation of modern contract law. Compared to the cases of sales examined above, which led to the provision of the right of withdrawal, the pre-contractual information duties have the common characteristic of aiming to ensure the actual autonomy of the contracting party when it comes to decision-making.

More generally, however, the rules – with their mandatory nature – which prescribe information duties are contrasted with all other mandatory rules that characterise the European contract law. In fact, they are designed to ensure actual freedom of contract, which is otherwise limited by the other mandatory rules as these represent an expression of State policy.

The issue regarding the great use of mandatory rules by the European legislator is, in fact, not (only) examined from the point of view of protecting the weaker contracting party, but also from the perspective of the relationship between market freedom – and therefore private autonomy – and State policy.

In this regard there is still a presumption of supremacy of private initiative and private autonomy unless there are specific reasons for an intervention intended to set limits through mandatory rules. This is because party autonomy has been considered to be the general principle of contract law in the European legal systems, but its limits have only been considered to be exceptions. Similarly, the freedom of contract, in all its forms, is considered one of the fundamental freedoms, which are the basic tools of the EC Treaty.

As far as the relationship between mandatory rules prescribing the context of the contract and (mandatory) information rules is concerned, it is confirmed that the latter must be favoured, as they provide for effective party autonomy based on transparency.[7]

A balance is thus required between mandatory rules on the one hand, which impose the content of the contract in order to ensure better functioning of the market and the protection of weak individuals like, for example, consumers, and, on the other hand, mandatory rules foreseeing information duties in order

[7] S. Grundmann, W. Kerber and S. Weatherill, n. 5 above, pp. 3 et seq.

to protect a contracting party with cognitive limitations, helping him in this way to avoid bad decisions.

The rules on information duties therefore tend to enhance the freedom of contract as, by removing the information asymmetries between producers and consumers, they favour the conclusion of contracts between contractual parties who are optimally informed and therefore able to express a consensus based on an effective evaluation of the convenience of the contract.

The question of the information duties is one of the most interesting aspects of modern contract law and, given its extent, cannot be dealt with exhaustively right now. However, it is worth pointing out the debate concerning the legislative technique as to the convenience of providing for a general provision rather than (or in addition to) the provision of individual rules prescribing specific information duties each time.

## VII. 'PETRIFICATION' OF THE LAW OR A NEW CONCEPTION OF THE FREEDOM OF CONTRACT

The significant increase of mandatory rules in the contract law of European origin is judged negatively by part of the doctrine that sees in this increase an unjustified sacrifice of the freedom of contract, which is a fundamental principle of the European civil codes.

In this sense a petrification of the right of sale or even a petrification of the private law has been discussed.

The two main topics of criticism are that (a) the consumer is not necessarily an ignorant or a person not being able to evaluate the convenience of the contract; and (b) furthermore, the mandatory rules are not necessary as the protection is ensured by means of the control of content of the contract.[8]

In this respect it can be observed very briefly that in some areas there are actually mandatory rules that impose a rethinking of the meaning of the freedom of contract. In fact, from the traditional meaning traced back to the freedom of contract one needs, at least in large part, to eliminate the content related to the freedom to determine the content of the contract.

Moreover, with reference to the thesis set forth above, considering the control of content to be sufficient for the purpose of protection, it should be noted that the two systems of control of content respond to two different conceptions and that, therefore, it does not only have to do with comparing the obtained or obtainable results.

---

8 G. Wagner, n. 6 above.

One just needs to reflect on the fact that the judge is entrusted with the control of content, with all the uncertainties connected to the single decision and in particular to the inevitable differences of evaluation in the different legal systems, disadvantages, of course, that do not exist in the case of mandatory rules.

On the other hand, it seems to me that the use of mandatory rules that impose the content of the contract should – because they limit the freedom of the contracting parties – be limited to cases in which the information duties do not appear to be sufficient. The information, in fact, is necessary and, as a rule, sufficient to protect the contracting party to ensure the advantages of the free market.

On the contrary, there can be no doubt about the opportunity of mandatory rules that foresee information duties. In fact, only a decision of the party that is based on adequate knowledge of all the characteristics of the economic transaction and the contractual regulation can ensure actual freedom of contract.

In doubt, however, the provision of a limit should be preferred instead of leaving the door open for abuse. In this respect the warning of O. von Gierke is still relevant, according to whom 'an unlimited freedom of contract self-destructs. A terrible weapon in the hands of the strong, a not-sharpened instrument in the hands of the weak one, becomes an instrument of submission of one due to the other one, to a shameless exploitation of a position of spiritual and economic strength'.[9]

9 O. von Gierke, *Die Soziale Aufgabe des Privatrechts*, Springer, Berlin 1889, pp. 28 et seq.

# GOOD FAITH AND REASONABLENESS IN EUROPEAN CONTRACT LAW

Emanuela NAVARRETTA

CONTENTS

I. The General Issue . . . 135
II. The European Perspective . . . 139
III. The Policy Dimension . . . 142
1. Form and Substance of Good Faith . . . 142
2. Role of the Reasonableness Standard Compared to the Principle of Good Faith . . . 144
IV. Coordination between Good Faith and Reasonableness . . . 146
V. The Politics of Harmonisation and a Final Remark . . . 148

## I. THE GENERAL ISSUE

In a speech given at the 1975 Conference on 'Europe and the unity of the law',[1] Alberto Trabucchi, who at that time was serving as a judge in the Luxembourg Court, referred to good faith as one of the general principles likely to be applied by the Court of Justice.

Five years on, the Vienna Convention on the contracts for the international sale of goods gave a prominent role to reasonableness alongside good faith.[2]

Since then, the use of good faith and of reasonableness[3] has spread relentlessly throughout European contract law: from the Directives[4] to the harmonisation

---

1 See F. POCAR, 'Il ruolo dei principi nel diritto comunitario' in *La formazione del giurista europeo, Quaderni della Rivista di diritto civile*, CEDAM, Padova 2008, p. 119.

2 See F. DIESSE, 'La bonne foi, la cooperation et le raisonnable dans la Convention des Nations Unites relative à la vente internationale de marchandises (CVIM)' (2002) 1 *Journal du droit international* 55 et seq. and S. TROIANO, *La 'ragionevolezza' nel diritto dei contratti*, CEDAM, Padova 2005, pp. 163 et seq.

3 S. TROIANO, n. 2 above, pp. 163 et seq.

4 For good faith see especially Directive 86/653/EC, Directive 93/13/EC, Directive 2005/29; for reasonableness see especially Directive 85/374/EC, Directive 93/13/EC, Directive 99/44/EC, Directive 2002/47/EC.

projects[5] and the DCFR,[6] up to the recent Proposal for a Regulation on a Common European Sales Law.

Their success,[7, 8] which has rapidly overshadowed twentieth-century critiques and concerns about the perils of a *Flucht in die Generalklauseln*, is mainly based on the *politics of harmonisation*.

European harmonisation enjoys rules that can easily be shared, due to their undetailed content and ubiquity in most European legal systems. On the other hand, the flexibility of the general clauses and standards satisfies the quest for uniform criteria as well as the need to preserve 'national and regional differences'.[9] Finally, the room which is left to the judge is common law, grounded in the authority of the precedent.

But why, then, choose to rely on the principles of good faith and reasonableness?

The answers to this question prompt our inquiry to move to the wider ground of legislative policy and technical legal reasons.

---

5 See C. Castronovo, 'Un contratto per l'Europa' in C. Castronovo, *Principi di diritto europeo dei contratti*, Guiffrè, Milan 2001, pp. XXX et seq.; C. Castronovo, 'Good Faith and the Principles of European Contract Law' (2005) *Europa e diritto privato* 589 et seq.; O. Lando and H. Beale (eds.), *The Principles of European Contract Law*: Part I, Martinus Nijhoff, Dordrecht 1995; A. Di Majo, 'L'osservanza della buona fede nei Principi Unidroit' in M.J. Bonell (ed.), *Contratti commerciali internazionali e Principi Unidroit*, Milan 1997, pp. 145 et seq.; S. Troiano, 'Clausole generali e nozioni giuridiche indeterminate nei Principi Acquis del diritto comunitario dei contratti' in G. De Cristofaro (ed.), *I 'princìpi' del diritto comunitario dei contratti*, Giappichelli, Turin 2009, pp. 189 et seq.

6 M. Mekki and M. Kloepfer-Pelèse, 'Good faith and fair dealing in the DCFR' (2008) 3 *European Review of Contract Law* 338 et seq.

7 See M. Auer, 'Good Faith: A Semiotic Approach' (2002) *European Private Law* 279 et seq.; C.M. Bianca, 'Buona fede e diritto privato europeo' in L. Garofalo, *Il ruolo della buona fede oggettiva nell'esperienza giuridica storica e contemporanea, Studi in onore di Alberto Burdese*, CEDAM, Padova 2003, pp. 201 et seq.; C. Castronovo (2005), n. 5 above, 589 et seq.; A. Di Majo, n. 5 above, pp. 145 et seq.; S. Grundmann and D. Mazeaud (ed.), *General Clauses and Standards in European Contract Law*, Kluwer Law International, The Hague 2006; M. Hoch, 'Is fair dealing a workable concept for European contract law?' (2005) *Global Jurist* 5; O. Lando, 'Is Good Faith an Over-Arching General Clause in the Principles of European Contract Law?' (2007) *European Review of Private Law* 841 et seq.; E. Navarretta, 'Buona fede oggettiva, contratti di impresa e diritto europeo' (2005) I *Rivista di diritto civile* 507 et seq.; E. Poillot, 'Influence du droit de l'Union Européenne et primauté de la loyauté: une protection incidente du consommateur?' (2011) *Petites Affiches* 34 et seq.; G. Vettori, 'Buona fede e diritto europeo dei contratti' (2002) *Europa e diritto privato* 915 et seq.; R. Zimmermann and S. Whittaker (eds.), *Good Faith in European Contract Law*, Cambridge University Press, Cambridge 2000, pp. 8 et seq.

8 There are also some signs of a possible decline of good faith. See in France Y.M. Laithier, 'Le décline de la bonne foi?' Annotation Cass. 2e civ., 25 févr. 2010, no 09-11352, and in Italy L. Cruciani, 'Clausole generali e principi elastici in Europa: il caso della buona fede e dell'abuso del diritto' (2011) *Rivista critica del diritto privato* 473 et seq.

9 M.E. Storme, 'Good Faith and the content of Contracts in European Private Law' (2003) *European Private Law* 13.

The success of the principle of good faith lies within a context of radical institutional changes and hints at the influence of several schools of thought. In the politics of the European Union the role of the market has gradually replaced the traditional statist organisation, characterised by a sharp division between the quest for social justice, left to the interventionism of the State into the domestic economy, and the regulation of private transactions and contracts, inspired by a laissez-faire approach to political economics.[10] The paradigm of market governance has prompted the idea of contract regulation as a tool for different political strategies.

Under the influence of ordo-liberal ideas akin to classical law and economic analysis,[11] good faith, once an unwelcome guest (*convitato di pietra*) in the market, was at first regarded mainly (but by no means only) in its procedural dimension, as a means for correcting the market, seen as an artificial output of the law,[12] through the imposition of duties of disclosure. Later on, well before the financial crisis cast an ominous shadow over the market and the whole system, the quest for justice brought about an expansion of the tasks assigned to good faith. Now it embodies the movement from a purely individualistic paradigm to a cooperative[13] (more than *stricto sensu* altruistic)[14] idea of contract, aimed at restoring its human and realistic dimension, and at affirming the value of the human being[15] and the commutative dimension of justice that only substantive equality can realise. Finally, according to some opinions,[16] even these boundaries were crossed

10 The laissez-faire approach is well represented by the famous observation of R. Brownsword, 'Positive, Negative, Neutral: the Reception of Good Faith in English Contract Law' in R. Brownsword, N. Hird and G. Howells (eds.), *Good Faith in Contract. Concept and Context*, Ashgate, Dartmouth 1998, p. 15, who says: 'Just as cricket without a hard ball is not cricket, so it is widely held that contract without tough self-interest dealing simply is not contract'.

11 J. Vickers, 'When is Trading Unfair?', speech to the David Hume Institute, Edinburgh 2001 (available from www.oft.gov.uk); J. Vickers, 'Economic for consumer policy', speech to the British Academy Keynes Lecture, 2003 (available from www.oft.gov.uk).

12 See N. Irti, *L'ordine giuridico del mercato*, 1st ed., GLF ed. Laterza, Roma-Bari 1998 (2nd ed. 2004), passim.

13 See T. Wilhelmsson, 'Good Faith and the Duty of Disclosure in Commercial Contracting' in R. Brownsword, N. Hird and G. Howells (eds.), n. 10 above, p. 181.

14 See D. Kennedy, 'La funzione ideologica del tecnicismo nel diritto dei contratti' (2002) *Rivista critica di diritto private* 333 et seq.

15 S. Rodotà, *Le clausole generali nel tempo del diritto flessibile, Lezioni sul contratto*, Orestano, Turin 2009, p. 116.

16 See M.W. Hesselink, 'CFR & Social Justice. A short study for the European Parliament on the values of underlying the Draft Common Frame of Reference for European private law: what role for fairness and social justice?' in *Centre for the Study of European Contract Law Working Paper Series* No. 2008/08, pp. 15 et seq., available at: http://ssrn.com/abstract=1270575.

and the need to reassert the demand for social justice, poured into contract law scholarship, affected the very role of good faith.[17, 18, 19]

When considering the reasons for the rise of the good faith clause, one might be struck by the contextual strength of the reasonableness standard. Those very reasons, in fact, unveil the false neutrality of a concept which – unlike good faith – actually conceals an individualistic, laissez-faire approach to contract law. Still, reasonableness endures in European law, providing the law of contract with the flexibility and openness required to in reality, namely the way in which contracts are drafted, particularly long-term contracts.[20, 21]

This scenario raises a number of questions that must be dealt with to understand whether the choice made by European law to favour good faith and reasonableness actually deserves our approval.

From a legislative policy perspective, we should ask what good faith can actually do, as this concept is attacked equally from both sides. It should be discussed whether good faith withstands the formal and institutional criticisms that see it as a sign of the 'sterilization of politics in western societies': a kind of compensation mechanism for the deficiencies of democracy and social policies in the European Union, brought about by the enlargement of judicial powers.

On the other hand, one should also consider whether good faith resists the substantive criticism that 'beyond the primacy of legislation, there is not a judge, who consults the justice and investigates the Good and the Evil, but [...] the automatism of a society depoliticized by the market'.[22] The principle of good faith is here seen as a 'whitewash' on a liberal-capitalist building, close to falling into ruin.

As regards the relationship between good faith and reasonableness, several interpretations might be proposed: a possible coexistence between opposing visions of contract; the enduring hegemony, through the standard of

---

17 See H. Collins, 'La giustizia contrattuale in Europa' (2003) *Rivista critica di diritto privato* 659 et seq. and 678 et seq.; H. Collins, *Social Market and the Law of Contract*, ARSP-Beiheft 49, Franz Steiner Verlag, Stuttgart 1992, pp. 85, 87.

18 A.T. Kronman, 'Paternalism and the Law of Contracts' (1983) *Faculty Scholarship Series Paper* 1065.

19 D. Kennedy, 'Distributive and Paternalist Motives in Contract and Tort Law, with special reference to compulsory terms and unequal bargaining power' (1982) 41 *Maryland Law Review* 563 et seq.; D. Kennedy, n. 14 above, 317 et seq.

20 See S. Troiano, n. 2 above, p. 166.

21 The success of the reasonableness standard can also be explained with the influence of the American law in international trade. See G. Weiszberg, *Le 'raisonnable' en Droit du Commerce International*, Paris 2003, p. 34.

22 M. Barcellona, *Clausole generali e giustizia contrattuale. Equità e buona fede tra codice civile e diritto europeo*, Giappichelli, Turin 2006, pp. 290–291.

reasonableness, of a laissez-faire, individualistic idea of contract; or finally a possible union, overcoming the apparent contradiction.

From a legal-technical point of view, some doubts can also be raised: the scepticism towards the imposition of categories likely to raise the reciprocal aversion of lawyers educated in different traditions; the suspicion raised by clauses, the meaning of which is controversial even within national legal orders; and the deep dislike for the contextual use of canons that, according to some, tend at best to overlap.

Finally, there are plenty of doubts concerning the *politics of harmonisation*, namely the fear that, through the concretisation carried out by the national courts,[23] the general clauses and standards might bring about a false harmonisation, resulting in a further process of judicial differentiation.

## II. THE EUROPEAN PERSPECTIVE

In order to deal with these three groups of problems, it should be preliminarily made clear how the passage from a national to a European perspective influences our way of understanding the concepts of good faith and reasonableness.

Firstly, the sharp functional difference between good faith, which leaves room for some flexibility in the statutory law systems, and reasonableness, which governs the application of the *stare decisis* by the courts,[24] tends to get lost in the European context. The statutory nature of European law, on the one hand, and the method of judicial precedent espoused by the ECJ and also followed by several domestic courts, on the other hand, make it difficult to draw a compelling distinction between good faith–civil law and reasonableness–common law.

Secondly, the relationship between these categories in European law can hardly match the range of reactions stirred up on a national level by whichever category is perceived as alien, spanning from refusal to intentional overlapping,

---

23 See J. Basedow, 'Der Europäische Gerichtshof und die Klauselrichtlinie 93/13: Der verweigerte Dialog' in G. Müller (ed.), *Festschrift für Günter Hirsch zum 65. Geburtstag*, C.H. Beck, Munich 2008, pp. 51 et seq.

24 See G. Weiszberg, n. 21 above, n. 34.

and even the adoption of the alien category in the place of the native category.[25, 26, 27, 28]

All too well known is the aversion of common lawyers, who blame good faith for being a dogmatic and indefinite concept, saturated with elusive ethics, at odds with the adversarial logic of contract and too general and generic not to compromise the pluralistic dimension of the contract. The proposal to turn the *test of unfairness* into a *test of unreasonableness* in the Unfair Contract Terms Bill, which will consolidate the 1977 Unfair Contract Terms Act and the 1999 Unfair Terms in Consumer Contracts Regulations clearly hints at this attitude.

Equally well known is the elusive character of reasonableness for civil lawyers, who see in it '*mille germes d'insécurité et d'imprévisibilité*',[29] a category that would leave the judge *legibus solutus*,[30] 'a bit like a swimmer in the ocean. In the open sea, with no earth visible in the distance, it is difficult to orientate oneself'.[31] This wariness is reflected in the attempts to translate reasonableness into more familiar categories, for example the clause of diligence in the law implementing the Directive on unfair commercial practices.

25 See the opinions of R. Goode, *The concept of 'Good Faith' in English Law*, Centro di studi e ricerche di diritto comparato e straniero, Rome 1992, p. 3; J. Steyn, 'Contract Law: Fullfilling the Reasonable Expectations of Honest Men' (1997) *Law Quarterly Review* 438 thinks that 'an overriding principle of reasonable expectation serves the same purpose as a general principles of good faith. The language might be different but the idea is the same' (R. Brownsword, N. Hird and G. Howells (eds.), n. 10 above, p. 30). Against see A. De Moor, 'Common and Civil Conceptions of Contract and European Law of Contract: The Case of the Directive on Unfair Terms in Consumer Contracts' (1995) *Revue européenne de droit privé* 260.

26 G. Criscuoli, 'Buona fede e ragionevolezza' (1984) *Rivista di diritto civile* 752 and C. Scognamiglio, *Interpretazione del contratto e interessi dei contraenti*, CEDAM, Padova 1992, pp. 352 et seq.; C. Scognamiglio, 'Abuso del diritto, buona fede, ragionevolezza (verso una riscoperta della pretesa funzione correttiva dell'interpretazione del contratto?)' (2010) 26 *La nuova giurisprudenza civile commentata* 139 read the good faith clause in the light of reasonableness. On the other hand, R. Brownsword, *Contract Law. Themes for the twenty-first century*, 2nd ed., Oxford University Press, Oxford 2006, p. 135 observes that in the modern law of contract in England there is a tendency 'for doctrine to reflect the expectations associated with good practices [...] in other words, we might expect that English Law will move towards the adoption of good faith as a requirement (in substance, if not in name)': the name will be reasonableness.

27 Favouring the idea of a close link between good faith and usages and practices, good faith could easily become reasonableness. Favouring the idea that 'the reasonable man represents after all no more than the anthropomorphic conception of justice' (*Davis Contractors Ltd v. Fareham UDC*. See Lord Hoffmann, 'Anthropomorphic Justice: The Reasonable Man and his Friends' (1995) 29 *The Law Teacher* 127, 128), reasonableness could become good faith.

28 The overlap is evident in the Dutch system, see Article. 2 of the Burgerlijk Wetboek – BW (1992) with its clause of '*redelijkheid en billijkheid*'.

29 G. Khairallah, 'Le raisonnable en droit privé français. Développements récents' (1984) *Revue trimestrielle du droit civil* 444.

30 F. Busnelli, 'Note in tema di buona fede ed equità' (2001) *Rivista di diritto civile* 555.

31 M. La Torre and A. Spadaro (eds.), *La ragionevolezza nel diritto*, Giappichelli, Turin 2002.

On the opposing side, there are opinions that are drawn by such an osmotic vision of the relation between these categories, such a profound attention to the foreign model, that they tend to replace the native with the alien category.

Indeed, if the axis of good faith is made to shift towards 'what is socially normal and regular', putting the accent on the *Verkehrssitten* rather than on *Treu und Glauben* in §242 BGB, good faith gradually tends to convert into reasonableness. Conversely, if we emphasise the part played by morality in defining the concept of proportionality and the standards that underpin social life – the reasonable man as 'a measuring rod of current morality and opinion'[32] or 'no more than the anthropomorphic conception of justice'[33] – reasonableness can easily drift towards good faith.

Finally, there is the idea of a latent overlapping, a tendency to virtually merge the concepts, seen as different ways to express the same needs in different contexts: 'An overriding principle of reasonable expectation serves the same purpose as a general principle of good faith. The language might be different but the idea is the same', observes a common lawyer,[34] whose opinion has been recently joined by the prediction that 'we might expect that English Law will move towards the adoption of good faith as a requirement (in substance, if not in name)': the name reasonableness would remain.[35]

But the close connection between the categories was expressed by Lord Steyn's words that 'there is not a word of difference between the objective requirement of good faith and the reasonable expectations of the parties'.[36] On the one hand this can be read as a sign that the mutual perception of extraneity is gradually being overcome; on the other hand if it is taken to the extreme it can be seen as logically inconsistent with the tendency of European law to avail itself of two categories and give voice to both traditions.

European law clearly cannot cope with either aversion and refusal or replacement and virtual indistinction, for both of these attitudes would in different ways lead to the repeal of one of the two categories. Their very co-existence should on the contrary prompt us to keep these concepts as much as possible distinct as regards their respective form and function, while preserving their coordination and capacity to interact.

At the same time, the criticism expressed at national level should not been be left unheard – and actually it has not been. It calls for an effort of clarity and reduction of the complexity that challenges even that well-known Latin maxim: *omnis definitio in iure civili periculosa est; parum est enim, ut non subverti*

---

32 M. Freeman, *The Legal Structure*, Longman, London 1974, p. 13.

33 This is the idea of Lord Hoffmann, n. 27 above, p. 128, who was inspired by Lord Radcliffe in *Davis Contractors Ltd v. Fareham UDC*.

34 See J. Steyn, n. 25 above, pp. 438 et seq. Similarly R. Goode, n. 25 above, p. 3. *Contra* cf. vice versa A. De Moor, n. 25 above, p. 260.

35 R. Brownsword, n. 26 above, p. 135.

36 J. Steyn, n. 25 above, p. 450.

*posset.*[37] Indeed, European law – especially its project – has plenty of definitions of good faith and reasonableness.

# III. THE POLICY DIMENSION

## 1. FORM AND SUBSTANCE OF GOOD FAITH

According to the Draft (Article I.-1:103, co. 1) and the Proposal for a Regulation on a Common European Sales Law (Article 2(b)), good faith is '*a standard of conduct characterised by honesty, openness and consideration for interests of the other party to the transaction or relationship in question*'.

European law therefore acknowledges the axiological connotation of good faith, setting the premise from which its difference to reasonableness can be drawn. This proves right Luigi Mengoni's insight that good faith and ethics do not need 'constitutional crutches' in order to interact.[38]

Yet the reference to ethics immediately revives the common lawyers' legitimate mistrust of a value-judgement that is likely to dissolve in the ethical pluralism dilemma: the '*china-shop of ethics*' mentioned by Powell.[39]

To avoid this criticism, there is nothing left for good faith to do but to turn to the legal system[40] to find the kind of justice contract law can achieve through good faith. Thence, if the relevant system is Europe, it is up to the Treaty to clarify the meaning of good faith, in its substantive as well as its formal dimension, concerning the impact of the clause of good faith on the constitutional dynamics and institutional relations.

On the other hand, since the Treaty is crowded with principles that are different in nature and even perhaps divided between economic freedoms and non-economic (i.e. personal) values, the elements of the definition of the concept of good faith are by no means useless. Honesty, loyalty and consideration of the interests of others easily go astray outside of the law, among different religious and secular ethical visions. Once they are conveyed in the dimension of the law, however, they can hardly lead to market freedoms – for if the market is regulated by good faith, it cannot regulate its rule. Quite to the contrary, honesty, loyalty and consideration for the others lead up to the principles expressing the

37 Giavoleno (D 50.17.202).

38 L. Mengoni, 'Autonomia privata e Costituzione' (1997) I *Banca, borsa e titoli di credito* 9.

39 R. Powell, 'Good Faith in Contracts' (1956) 9 *Current Legal Problems* 38.

40 We must remember, on the one hand, that 'in the Nazi period, the Courts applied *the principle [of good faith] to discriminate against the Jews*' (O. Lando, n. 7 above, p. 845) and, on the other hand, that the modern idea of good faith has emerged from the new Constitutional Principles. That is why in Italy it was refused the proposal (see the *Relazione avente a oggetto le proposte di riforma del codice avanzate dalla Commissione costituita nel 1944*) to revoke the clause of good faith of Article 1375 Civil Code after the Fascist period: see U. Natoli, *L'attuazione del rapporto obbligatorio*, I, Guiffrè, Milan 1974 (1st ed. 1961), p. 33.

primacy of the human being in Articles 2 and 6 TEU and in the EU Charter of Fundamental Rights: solidarity, equality and protection of human rights.

These references are by no means generic. Solidarity is more than trivial altruism. It drives the quest for a balance between self-interest and deference to others' interests, which good faith commits to the judge, and for the consideration of which the involvement of a personal element may have an influence. This quest would not cause a breach of the institution of contract. Quite to the contrary, the contract can be enriched, managed and moulded by good faith in its *construens* dimension. On the other hand, even the *destruens* dimension of good faith does not mark a breach of the institution of contract, provided that it steps in only when the principle of equality is betrayed by a legally relevant substantive inequality, which justifies a control on the merits of the bargain.

Good faith thus has the twofold aim of rationalising and correcting the market: *market-rational regulation* and *market-rectifying regulation* according to the sophisticated classification proposed by Wilhelmsson.[41] The former prompts a substantive reaction to the problem of asymmetric information, entrusted to the principles of solidarity and consideration for the other party's position. It is about the actual capacity of the weaker parties to understand the essential and relevant information, rather than the crowding of procedural information disclosure requirements,[42] that so often mystify them. The latter – *market-rectifying regulation* – aims to correct the asymmetries brought about by the exercise of private autonomy within the market and to promote a synergy between private autonomy and substantive equality. It is about to open the institution of contract to the consideration of personal, non-economic values.

These tasks are epitomised by the concept of contractual justice, justice within the contract or commutative justice, which has nothing to do with the arithmetical correction of the price. Contractual justice embodies the seeming paradox of a principle – such as private autonomy – which in order to fully realise itself, and maintain its human dimension, must in part scale itself down.

But can good faith also attain social justice, or distributive justice?

It is difficult to deny that contract law, particularly when it works with general categories – such as consumers, firms, etc. – has distributive effects.[43, 44] Quite another thing is to hold that redistribution through contract regulation

---

41 T. Wilhelmsson, 'Varieties of Welfarism in European Contract Law' (2004) 19 *European Law Journal* 718.

42 See R. Brownsword, N. Hird and G. Howells (eds.), n. 10 above, pp. 30 et seq. and H. Collins, 'Good Faith in European Contract Law' (1994) 14 *Oxford Journal of Legal Studies* 229 et seq. on the different views of good faith.

43 G. Calabresi, 'The Pointlessness of Pareto: Carrying Coase Further' (1991) 100 *Yale Law Journal* 1211.

44 D. Kennedy, n. 19 above, pp. 563 et seq.; D. Kennedy, n. 14 above, pp. 317 et seq. See also H. Collins (2003), n. 17 above, pp. 659 et seq.

can effectively attain definite social policies. And definitely another thing is to maintain that the goal of redistribution can guide the judge who applies the general clauses.[45] Charging the general clauses – good faith and *a fortiori* the principles of public policy and morality – with distributive tasks would result in an uneven, erratic repartition of the burdens of social justice and would eventually trigger the exclusion of the poorest and weakest classes from the market.

This is not to say that contractual justice cannot have positive distributive effects, but that it does not need to draw its legitimacy from that goal. Above all, distributive ends should not guide the judicial enforcement of the general clauses, in the attempt to make up for the absence of governance in the implementation of social policies.

Good faith therefore draws an institutional boundary between the respective tasks of the judiciary and the legislature in the enforcement of social justice. In this sense, it stands against the background of the ideal of a social market economy (cf. Article 3(3) TEU). In other words, trust in the virtues of regulated markets is tempered by awareness of its limits and the acknowledgement that social policies are needed that are not spontaneously provided by either market or judicial intervention.

The institutional meaning of good faith thus lies in the fact that it gives the judge the power to implement commutative justice, with an advertency to its relevance as a free-standing concept and its limits as well. Judicial intervention cannot substitute for specific social policies. This should also be taken on by the EU, so as to protect the weakest social categories and guarantee access to particular goods. These policies need in fact to be defined *a priori* and equally affect all those who are concerned, in a way that only statutory law (be it aimed at the contract's content or not) can perform.

## 2. ROLE OF THE REASONABLENESS STANDARD COMPARED TO THE PRINCIPLE OF GOOD FAITH

The digression on the role of good faith makes the enquiry into the function of reasonableness somewhat easier.

Contrary to the common law, which is silent on this point, European law tries to define the concept of reasonableness: a more subjective attempt in the Lando Principles (Article 1:302); and a definitely objective one in the DCFR (Article I.-1:104) and the Proposal for a Regulation on a Common European Sales Law (Article 5, Annex I). Neither get directly to the point. Instead, they identify the elements, concerning respectively factual indices (*the nature and purpose of what*

45 See H. Collins (2003), n. 17 above, p. 679.

*is being done and the circumstances of the case*) and the social dimension (usages and practices).

The very obscurity of the technique of indirect definitions calls for the help of political philosophy.

According to Thomas Scanlon, making normative judgements requires thinking about 'what could be *justified to others* on grounds that they, if appropriately motivated, could not reasonably reject'.[46, 47]

Philosophical analysis therefore focuses on social acceptance, which is actually also what the legal indices ultimately refer to, as a suitable paradigm to draw the fundamental distinction between rational and reasonable choices.

The former is 'a matter of basing our choices [...] on reasoning that we can effectively *sustain* if we subject them to critical scrutiny':[48] here rationality is basically congruity between the action and the realisation of an egoistic interest. A choice prompted by either a flawed critical examination (bounded rationality) or by a weakness of the will (which the Greeks termed *akrasìa*) is therefore irrational. The relation to an egoistic interest does not exclude altruistic interests (even for Adam Smith, according to Amartya Sen's reading),[49] provided that the latter also become an interest of the agent.

On the other hand, if the array of reasons that prompt (or direct) the action encompasses the adequacy of the choice in relation to reasons that go beyond self-interest and include its social acceptability and consensus, we are moving from the dimension of rational choice to the domain of reasonable judgements. Reasonableness adds to rationality the reference to grounds that rise above personal interests and are justified by the others' acceptance, which is the basis of society.

These remarks may help clarify the interpretation of the reasonableness standard in European law.

If reasonableness is taken as the measure of what a subject can know, expect or foresee, and if, *a fortiori*, it is taken as the measure of what is due or can be claimed, then the model of reasonable subject assumed by the standard is moulded by the circumstances of the case, including the conditions acted upon by the agent, who must consider the reasons which made her choice acceptable. It is clear that these reasons encompass legal rules, including the principle of good faith, as well as social conventions and customs: '*any relevant usages and*

46 T. Scanlon, *What We Owe to Each Other*, Harvard University Press, Cambridge MA 1998, p. 5.

47 According to Josef Esser the interpretation should make clear 'the relation of the meaning with a solution which is *acceptable* according to reasonableness': J. Esser, *Precomprensione e scelta del metodo nel processo di individuazione del diritto*, translated by S. Patti and G. Zaccaria, Edizioni scientifiche italiane, Naples 1983. This sentence is a starting point in the excellent essay of S. Patti, *La ragionevolezza nel diritto civile*, Editoriale Scientifica, Naples 2012, p. 9.

48 A. Sen, *L'idea di giustizia*, Mondadori, Milan 2010, p. 191 (A. Sen, *The Idea of Justice*, ch. VIII, Kindle ed., 2009).

49 A. Sen, n. 47 above, pp. 195 et seq.

*practices*', reads Article 5, Annex I of the Proposal for a Regulation on a Common European Sales Law.

On the other hand, when reasonableness is taken as the measure of objective elements – the reasonable deadline, the reasonable price, the reasonable content – the reference to the relevant usages and practices according to the circumstances of the case is all the more justified.

The detachment of reasonableness from economic rationality, namely as individualistic agency, dispels the fear that the concept of the former might rest upon a purely egoistic vision of the bargain, which would clash with the solidaristic stances taken by the principle of good faith towards the institution of contract.

Legal rules, along with social practices, are indeed among the reasons that concur in the name of social acceptability to establish the logical coherence of reasonable acting. Good faith and reasonableness are thereby joined together without overlapping, just as the diligence standard and the general clause of good faith interact in the national legal orders.

The submission of (the law of) contract to the market does not follow from the openness to social practices and customs brought about by the reasonableness standard, for the idea of reasonableness is flanked by that of good faith. An 'improper practice' would not pass the acceptability test. Unfair *Verkehrssitten* cannot prevail against *Treu und Glauben*.

## IV. COORDINATION BETWEEN GOOD FAITH AND REASONABLENESS

Moving from the policy dimension to technical legal considerations, several elements suggest that the relationship between reasonable practices and the objective standard of good faith does not imply a conflict, nor the subordination of good faith to what is normally practised. Indeed, it is better conceived as a relationship of coherence, premised on the fairness of relevant practices.

Article 86 and Article 170 Annex I of the Proposal for a Regulation on a Common European Sales Law, concerning asymmetric (B2B) contracts and overdue interest respectively, read that a contract term is unfair if 'its use grossly deviates from good commercial practice, contrary to good faith and fair dealing'.

If good faith and reasonableness interact without overlapping when the elements of the reasonableness test fit in the test of good faith, they can all the more easily co-exist without losing their identities or experiencing friction with other realms of European law.

Apart from this case, European law in its *destruens* dimension, aimed at restraining the content of the contract, prefers good faith to the reasonableness test. Good faith is in fact expressly called forth by Directive 93/13 and by the Annex I of the Proposal for a Regulation on a Common European Sales Law. Moreover, it is also implicitly called upon in the judgement on the unfair exploitation that moves the fairness control from macroeconomic to so-called microeconomic asymmetries (Draft Articles II.-7:207; IV.H.-2:104 and Annex I, Article 51).

Whilst European contract law in its *destruens* function takes a stand in favour of good faith, in its *construens* dimension it admits to the possibility of good faith and reasonableness coexisting and even coordinating.

Due to their different but not conflicting criteria, good faith and reasonableness concur in the interpretation and construction of contract. Good faith brings in a value-laden stance, while reasonableness acts as a measure of what was intended by the other party (Annex I, Article 58(2) and Draft Article II.-8:101) and as a parameter to construct the objective meaning of contract with a further and obvious reference to the circumstances, the uses and trade practices, and the nature and scope of the contract (Annex I, Article 67; Draft Article II.-8:102), elements from which implicit terms can also be inferred (Annex I, Article 68(a) and (b) and Draft Article II.-9:101).

The coordination of the coexistence evolves when the judgement pertains to the conduct of the parties. The concept of good faith, in fact, sets out rules of conduct, reasonableness measures and what can be expected by the agent, taking into account the standards set by rules of conduct, *quarum* fairness (see for a paradigmatic instance: Annex I, Article 88 concerning excused non-performance).

This dialectic clearly mirrors itself in the dogmatically complex, but substantively coherent Directive 2005/29/EU on unfair commercial practices. Here a standard of conduct (what 'may reasonably be expected') is identified and ascribed to the concept of diligence (not surprisingly, for reasonableness as a measure of conduct easily fades into diligence). On the other hand, 'the general principle of good faith' and 'the honest market practices' jointly and not alternatively[50] represent the metric by which what can be expected is measured (Article 2(h) Directive).

The Directive on unfair commercial practices, therefore, also clearly testifies to the ability of reasonableness to extend the range of reasons bearing on the evaluation of conduct to commercial practices, i.e. to social rules that by virtue of reasonableness acquire legal relevance, in coordination with, and not against, good faith.

Different models of enforcement stand out against the background of so many operational offshoots.

Reasonableness is pervasive, but its enforcement follows the ramifications of the several disciplines that provide for it. This means that it cannot be

---

[50] G. De Cristofaro, 'Il divieto di pratiche commerciali sleali. La nozione generale di pratica commerciale "sleale" e i parametri di valutazione della "slealtà"' in G. De Cristofaro (ed.), *Le 'pratiche commerciali sleali' tra imprese e consumatori. La direttiva 2005/29/Ce e il diritto italiano*, Giappichelli, Turin 2007, p. 121.

extended beyond the possibility of understanding 'any reference to what can be expected of or by a person, or in a particular situation, [as] a reference to what can reasonably be expected' (Article 5, Annex I, Proposal for a Regulation on a Common European Sales Law). Conversely, the concept of good faith has a wide-open scope, expanding from the pre-contractual stage of commercial practices and advertising to the whole life of the contract and the so-called post-contract. This is evident in the Draft and its legacy: the Proposal for Regulation on a Common European Sales Law, at Articles 2 and 3 of Annex I. Other Directives, on the other hand, like the disappointing Directive 2011/83 on Consumers' Rights and the Directive 2008/48 on Consumer Credit, take a procedural stance to the propagation of information disclosure requirements, which are not backed by a general clause like Article 28, Annex I, Proposal for a Regulation. In spite of that, and perhaps *a fortiori*,[51] we must reassess the substantive and general breadth of the concept of good faith, as it is mirrored by its very bilateral character, felicitously acknowledged by the ECJ in *Messner*.[52] Nor should this worry the common lawyer, apprehensive of the possibility of betraying the actual complexity of contract.[53] Good faith, in fact, shows a peculiar ability to adjust to different operational contexts, as recital 31 of the Proposal for a Regulation positively reasserts, as well as to the capacity to play different functions, thereby acting through different remedies: from the invalidity brought about by good faith in its *destruens* dimension, to the pre-emption of the exercise of a right, remedy or exception, to the damages (see Article 2(2) Annex I).

## V. THE POLITICS OF HARMONISATION AND A FINAL REMARK

The argument developed so far aimed at stressing the possibility of exploiting and making the most of the wealth of good faith at civil law and the legacy of reasonableness at common law.

The solidarity perspective brought by good faith to the contract 'is not at odds with the classical law of contract'.[54] It does not imply 'a Franciscan renunciation

---

51 Just in order to guarantee an '*information circostanciée et personnalisée*', see S. Pagliantini, 'Il contratto di credito al consumo tra vecchi e nuovi formalismi' in G. De Cristofaro (ed.), *La nuova disciplina europea del credito al consumo. La direttiva 2008/48/106*, Giappichelli, Turin 2009, p. 106.

52 Case C-489/07, *Messner* [2009] ECR I-7315.

53 Other than the idea of an adaptation to different context of good faith is the idea of diversifying the conceptions of the clause according to the context. See J. Wightman, 'Good Faith and Pluralism in the Law of Contract' in R. Brownsword, N. Hird and G. Howells (eds.), n. 10 above, pp. 41 et seq.

54 A. De Vita, 'Buona fede e common law. Attrazione non fatale nella storia del contratto, Il ruolo della buona fede oggettiva nell'esperienza giuridica storica e contemporanea' in L. Garofalo (ed.), n. 7 above, p. 482.

to pursue one's own interests in order to help a rival'.[55] Rather, it recalls the Kantian idea that to act justly is something we want to do as rational, free and equal agents. This idea is not unknown to the logic of the common law, though there it has taken different routes, with different legal institutes and perhaps a disposition more sympathetic to personal responsibility than to command-and-control regulation. At any rate, the detachment of the Anglo-Saxon approach from the concept of good faith is formal more than substantial and it is lessened by other common law jurisdictions' familiarity with it.

The positive contribution made by the reasonableness standard to contract consists, for its part, in its very capacity to appreciate the value of personal responsibility as well as its coherence with the societal context in which contracts are made. Its disarming intuitive character, on the other hand, due to that flat and unstructured *modus argumentandi* characteristic of the Anglo-Saxon thought, no longer confronts civil lawyers with an enigma, since it can be reconciled with an effort of reflective reconstruction. Reasonableness indeed offers two faces: that of rationally justified expectations, the understanding of which does not need to be conveyed by the concept of diligence, and that of the capacity to fulfil, through its reference to social practices and customs, a whole array of reasons on which social acceptance is built.

As long as the two traditions can converse, understand each other and interact, the methodological choice of European lawyers remains contingent on the assessment of the opportunity to adopt a technique that significantly broadens the discretion of the judge faced with the legislature.

From the point of view of the politics of the harmonisation, the fear that a further process of differentiation might follow, triggered by the concretisation of general clauses and standards, has been – I believe – dispatched by the ECJ doctrine, especially in the judgment given by the Grand Chamber on 9 November 2010 (C137/08), *Pènzügyi Lizing Zrtt. v. Ferenc Schneider*. The judgment leaves it to the Court to interpret 'the concept of "unfair term" [... and to define] the criteria which the national court may or must apply when examining a contractual term in the light of the provisions of that Directive, bearing in mind that it is for that court to determine, in the light of those criteria, whether a particular contractual term is actually unfair in the circumstances of the case'. The important tasks assigned to the ECJ are made clear in this judgment with more accuracy than the famous precedent *Freiburger Kommunalbauten*,[56] which was in my view unfairly criticised.[57]

It cannot be denied that the European Court of Justice is confined to the interpretation of the law, whereas the application of the general rules to

55 Ibid.

56 Case C-237/02, *Freiburger Kommunalbauten* [2004] ECR I-3403.

57 See M.W. Hesselink, 'Case Notes. Case: ECJ – Freiburger Kommunalbauten v. Hofstetter' (2006) 3 *European Review of Contract Law* 372 et seq. and L. Cruciani, n. 8 above, p. 482.

particular cases is up to the national courts. But this does not necessarily strengthen the risk of a national jurisdiction-driven process of divergence. First of all, the reference to interpretive criteria leading the application of the rules suggests that the Court of Justice retains for itself the capacity to go beyond the pure explanation of the norms, in order to steer the process of application by national courts. Moreover, in the light of the claims made by the Court the possibility can hardly be ruled out that the concretisation carried out at national level may in turn be the object of a reflexive synthesis by the ECJ, through a feedback relation between national and supranational levels. Indeed, through the comparison of the national doctrines the ECJ might eventually extract typical groups of cases (*Fallgruppen*) so as to make its hermeneutic criteria progressively more specific. In this way it would be possible to accomplish the goal of flexible harmonisation in which Member States participate more, which would ensure uniformity in the application of the law while at the same time respecting national legal identities.

To conclude, the use of general clauses and standards should also be positively – though prudently – valued from the point of view of the politics of harmonisation, after having been approved on broader policy and legal-technical grounds. Indeed, general clauses and standards not only outline the possibility of a fitting institutional compromise between civil law systems and common law systems, they might also provide the best frame of reference at substantive level.

Reasonableness guarantees the deepest coherence of contracts with the economic and social dimension in which it is brought about by self-responsible parties. Good faith bestows humanity upon contracts, which makes them consistent with the ends of justice. There is no reason to doubt that the axiological dimension would jeopardise the contract, as long as it stays within the boundaries of commutative (contractual) justice, which set the limits of judicial intervention. This does not mean that we should renounce the quest for social justice. It means that this quest is entrusted to the legislature, possibly also to the European legislature, thereby involving all the powers of the state in the task of enforcing the ends of justice.

Contractual justice cannot make up for social justice, though it can join it, and both – each with its characteristic institutional competence – must assert their legitimacy, quite independently from efficiency grounds.

According to John Rawls, '[j]ustice is the first virtue of social institutions, as truth is of systems of thought. A theory however elegant and economical must be rejected or revised if it is untrue; likewise laws and institutions must be reformed if they are unjust'.[58] Similarly they must be preserved and protected – we should add – when they are just.

58 J. Rawls, *A Theory of Justice*, Harvard University Press, Oxford 1971 (*Una teoria della giustizia*, Feltrinelli, Milan 2010, p. 25).

# BENEFITS TO THE DEFENDANT AS A MEASURE FOR RELIEF

## Toward a Specific Rule in European Contract Law?

Carlos GÓMEZ LIGÜERRE

CONTENTS

I. Restitution and Unjust Enrichment . . . . . . . . . . . . . . . . . . . . . . . . . . . . . . 151
II. Profits as Enrichment. . . . . . . . . . . . . . . . . . . . . . . . . . . . . . . . . . . . . . . . . 154
III. Disgorgement of Profits Made by Breach of Contract . . . . . . . . . . . . . . . . 157

## I. RESTITUTION AND UNJUST ENRICHMENT

In a general and broad sense, 'restitution' means restoration, i.e. returning something lost or stolen. From a legal point of view, 'restitution' refers to a specific set of remedies designed to restore what the defendant has gained at the plaintiff's expense to the plaintiff.[1] By their very nature, restitutionary remedies always entail something wrong that therefore has to be redressed.

Restitution is applicable to a wide range of different situations, from contracts made by mistake to uses of another's assets without the owner's consent.[2] In all such cases, the legal system tries to restore things to the scenario of nothing wrong having even happened by returning everything to the right place, as it was before the wrongful conduct that triggered restitution. In doing so, all possible restitutionary solutions share a common goal: preventing unjust enrichment.[3]

---

1 See D. LAYCOCK, *Modern American Remedies*, 3rd ed., Aspen Publishers, New York 2002, p. 4.

2 'Restitution is a simple word but a difficult subject, partly because restitutionary ideas appear in many guises.' See D.B. DOBBS, *The Law of Remedies*, 2nd ed., Hornbook Series, West Group, St. Paul MN 1993, p. 366.

3 In his seminal work Peter Birks wrote that 'Restitution and unjust enrichment identify exactly the same area of law. The one term quadrates with the other.' See P. BIRKS, *An Introduction to the Law of Restitution*, Clarendon Press, Oxford 1985, p. 17. The author goes on stating: 'Restitution is not the only mechanism against unjust enrichment. If we take prevention

What we currently know as the law of restitution and unjust enrichment was developed from a number of more specific remedies and causes of action that have been identified by common law and civil law systems in different ways. Quasi-contracts, constructive trusts, accounting for profits, rescission, equitable lien, subrogation, indemnity and contribution, among others, are legal responses in situations in which someone does not rightfully gain the right to hold another's assets or to get profit from them.

Legal systems have tried to identify a general principle on which these separate remedies are based, and they have found it in the general prohibition on unjust, or unjustified, enrichment. In fact, it is generally acknowledged that no one is entitled to retain unjustified enrichment. In all legal systems the law on unjust enrichment is largely devoted to distinguishing between unjust and not unjust enrichment.[4] Transfers of money or assets made in performance of valid contracts or as a valid gift are deemed justified, while transfers made by mistake or as a consequence of void contracts or invalid gifts are not justified. The former allow the money to remain; the latter require restoration, as noted above.

The principle seems to be universally recognised, even in the absence of any express provision in some European civil codes, specifically in the French Civil Code and the Codes that followed its structure. However, such civil codes expressly foresee specific remedies for management of another's assets and remedies for undue payments, as solutions for certain situations embraced under the umbrella of 'quasi-contracts', following the Roman tradition.

By contrast, other civil codes expressly mention the consequences following unjust enrichment as a specific remedy being used in the event of enrichment unduly obtained by the defendant. This is the case of the German Civil Code, whose §§812–822 deal with the claim for the restitution of unjustified enrichment. §812 defines the cause of action as follows:

> '*(1) Wer durch die Leistung eines anderen oder in sonstiger Weise auf dessen Kosten etwas ohne rechtlichen Grund erlangt, ist ihm zur Herausgabe verpflichtet. Diese*

---

as the genus we can distinguish under it three different species: deterrence, anticipation and reversal. Alternatively, it might equally be said that prevention (by deterrence and anticipation) should be contrasted with reversal (by restitution). [...] Unjust enrichment is deterred most obviously by those parts of the criminal law which punish acquisitive dishonesty. The law of theft and related offences is all about trying to curb the temptation to acquire wealth in modes of which society disapproves. The same can be said of blackmail; and there are many specialized cases, for instance insider-dealing in company securities. In civil law the torts of conversion and deceit can be seen as part of the same picture' (p. 25).

4 Cf. J. Gordley and A.T. von Mehren, *An Introduction to the Comparative Study of Private Law*, Cambridge University Press, Cambridge 2006, p. 555: 'While the principle against unjust enrichment seems to be universally recognized, despite the recalcitrance of the English and the absence of any express text in France, many jurists doubt whether it means anything definite. Even the Romans recognized a few limited cases in which a plaintiff would be entitled to relief.'

*Verpflichtung besteht auch dann, wenn der rechtliche Grund später wegfällt oder der mit einer Leistung nach dem Inhalt des Rechtsgeschäfts bezweckte Erfolg nicht eintritt. (2) Als Leistung gilt auch die durch Vertrag erfolgte Anerkennung des Bestehens oder des Nichtbestehens eines Schuldverhältnisses.'*

The Italian Civil Code also addresses the matter specifically in its Articles 2041 and 2042. Article 2041 defines the unjust enrichment claim as follows:

*'Chi, senza una giusta causa, si è arricchito a danno di un'altra persona è tenuto, nei limiti dell'arricchimento, a indennizzare quest'ultima della correlativa diminuzione patrimoniale.*

*Qualora l'arricchimento abbia per oggetto una cosa determinata, colui che l'ha ricevuta è tenuto a restituirla in natura, se sussiste al tempo della domanda.'*

The Common Frame of Reference, while trying to establish a common core on the topic among the European legal systems, devotes a specific book to unjust enrichment and sets forth:[5]

'Article VII.–1:101: Basic rule
(1) A person who obtains an unjustified enrichment which is attributable to another's disadvantage is obliged to that other to reverse the enrichment.'

In fact, the Common Frame of Reference takes a wide perspective on the issue and considers the use of another's assets as a general source of obligations that can justify the condemnation of paying benefits unduly obtained to the person vested with the infringed right. Article VII.-3:101[6] includes the use of another's assets as an specific way of enrichment, and Article VII.-3:102[7] includes such use in the disadvantages that trigger the application of the rules on unjust enrichment.

---

5 Annex 1 to the Common Frame of Reference containing definitions of legal terms defines 'unjust enrichment' in the following way: 'An "unjustified enrichment" is an enrichment which is not legally justified, with the result that, if it is obtained by one person and is attributable to another's disadvantage, the first person may, subject to legal rules and restrictions, be obliged to that other to reverse the enrichment.' This is a very broad understanding of what unjust enrichment is, and therefore of the legal basis for a claim for unjust enrichment. As Jan Smits and Vanessa Mak concluded: 'we must criticize the very broad playing field for unjust enrichment: in the DCFR any increase in assets or decrease in liabilities counts as enrichment. This means that enrichment is not a normative concept: any change in someone's financial position as a result of the act of another can count as an enrichment.' See J. Smits and V. Mak, 'Unjustified enrichment' in L. Antoniolli and F. Fiorentini, *A Factual Assessment of the Draft Common Frame of Reference*, Sellier, Munich 2011, p. 265.

6 Article VII.–3:101: Enrichment. (1) A person is enriched by: (a) an increase in assets or a decrease in liabilities; (b) receiving a service or having work done; or (c) use of another's assets.

7 Article VII.–3:102: Disadvantage. (1) A person is disadvantaged by: (a) a decrease in assets or an increase in liabilities; (b) rendering a service or doing work; or (c) another's use of that person's assets.

In the same context, the recently published Restatement of the Law (Third) on Restitution and Unjust Enrichment[8] contains the following general clause:

> '§1. Restitution and Unjust Enrichment
> A person who is unjustly enriched at the expense of another is subject to liability in restitution.'

## II. PROFITS AS ENRICHMENT

It is generally understood that the claim of action for unjust enrichment requires that the plaintiff suffered an impoverishment that corresponds to the equivalent enrichment gained by the defendant.

Problems arise in a specific set of claims in which the enrichment may be deemed unjust despite the plaintiff not suffering any loss. This is the case when the enrichment has been gained by breaching fiduciary duties or in cases of some statutory torts such as infringements of intellectual property. What these situations have in common is the existence of an unduly obtained enrichment, although it does not correspond to any impoverishment suffered by the plaintiff.

Two leading decisions illustrate the problem. The first, rendered by the Supreme Court of the United States, is *Snepp v. United States*.[9] The court decided the claim of the American Central Intelligence Agency (CIA) against one of its former employees, Frank Warren Snepp.

Snepp was an analyst in charge of some tasks during the Vietnam War and was one of the last Americans to leave the US Embassy in Saigon. Years later, once Snepp was no longer in active service, he published *Decent Interval*, a critical overview of the activities of the Agency in Vietnam based on the author's personal experiences. The CIA tried to prevent the publication of the book and sued Snepp for breaching an obligation contained in the contract he made with the Agency, according to which he had agreed not to publish any information relating to the Agency without prepublication clearance. Snepp appealed on the grounds that his actions were covered by his first amendment right to freedom of speech. The Supreme Court decided that Snepp had acted wrongfully, and he was ordered to pay to the CIA the profits obtained by selling the book. Thus, the Agency did not suffer any monetary loss.

The second case, which resembles the first one, was decided by the English House of Lords. It is *Attorney General v. Blake*.[10] George Blake was an agent of the English Secret Intelligence Service who secretly worked as a double agent

---

8 Published by the American Law Institute in 2011. American Law Institute, *Restatement of the Law (Third) of Restitution and Unjust Enrichment*, 2011.

9 444 U.S. 507 (1980).

10 [2000] UKHL 45.

for the Soviet Union. When his function as a double agent was detected, he was condemned as a traitor and imprisoned. However, he escaped and fled to the Soviet Union, where he lived for the rest of his life. In 1990, once the Soviet regime fell, Blake wrote his autobiography, *No Other Choice*, describing his life as a double agent. The British Government sued Blake over the publication and it was ruled that Blake must pay to the Crown all the profits he made from the book.

Putting aside the details, in both cases the activities at stake were wrongful and Snepp, as well as Blake, became enriched having breached contractual and fiduciary duties. The problem is that in both cases it was not clear to what extent the plaintiffs had suffered an impoverishment that should and could be restored by the defendant. In spite of the unjust condition of the enrichment, the principles of restitution hardly apply to such cases.[11]

In such cases the calculation of the measure of restitution is sought in the benefits obtained by the wrongdoer, who is obliged to disgorge profits independently of the losses suffered by the plaintiff. It has traditionally been said in cases of enrichment by wrongdoing that the key remedy to restitution is disgorgement, or 'accounting' as it is sometimes called. This form of liability is ordinarily limited to cases of intentional or conscious wrongdoing. The remedy recalls the classical rule *nemo propriam turpitudinem allegans auditur* and is well captured by §3 of the Restatement (Third) of Restitution and Unjust Enrichment:[12]

> 'A person is not permitted to profit by his own wrong.'

Cases like the aforementioned show the limits of the traditional explanation of unjust enrichment and restitution doctrines[13] and recall cases on torts, which are different to the problems usually faced by unjust enrichment remedies.

---

11 'At this point we cross a major divide. Hitherto we have been concerned with plaintiffs whose prima facie claim to restitution is that they have lost what the defendant has gained. That is to say, they put themselves within the subtraction sense of "at expense of" and then, having shown that the defendant has been enriched at their expense in that sense, they go on to identify a factor which calls for restitution and thus shows that the enrichment is "unjust". We have seen that such plaintiffs never need to rely on the wrong as the factor calling for restitution. They point instead to vitiated voluntariness, qualified voluntariness, free acceptance, or an identifiable policy favoring restitution in the given circumstances. By contrast [...] title to restitution rests on the statement that the defendant has enriched himself by committing a wrong'. See, P. Birks, n. 3 above, p. 313.

12 The previous version of this provision was §3 of the Restatement of Restitution, which foresaw that '[a] person is not permitted to profit by his own wrong at the expense of another'. The current version avoids establishing that the wrong has to cause enrichment 'at the expense of another'. The cause of action is defined in wider terms allowing for disgorgement of profits since the remedy is designed to redress enrichments by wrongs that usually are not made 'at the expense of another'.

13 '[T]here are significant instances of liability based on unjust enrichment that do not involve the restoration of anything the claimant previously possessed. The most notable examples are

In fact, disgorgement has little in common with the general unjust enrichment doctrines, although it has traditionally been considered to be a part of them.[14] By disgorging profits the legal system is seeking another solution, something different from restoring gains owed to the rightholder. Because such gains do not correspond to the loss suffered by the holder of the infringed right, its restoration is far from the goals pursued by the law of restitution. In the end, restitution is based on losses suffered by the plaintiff, not in gains made by the defendant.

The point here is to make the surreptitious use of another's right and the infringement of duties economically unprofitable. By condemning the wrongdoer to repay the benefits obtained, the law promotes incentives to agree in advance the price for using the right or for breaching the duty.

The economic preference for voluntary transactions helps explain the disgorgement of unduly obtained profits. By preventing infringers from obtaining any profit, the law promotes a negotiation directly with the person vested with the right that the potential infringer wants to use or to enjoy to some extent. Disgorging benefits promotes negotiation rather than ignoring the market by stealing rights and forcing the owner to seek compensation from the court for his loss.[15]

The economic justification of disgorgement of profits is that it forces defendants to obtain what they want through voluntary transactions. Thus, disgorging profits serves a prophylactic function.[16]

Some legal systems have solved the problem of disgorging profits as an implied and fictional promise to pay for the benefits received by defendant. Such device has been called a 'quasi-contract'. In doing so, the law uses disgorgement of profits as a remedy for situations equivalent to 'implied contracts', by forcing the wrongdoer to repay to the rightholder what the wrongdoer would have paid if the undue use of the right had been negotiated in advance.[17] Article 1371 of the French Civil Code is the best example of such a solution:

---

cases involving the disgorgement of profits, or other benefits wrongfully obtained, in excess of the plaintiff's loss.' See American Law Institute, n. 8 above, Comment c) to §1.

14 'Under the heading of restitution of wrongs, disgorgement is usually a remedy to punish wrongs and vindicate rights that exist and are enforced outside of the law of Restitution.' See M.P. Gergen, 'What Renders Enrichment Unjust' (2001) 79 *Texas Law Review* 1927, 1935.

15 See D. Laycock, n. 1 above, p. 603.

16 'One prophylactic technique is to impose a duty not bring about a situation in which the mischief in question might happen. The sanction for such a duty cannot ever be compensatory damages, since *ex hypothesi*, you are not waiting for the loss to supervene. [...] Such a duty would have to be sanctioned by injunctions or fixed penalties or in some other way, but at all events not by compensatory damages: to wait for the loss to happen would simply be to abandon the prophylactic approach.' See P. Birks, n. 3 above, p. 332.

17 This fiction was already used by Roman law. 'Under the heading of "obligationes quasi ex contractu" we find, most importantly, indebitum solutum; furthermore, negotium gestum, tutela, communion and legatum per damnationem (i.e. obligations arising from unjustified enrichment, from (unauthorized) management of (another's) affairs, from the tutor's conduct of his ward's affairs, from the relationship between co-owners and from specific instructions contained in a will).' See, R. Zimmermann, *The Law of Obligations. Roman Foundations of the Civilian Tradition*, Clarendon Press, Oxford 1996, pp. 15–16.

> *'Les quasi-contrats sont les faits purement volontaires de l'homme, dont il résulte un engagement quelconque envers un tiers, et quelquefois un engagement réciproque des deux parties.'*

Thus, disgorging profits is a way to 'contractualise' the consequences created by the wrongdoing. When understood that way, the duty to disgorge profits has two main implications.

The first would entail a change in the way the legal system protects the right and grants remedies for the rightholder. The remedies granted to the person vested with the infringed right change dramatically *ex ante* and *ex post*. Before being confronted with undue use of the right or breach of contractual or statutory duties, the person vested with the right can freely decide how to manage his right. He is entitled to sell the right or to prevent its being sold by filing for an injunction against non-agreed uses by third parties. However, once the right has been unduly used by third parties, the rightholder is only entitled to ask for the benefits obtained by the wrongdoer.[18]

The second implication of disgorgement as a mechanism of 'contractualising' profits unduly obtained by the use of another's assets deals with the use of disgorgement as a measure for damages in cases of breach of contract. The next section touches upon the issue.

## III. DISGORGEMENT OF PROFITS MADE BY BREACH OF CONTRACT

It is generally understood that profits gained by breach of contract do not count as a measure for relief. Breach of contract has not been considered a wrongdoing, in the sense of the undue use of another's assets. Therefore, breach of contract has not traditionally been understood as a source of enrichment or wrongful gain. More technically, the contract itself provides a framework for compensation in the event of non-performance. Compensatory damages should be calculated according to the risks and costs assumed by the parties, instead of taking into account the benefits obtained by the non-performer.[19] In spite of such considerations, it seems clear that disgorging profits would be an effective threat against opportunistic breaches.

In fact, no legal system generally allows for disgorgement in cases of breach of contract. The remedy has usually been limited to cases in which the

18 Cf. M.P. Gergen, n. 14 above, 1934: 'Ex ante, the law protects property through injunction. Ex post, the argument goes, the law protects property through a right to the infringer's profit, among other ways.'

19 See A. Farnsworth, 'Your Loss or May Gain? The Dilemma of the Disgorgement Principle in Breach of Contract' (1984–1985) 94 *Yale Law Journal* 1339. For a very interesting and complete comparative overview, see, M. Siems, 'Disgorgement of Profits for Breach of Contract. A Comparative Analysis' (2003) 7 *Edinburgh Law Review* 27.

wrongdoer affected property rights.[20] The legal system normally grants the holder of the right the monopoly for the gains derived from the asset and entitles him to recover the benefits unduly obtained by the wrongdoer. Specifically, disgorgement of profits has been foreseen by Article 13 of Directive 2004/48/EC of the European Parliament and of the Council of 29 April 2004 on the enforcement of intellectual property rights:

> '1. Member States shall ensure that the competent judicial authorities, on application of the injured party, order the infringer who knowingly, or with reasonable grounds to know, engaged in an infringing activity, to pay the rightholder damages appropriate to the actual prejudice suffered by him/her as a result of the infringement. When the judicial authorities set the damages:
> (a) they shall take into account all appropriate aspects, such as the negative economic consequences, including lost profits, which the injured party has suffered, any unfair profits made by the infringer and, in appropriate cases, elements other than economic factors, such as the moral prejudice caused to the rightholder by the infringement; or
> (b) as an alternative to (a), they may, in appropriate cases, set the damages as a lump sum on the basis of elements such as at least the amount of royalties or fees which would have been due if the infringer had requested authorization to use the intellectual property right in question.
> 2. Where the infringer did not knowingly, or with reasonable grounds know, engage in infringing activity, Member States may lay down that the judicial authorities may order the recovery of profits or the payment of damages, which may be pre-established.'

However, some recent legal proposals seem to comprehend disgorgement of profits in a wider way that could allow disgorging the profits made by the breach of contract. The Common Frame of Reference considers disgorgement as an alternative remedy in cases in which full reparation is sought. Article VI.-6:101 (Aim and forms of reparation) sets forth:

> '(1) Reparation is to reinstate the person suffering the legally relevant damage in the position that person would have been in had the legally relevant damage not occurred.
> [...]
> (4) As an alternative to reinstatement under paragraph (1), but only where this is reasonable, reparation may take the form of recovery from the person accountable for the causation of the legally relevant damage of any advantage obtained by the latter in connection with causing the damage.'

Article 174 of the Proposal for a Regulation of the European Parliament and of the Council on a Common European Sales Law (CESL) also foresees

20 These cases recall the logic of tort law. In such situations, disgorging profits is presented as a proxy of compensation.

disgorgement as a way to effectively grant restitution. Article 174 deals with 'Payment for use and interest on money received' and sets forth:

> '1. A recipient who has made use of goods must pay the other party the monetary value of that use for any period where:
> (a) the recipient caused the ground for avoidance or termination;
> (b) the recipient, prior to the start of that period, was aware of the ground for avoidance or termination; or
> (c) having regard to the nature of the goods, the nature and amount of the use and the availability of remedies other than termination, it would be inequitable to allow the recipient the free use of the goods for that period.'

The last version of the Restatement (Third) on Unjust Enrichment and Restitution has gone a little bit further. Its §39 (Profit from Opportunistic Breach) expressly foresees disgorgement in cases of conscious, deliberate and profitable breach of contract:

> '(1) If a deliberate breach of contract results in profit to the defaulting promisor and the available damage remedy affords inadequate protection to the promisee's contractual entitlement, the promise has a claim to restitution of the profit realized by the promisor as a result of the breach. Restitution by the rule of this section is an alternative to a remedy in damages.
> (2) A case in which damages afford inadequate protection to the promisee's contractual entitlement is ordinarily one in which damages will not permit the promisee to acquire a full equivalent to the promised performance in a substitute transaction.
> (3) Breach of contract is profitable when it results in gains to the defendant (net of potential liability in damages) greater than the defendant would have realized from performance of the contract. Profits from breach include saved expenditure and consequential gains that the defendant would not have realized but for the breach, as measured by the rules that apply in other cases of disgorgement.'

The comment to this section recognises: 'The purpose of the disgorgement remedy for breach of contract is to eliminate the possibility that an intentional and opportunistic breach will be more profitable to the performing party than a negotiation with the party to whom such performance is owed. For this reason, "profit realized [...] as a result of the breach" includes the gains that motivated the promisor's decision to breach the contract. If the defendant's liability in restitution were limited to the amount that might have been paid to obtain the necessary contractual modification in a voluntary transaction, there would be inadequate incentive to bargain over the entitlement in question.'[21]

Thus, disgorgement is regarded as a remedy aimed at making the breach of contract unprofitable. This result could be achieved under the most recent proposals on European contract law.

[21] American Law Institute, n. 8 above, Comment e) to §39.